P9-BJL-831

RISKING FREE TRADE

Pitt Series

in Policy and

Institutional

Studies

Bert A. Rockman

Editor

RISKING FREE TRADE

The Politics of Trade

in Britain,

Canada, Mexico,

and the

United States

Michael Lusztig

University of Pittsburgh Press

AUGUSTANA UNIVERSITY COLLEGE
LIBRARY

Published by the University of Pittsburgh Press,
Pittsburgh, Pa. 15260
Copyright © 1996, University of Pittsburgh Press
All rights reserved
Manufactured in the United States of America
Printed on acid-free paper

10   9   8   7   6   5   4   3   2   1

Library of Congress Cataloging-in-Publication Data
Lusztig, Michael, 1962–
    Risking free trade : the politics of free trade in Britain, Canada,
Mexico, and the United States / Michael Lusztig.
        p.   cm. — (Pitt series in policy and institutional studies)
    Includes bibliographical references and index.
        ISBN 0-8229-3932-0 (acid-free paper). — ISBN 0-8229-5589-x (pbk.:
acid-free paper)   1. Free trade. 2. Free trade—Great Britain. 3. Free
trade—Canada. 4. Free trade—Mexico. 5. Free trade—United
States. I. Title. II. Series.
HF1713.L87   1996   96-25208
382'.71—dc20
A CIP catalog record for this book is available
from the British Library.

Part of chapter 2 first appeared as "Solving Peel's Puzzle: Repeal of the
Corn Laws and Institutional Preservation," *Comparative Politics*, 1995.
I would like to thank *Comparative Politics* for allowing me to use this
material.
    Grateful acknowledgment is also made to the J. B. Smallman Publi-
cation Fund, Faculty of Social Science, University of Western Ontario,
for assistance in constructing the index of this book.

To Chrissy and my parents

CONTENTS

ACKNOWLEDGMENTS

Like so many books, this one could not have been completed without the generous assistance and support of family, friends, and colleagues. Intellectually, the largest debts I owe are to Hudson Meadwell, who first sparked my interest in trade, and Patrick James, who also has provided support and inspiration throughout. In addition, I owe debts of gratitude to the many individuals who read this manuscript, in whole or in part, or who helped me grapple with the ideas it expresses. I alone am responsible for the book's contents, and any errors contained within. Thanks are due to Ruth Abbey, Donald Abelson, James Booth, Paul Brace, Mark Brawley, Ian Brodie, David Carment, Allan Castle, William Claggett, Catherine Fieschi, Frank Harvey, John Ikenberry, Peter Johnson, HeeMin Kim, Douglas Lemke, Cameron Lusztig, Mary Mackinnon, Christopher Manfredi, Pierre Martin, Jeremy Moon, Philip Oxhorn, James Lee Ray, Liliana Riga, Evan Ringquist, and Richard Vernon. The criticisms made by the anonymous reviewers for the University of Pittsburgh Press made this a far better book. Jane Flanders, Pippa Letsky, Kathy McLaughlin, Cynthia Miller, and Mary Ellen Pearl guided the manuscript through the editing process at the University of Pittsburgh Press. Helen Drokin at the University of Western Ontario provided much needed assistance in the preparation of the manuscript. Finally, Christine Carberry, Miriam Desjardines, and Laura Stephenson assisted in proofreading the final draft.

Much of the financial support for this book was provided by the Social Science and Humanities Research Council of Canada. I would also like to thank the J. W. McConnell Foundation for financial support in the early stages of the project. I am grateful to the political science departments at McGill University and the University of Western Ontario for providing institutional support. Much of this work was undertaken while I was a postdoctoral fellow at the Department of Political Science at Florida State University. Special thanks are due to the department as a whole for logistical and intellectual assistance.

Some of my previously published work has been modified for inclusion in this work. I am grateful for permission to incorporate material from "Solving Peel's Puzzle: Repeal of the Corn Laws and Institutional Preservation," *Comparative Politics* 27 (1995): 393–408.

Finally, I wish to thank my parents as well as my wife, Christine Carberry, for their unfailing support, which has seen me through this project, and indeed my academic career. It has been a long process in which they have shared my triumphs and helped me deal with my defeats. This book is dedicated to them.

RISKING FREE TRADE

1

OVERVIEW

Why Governments Enact Free Trade

Why do countries enact free trade? This question might, at first blush, be considered a purely economic one. Governments identify their economic objectives (presumably the maximization of the country's aggregate wealth) and adopt trade policies that promise to advance those objectives most efficiently. The problem is that whereas trade liberalization is almost always in each country's aggregate economic interest, it is rare to find instances in which countries have sought sharp, sudden reductions in rates of import protection. The reason, as much of the extant literature on trade liberalization has emphasized, is that the political costs of free trade outweigh the economic benefits. The puzzle that brings politics into the realm of trade policy, therefore, is to determine under which circumstances governments will risk policies of free trade.

. . .

It is widely accepted among political economists that, ceteris paribus, countries maximize aggregate wealth through policies of liberal trade.[1] As Rodrik notes: "There is probably no area in economics where professional opinion is so united: warts and all, free trade is seen as superior to protection by the vast majority of the economics profession." According to classical liberal theory, free trade benefits all countries. One important qualification is that "infant" industries often require import protection for the first few years of their existence in order to establish a position in the world economy. Similarly, security considerations can militate against the incentive to liberalize trade in key strategic sectors. Finally, some have argued that it is collectively rational for risk averse actors to seek to shield themselves from the volatility of the international economy through the creation of protectionist structures.[2]

The logic of comparative advantage suggests that countries will maximize wealth by producing the goods they can manufacture most efficiently, and importing the goods that they are less efficient at producing. The benefits that accrue to the liberalizing country are such that even unilateral elimination of trade barriers is efficient. This is because protectionist devices such as tariffs, quotas, and import licenses impose deadweight costs onto society as a whole. By skewing incentive structures within the marketplace, import protection diverts resources from sectors enjoying comparative advantage toward those that operate less efficiently. Moreover, in the long run, the logic of comparative advantage dictates that unilateral liberalization also may create incentives for tariff reduction abroad.[3]

In its simplest form, this logic suggests that unilateral liberalization creates a disincentive for interests in other countries to allocate resources in inefficient sectors, because increased market potential (through the possibility of exporting to the liberalizing country) motivates actors to allocate resources into more efficient sectors. The benefits of free trade, therefore, are twofold. In the short term, advantages include lower consumer prices, wider consumption potential, and investment in sectors that enjoy comparative advantage, thereby lowering deadweight costs. In the longer term, free trade has the potential to create expanded markets for the export sector.

For the classical theory to operate as described, resources have to be completely mobile. In reality they are not. Many factors of production (agricultural land, factories, and so on) tend to be sector-specific, and resources cannot easily be diverted from inefficient sectors. Given this sector-specificity it is recognized that, although free trade has numerous economic advantages, it imposes severe costs on certain segments of the domestic economy.

Thus, the enactment of free trade policies entails a considerable political dimension and may be considered politically problematic insofar as it promises to alienate rent-seeking interests within society.[4] Due to differentials in intensity of preferences, free trade constitutes an asymmetric public good whereby the benefits are widely distributed and often latent while the costs are concentrated and manifest. Although free trade is beneficial in the aggregate, differential marginal utilities dictate that those bearing the costs have proportionally greater interest in the issue than do those reaping the benefits. The former mobilize to generate pressure on governments to retain inefficient, but narrowly lucrative, policies. As Arnold notes, with respect to the United States:

> Even when these concentrated interests are not well organized, legislators know that the affected publics are both more attentive to Washington action and more likely to show their appreciation at the polls than are those citizens who have less at stake and who are less attentive to what happens in Congress. These simple arguments help to explain why Congress erects trade barriers to protect specific industries, creates an endless stream of special tax provisions, maintains price supports for many agricultural commodities, and refuses to enact restrictions on the ownership of guns.[5]

Indeed, in many cases, the marginal utility differential between rent-seeking producers and consumers in general is so great that it is not politically feasible for governments to enact policies of trade liberalization.

Another important political factor favoring protectionism over free trade is that protectionist rent-seekers find it easier to generate public support for their position than do free traders. The former are able to point to tangible costs of trade liberalization such as job loss, business failure, and general economic dislocation. By contrast, free traders are reduced to explaining the more abstract benefits of concepts such as comparative advantage, economies of scale, and the potential for greater long-term economic growth. As Tullock suggests: "the arguments for a protective tariff are simple and superficially obvious, while the arguments against it are unfortunately complicated and indirect. Granted that the voter has no motive for becoming well informed, he or she will buy the simpler of the two explanations."[6]

Yet another consideration benefiting protectionists is that groups seeking tariffs often can count on support from other groups seeking to create a climate conducive to rent-seeking. Unaffected groups may support another's tariff claim because they "think that such action will increase their own chances of receiving tariff protection in the future; in effect, they endeavour to bring about a type of political exchange." Pressure group activity during the Smoot-Hawley tariff debates of the late 1920s and early 1930s is perhaps the best-documented example of such a phenomenon.[7]

Finally, psychological variables may come into play. Prospect theory, for example, proposes that individuals assign greater value to the loss of existing utility than to the gain of an equal amount.[8] As a result, individuals in groups losing existing tariff protection can be expected to feel a sense of loss greater than the sense of gain experienced by individuals in groups that reap proportional benefits through tariff reduction. By extension, this makes it more likely that groups will mobilize in support of continued protectionism than in support of trade liberalization.

In addition to the costs associated with alienating rent-seekers, there are other factors that might inhibit the enactment of free trade policies. A second source of intractability emanates from within the state itself. Some actors in the public sector, for example, may benefit from inefficient trade policies. State agencies (which constitute bureaucratic advancement streams) often form clientelistic affiliations with rent-seeking societal interests at the expense of efficient government. Policy reforms that jeopardize this clientelistic relationship typically are resisted.[9] Moreover, regardless of how socially inefficient, most policies create legacies that remain part of the bureaucratic agenda.[10] This is largely because senior civil servants throughout government have a preference for the system that makes them most knowledgeable. Since knowledge is a great source of bureaucratic power, high-ranking officials actively oppose changes to the status quo, even if such changes are demonstrably more efficient.[11]

Finally, states may contribute to the intractability of free trade as a matter of government policy. Governments rely on institutionalized power bases that tend to constitute minimum winning coalitions. They do not necessarily have an incentive, therefore, to serve the aggregate interest. Rather, they may seek to distribute resources selectively in order to ensure the continued support of key interests for the ruling coalition.[12]

In sum, societal rent-seekers not only have logistical advantages in mobilizing politically against trade liberalization, but also greater incentives to do so. By the same token, governments have great incentive to heed the demands of rent-seekers. Because protection-seekers tend to derive greater marginal utility from the status quo than reformers derive from reform, rational government leaders rarely will risk alienating such a motivated lobby. As Rodrik notes: "From the perspective of policymakers, the pure reshuffling of income must be counted as a political cost. In politics, rents and revenues that accrue on a regular basis create entitlements. Whether viewed as desirable or not, taking income away from one group is rarely easy for a politician to accomplish. And while most policy reforms under-cut such entitlements, trade reform does so with a vengeance."[13] Finally, it is not always in the interest of state actors to maximize the aggregate level of wealth within society. Elected and nonelected state actors alike may de-termine that inefficient trade policies serve their narrow political interests more effectively than do policies of free trade.

The question that naturally emerges, therefore, is: Why free trade? Why do government leaders, even if they desire lower barriers to imports, run the risk of alienating entrenched societal (and even bureaucratic) rent-seekers?

. . .

For present purposes, the term *trade liberalization,* or free trade, is defined narrowly. It refers only to policies aimed at removing direct barriers to im-ports. Thus, changes in monetary policy, even if they serve to stimulate im-ports, are not at issue. Instead, operationally, trade liberalization conforms to three criteria. First, it constitutes a break with past trade practices, that is, it represents a new direction in trade policy by eliminating a long-stand-ing policy or tradition of protectionism in favor of rapid (or the promise of rapid) reductions in the level of import protection. Second, it is com-prehensive. It involves a commitment to significant tariff reductions affect-ing at least one-third of the liberalizing country's total trade volume. Third, it is politically controversial. Free trade is not, in other words, taken to entail mere backroom adjustments to the tariff schedule. It is highly vis-ible, and of sufficient economic significance to trigger the mobilization of political opposition.

This book seeks to address the question of why government leaders as-sume the political risk of passing free trade policies. It does not seek to ex-plain all instances of trade liberalization. Rather, it attempts to provide one explanation of circumstances under which governments overturn long-standing traditions of protectionism in favor of fairly rapid reversals to-ward free trade policies. In doing so, this study develops a model that con-ceptualizes free trade not as a first-order objective of the liberalizer, but rather as the *by-product* of a pursuit of larger, more politically rewarding, objectives.

In its briefest form, the model relies on the following logic. As a rule, governments must assemble a coalition of interests that permits realiza-tion of most legislative goals. Occasionally, however, government leaders seek objectives that cannot be achieved through regular legislative channels. Such objectives typically involve significant transformations of the polity. Such transformative politics are styled *alignment games* and entail attempts to effect electoral realignments or, alternatively, to prevent impending realignments from occurring. Realignments, it may be argued, may be stimulated by altering the regime-defining—or institutional—structure of the polity. Because the political payoffs derived from alignment games tend to be large, the model turns on the assumption that under certain conditions first-order objectives of state actors may involve attempts to reform (or preserve in the face of threat) the regime-defining characteristics of the polity.

Leaving aside a detailed description for the moment, the model suggests that a particular outcome in the alignment game—realized through either institutional innovation or institutional preservation—is the overarching objective of a policy innovator, or political entrepreneur. In order to realize their institutional objectives, political entrepreneurs must have the support of all actors—state and societal—with the ability to block the institutional initiative. Where such actors are neutral, or even hostile, to the political entrepreneurs' overarching objectives, their support must be attracted through incentives such as direct subsidies, grants, tax incentives, or policy reforms. Of current interest are instances when a specific type of policy reform—trade liberalization—is logrolled with the political entrepreneurs' institutional objectives.

The idea of free trade as being a by-product of the quest for institutional innovation or preservation provides an interesting contrast with the way existing theories from comparative and international political economy treat trade liberalization. As noted, unlike prevailing explanations, the model outlined in this book does not assume that free trade is a first-order preference of government. This approach suggests that governments are not hostage to economic or systemic political forces. Leaders are assumed to be rational actors who willingly assume the political risks associated with trade liberalization and construct logrolling scenarios that optimize on the basis of perceived preference orderings among those included in such scenarios.

The extant literature provides important insights into the ways that countries liberalize trade, but it is incomplete. By focusing too narrowly (that is, conceptualizing free trade as an end for governments), existing theories ignore the possibility that free trade is often merely a means to the realization of other objectives. This leads to a second problem. Why do governments undertake action that is politically harmful? Existing theories reconcile the political nonrationality of free trade policies in one of two ways. On one hand, many theories treat trade liberalization as action that is structurally determined, or imposed by external (systemic) or internal (societal) forces. Even some statist explanations envision trade liberalization as something that is possible only in the absence of constraints. The existing literature may, on the other hand, reify the state to the extent that it possesses a mandate to act in the national interest. Neorealists and state autonomists are guilty, to varying degrees, of assuming that the "state" (or components of the state) are unified and capable of acting in defiance of societal resistance.

The model outlined in this book reconciles trade liberalization with political rationality in a way that does not need to be structurally determined, or to rely on reification of the state. This model is intended as a complement, not necessarily a rival, to existing theories.

Systemic-Level Theories

A large body of literature on the determinants of foreign economic policy is dedicated to the study of the international environment in which states operate. This environment typically is regulated by international regimes, defined in the literature as social institutions: norms, rules, and decision-making procedures around which actor expectations converge in a particular issue area.[14]

Perhaps the most influential explanation of the means by which regimes regulate trade policy is hegemonic stability theory, first articulated by Kindleberger. According to this schema, hegemons underwrite a stable liberal international trade and monetary order. Hegemons provide the impetus for free trade regimes by lowering tariffs, in exchange for trade liberalization on the part of their partners, and resolve collective action problems by ensuring compliance with the regime. Britain, after the repeal of the Corn Laws, and the United States in the post–World War II era are the most widely cited examples of hegemonic leadership, although some theorists also point to the Netherlands in the eighteenth century as an example.[15]

From this neoliberal perspective, states are conceptualized as rational, egoistic utility maximizers. States participate in the regime, not because they are coerced, but because it is in their best interest to do so. All states, it is assumed, prefer free trade but are reluctant to maintain open markets for fear that others will not.[16] In order to overcome states' rational predilection to free trade, coordination of trade policies is required, and regimes, underwritten by hegemons, provide this coordination. Regimes consist of strict rules and sanctions to ensure that no state cheats by maintaining tariffs on imports while enjoying tariff-free markets for exports. As long as actors realize that the costs of defection outweigh those of cooperation, they will continue to cooperate.

From the neorealist perspective, other hegemonic stability theorists (such as Krasner) suggest that regimes are not so much negotiated as imposed. Young suggests that hegemons impose regimes upon their partners, either overtly or implicitly. Acting overtly, the hegemon coerces others into compliance by any number of weapons at its disposal, the most common of which is the imposition of trade sanctions. Over time, this coercion becomes self-enforcing. Habits of obedience tend to be cultivated, usually in the form of a Gramscian-style ideology. The period of reconstruction after World War II, for example, provided the United States with the opportunity to export its ideological commitment to international liberalism to France, West Germany, Italy, and Japan.[17]

Implicit imposition occurs when the hegemon acts unilaterally to alter the incentive structures of other states within the system. By virtue of the hegemon's power in the international marketplace, unilateral tariff reductions affect worldwide factor returns and commodity prices. In turn, this alters the balance of power among domestic interest groups in other states, empowering positively affected groups to mobilize in support of free trade. In short, the unilateral action of the hegemon empowers free trade lobbies in other states and creates internal pressures for these states to comply with the international regime.[18]

Hegemonic stability theory is compelling because it is comprehensive and parsimonious. Eras of trade liberalization correspond to those of hegemonic ascendance, whereas protectionism and hegemonic decline occur in tandem. Moreover, the emergence of a free trade regime at once explains decisions to embrace trade liberalization in numerous states. Trade policy is depoliticized domestically because governments are constrained in their policy choices by their commitment to the international regime. The success of the General Agreement on Tariffs and Trade (GATT) is testimony to such logic.

On the other hand, the very parsimony that makes hegemonic stability theory so attractive, stands up poorly to rigorous analysis. Closer inspection reveals conceptual flaws. Perhaps the greatest is that the theory relies on the assumption that states are rational and unitary actors, motivated to act in some vague, undefined "national interest." This macropolitical conceptualization, while methodologically appealing, subordinates (and indeed, in some cases even ignores) subsystemic phenomena. Moreover, there is no logical basis for assuming that state actors will perceive or reflect the national interest.[19]

Hegemonic stability theory turns on the premise that hegemons are required to overcome collective action problems in the otherwise anarchic international system. However, in treating states as cohesive and unitary actors, the theory ignores that states themselves represent collective entities. Thus, in addition to resolving collective action problems at the international level, hegemons are assumed to have solved their own internal collective action problems; that is, to have constructed a domestic coalition seeking to advance the "national interest." What is the basis for this assumption? Hegemonic stability theory provides few answers.[20]

In short, the theory seems to embrace not only a "black box" theory of government decision-making, but an "invisible hand" conceptualization of domestic interest group behavior within the hegemon. As such, the theory's strength lies more in the correlation between hegemonic ascendance and economic openness than in the demonstration of causality. As McKeown notes, the theory

> is not very helpful in telling us what actors did in order for a system to move from point A to point B. The linkage between shifts in capabilities and shifts in regimes or other outcomes is inferred by noting covariations (generally in a low-N setting), without any attempt to trace the process whereby changes in capabilities translate into different outcomes.[21]

Despite the conceptual problems associated with hegemonic stability theory, the role of systemic variables such as international regimes is important to the study of trade liberalization. Regimes constrain and structure the behavior of domestic actors and facilitate liberal trade by compelling states to devolve a degree of foreign economic policy autonomy to international institutions created to administer the regime. Once committed to the regime, governments are afforded a degree of protection against domestic interests hostile to the existing trade policy. Liberal trade is perceived less as a policy choice of government, as of compliance to the dictates of the regime. By the same token, incremental reductions in the level of import protection are seen as supragovernmental decisions. As long as the regime is understood to be widely beneficial (as was the GATT, for example), governments can maintain that incremental trade liberalization is the only course of action available to them.

In sum, systemic theories appear to explain some, but not all, of the factors leading to free trade. They help to explain, for example, structural determinants of trade liberalization. However, where actors (such as the hegemons themselves) are not constrained by the international system, systemic theories prove unable to explain shifts toward free trade.

Societal-Level Theories

A second classification focuses on societal-level, or general equilibrium, explanations of trade liberalization. General equilibrium theories also tend to be structurally derived, but these theories turn on economic, rather than political, considerations. They suggest that countries will arrive at the most efficient levels of protection by encouraging or facilitating resource allocation into sectors that enjoy comparative advantage. Competition among those with different factor endowments (labor, capital, and land) creates a tariff level at equilibrium. Changes in tariff levels are the result of exogenous changes: the most obvious are technological advances, but others such as cycles in the world economy are also important. These exogenous changes alter the balance of political influence, or equilibrium, among factor owners, thereby facilitating changes in trade policy toward either greater protectionism or greater liberalization.

An example of general equilibrium theories is the Stolper-Samuelson theorem, which holds that trade liberalization empowers (whereas protectionism harms) owners of factors with which—relative to the rest of the world—a country is generously endowed. (Similarly, the reverse holds true. Owners of scarce factors benefit from protectionism, whereas owners of abundant factors suffer.) Rogowski suggests that exogenous variables affect levels of international trade, thereby altering the relative power of domestic groups.[22] New coalitions are formed as the interfactoral balance of power weakens certain actors while strengthening others. Changing domestic coalitions, in turn, explain why states radically alter trade policies toward either protectionism or free trade. The state is afforded no role in the process. It merely responds to policy preferences of the societal forces temporarily empowered by exogenous conditions.

Rogowski's argument is similar in many ways to the model developed in this book. The principal difference is that, in this book, causality is reversed. Trade does not affect coalition construction; rather, coalition construction is a function of trade policy. Another difference is that, according to the model developed in this book, the elements of the winning coalition are not structurally determined. Instead, they are the product of rational calculation by actors within the state.

The Stolper-Samuelson theorem—while empirically sound (Rogowski's comprehensive study uses the theory to explain trade policy change in all regions of the world across a number of different eras)—rests on assumptions that are logically less impressive. For example, the theory turns on the premise that factor ownership constitutes the dominant line of economic cleavage within society. However, this assumption ignores the wide potential for intrafactoral conflict and interfactoral alliances.[23] Indeed, within factors, interests are more likely to align according to industry or sector than according to factor-wide groupings. Similarly, regional considerations are better indicators of trade preferences than are factor endowments.[24]

A more telling criticism of general equilibrium theories writ large is that they suffer from the same problem that afflicts pluralist political thought—they fail to account for power and resource differentials among competing groups.[25] Groups differ in their ability to overcome collective action problems in the mobilization of trade lobbies. As noted, the ability of rent-seeking interests to mobilize more effectively than other groups means that protectionism is more likely to be pursued than is free trade. While export-oriented lobbies do emerge to seek free trade, this rarely is a sufficient condition for trade liberalization.[26]

State-Level Theories

State-level theories of trade liberalization focus on the supply side of trade policy. Statist theories are analytically distinctive because they posit at least a degree of autonomy on the part of state actors in the process of making trade policy. Krasner was among the first to explore the possibility that states pursue trade policy independently of systemic and societal pressure. Drawing on neoclassical economic theory, Krasner suggests that states prefer free trade to protectionism because aggregate welfare maximization is in the "national interest." However, states will not always be free to pursue the national interest, because of countervailing pressure from domestic rent-seekers. Trade policy choice, according to Krasner, therefore becomes a struggle between powerful societal interests, and relatively autonomous state actors (in the case of the United States, this entails the White House and the State Department).[27]

Lake explores this theme further, distinguishing two functionally distinct components of the liberal democratic state, which he calls respectively the "representative component" and the "foreign policy executive." The representative component consists of the legislature and the constituent agencies of government (such as departments of agriculture, labor, commerce, and so on). Because legislators tend to be motivated by a desire for reelection, and constituent agencies are susceptible to clientelistic capture, the representative component constitutes the principal target of domestic rent-seekers.[28]

The foreign policy executive, on the other hand, consists of nationally elected executive officials and high-ranking bureaucrats in charge of defence and foreign policy and is shielded from many of the rent-seeking pressures faced by the representative component. The logic is that nationally elected officials have a greater interest in the aggregate welfare than do more parochial representatives, while departments such as defense and foreign affairs are less clientelistic than other departments. Obviously these points must be qualified. Nationally elected officials are not immune from the influence of powerful lobbies.[29] Moreover, in parliamentary forms of government, the legislative and executive roles of elected officials are conflated, thus mitigating the insulation of these officials from domestic rent-seekers. As for bureaucrats in the foreign policy departments, long-standing and widespread allegations of venality within the U.S. military-industrial complex, for example, undermine the contention that the foreign policy executive is free from clientelistic pressures. However, in general, the foreign policy executive serves the "national interest" and is dedicated to "husbanding the nation-state's wealth and power, given the interests and actions of other countries."[30]

In addition to distinguishing among degrees of autonomy within states, Krasner, in *Defending the National Interest,* also notes differences in levels of state autonomy across states. He suggests that countries can be classified according to how "strong" or "weak" they are—that is, according to how much autonomy state actors enjoy from societal pressures. Strong states, according to this logic, are more capable of resisting pressure from rent-seeking special interests.

Katzenstein suggests that state strength is a function of the degree of centralization of state institutions and societal organizations, especially labor and the industrial and banking sectors. Degree of centralization is conditioned, in large part, by the pace and timing of modernization. As a rule, Katzenstein argues, centralized bureaucracies tend to emerge in countries where powerful administrative machines were put in place prior to the establishment of democratic institutions. Thus, for example, one sees stronger, more centralized states in Germany, France, and Japan than in Britain or the United States. At the societal level, following Gerschenkron, Katzenstein argues that unlike firms in early developers (the United States and the United Kingdom, for example), firms in late developers were unable to compete internationally without state assistance.[31] This led to sectoral concentration and the development of peak associations, facilitating the creation of a leading role for the state within the domestic economy. The tradition of strong state presence in the economies of late developers has afforded actors in these states greater proactive capacity than is enjoyed by actors in weak states or early developers. Moreover, administrative efficiency in more centralized states provides actors in strong states with a wider range of policy instruments in the making of trade policy.

State-centered explanations are more sensitive to explanations along other levels of analysis than are systemic or societal explanations. However, they tend to suffer from two principal problems. First, if not guilty of the unitary-actor assumption per se, many statists postulate a foreign policy executive that acts in a coherent way consistent with the national interest. This is a dubious claim. It is risky to assume, for example, that the foreign policy executive is much more cohesive than any other branch of government. The well-documented accounts of infighting within the Roosevelt administration alone make this point. Similarly, the notion that the foreign policy executive acts in the national interest is questionable. As Frey argues: "'Countries' or 'nations' do not behave as such; there is no imaginary 'benevolent dictator' who maximizes social welfare; rather, what we observe countries doing is the result of decision-makers acting according to their own advantage. . . . [T]he interests of the government (even if democratically elected) do not necessarily coincide with those of the country as a whole."[32]

The second principal problem with statist theories is that the distinction between weak and strong states does not hold up well empirically with respect to trade policy. According to this theory, early developers or weak states—such as Britain, the United States, and maybe Canada—should have had relatively little policy autonomy vis-à-vis societal interests. Yet in each of these cases, the state's role in the passage of trade policy was proactive. Moreover, as Doner suggests, state strength is of questionable utility in determining the range of policy options available to state actors. State strength is also a poor indicator of cohesion at the executive level, and such strength even may enhance predatory behavior on the part of state officials seeking to expand policy jurisdiction. Ikenberry too is critical of the weak state/strong state dichotomy, maintaining that all states, weak or strong, are bound by past policy decisions that create vested interests and constrain state action. He argues that policy flexibility is a far more telling indicator of state capacity than is state strength. Indeed, by virtue of past policy decisions, states that are strong in one policy domain may find themselves weak in another. Cairns makes a similar point, suggesting that past policy decisions create a network of interests that "embed" the state into a position of inflexibility and stasis.[33]

Although the various determinants of state capacity are important, analysis that places too great an emphasis on state capacity—setting up state and societal power as rival explanations of determinants of trade policy choice—is in danger of becoming overly reductionist. In creating trade policy, state actors do not operate in an environmental vacuum. Thus, an important component of the literature in state-centered analysis focuses on the interaction between state and societal actors. From a statist perspective, the making of trade policy involves state actors constructing coalitions with societal actors. Lake, for example, makes this point in suggesting that the foreign policy executive, in seeking to liberalize trade, attempts to mobilize latent or neutral groups. More systematically, Frey and Borchardt suggest that a political market for trade policy exists. Demand arises from societal interests. In return, state actors are offered political support for reelection bids, legislative endeavors, institutional expansion, and budget problems.

In short, political coalitions are forged among state and societal actors, with trade policy and political support as the media of exchange.[34] As Gourevitch notes:

> Economic actors begin with an economic situation, to which they link an economic policy preference, and then seek out a political strategy to make that preference prevail. Politicians begin with a political situation, for which they need support, and then seek economic policies which provide that support. . . . Hence, economic actors and politicians interact. Each

needs the other. Politicians need the support of economic actors to win office and to govern. Economic actors need the support of politicians to construct winning coalitions for getting their policy preferences accepted.[35]

Once dominant political coalitions are forged between state and societal actors, they remain stable over time and are resistant to radical departures from the status quo. This accounts for the relative stability observable in states' trade policies. However, in times of crisis, even stable coalitions become susceptible to change. It is during periods of crisis, Gourevitch argues, that stable coalitions break down and are replaced.[36] For Gourevitch, who focuses on economic crises, hard times highlight sources of tension within the dominant coalition that were less evident or important during stable periods. Eventually these sources of friction grow to overwhelm the dominant coalition, which crumbles and is replaced by a new one. It is the creation of a new dominant coalition, he argues, that accounts for radical changes in trade policy.

From Gourevitch one can extrapolate that free trade is a function of abrupt disruptions within the dominant political coalition. However, while this explanation makes an important start, it begs a vital question. Why do utility-maximizing state actors seek to align with societal free traders, given the limited political capital such a position traditionally yields?

The High-Risk Strategy

This book provides a contrast to the extant literature by suggesting that free trade often emerges as a by-product of other political considerations. The model driving this project may be thought of as the high-risk strategy to trade liberalization. (The high-risk model is presented in summary form in Figure 1.) Elected policy-makers will choose the high-risk strategy only if the long-term payoffs promise to exceed the short-term costs associated with policy innovation. As noted, policy-makers who enact trade liberalization under these circumstances are styled political entrepreneurs whose first-order objectives typically entail transformative politics such as electoral realignments, or alternatively, preservation of existing alignments.[37]

Political entrepreneurs typically are heads of government, because alignment games are of most benefit to government leaders (or potential leaders), and because achieving these first-order objectives requires at least some control or influence over all organs of the state. It is possible to identify four distinct roles undertaken by political entrepreneurs. First, they are

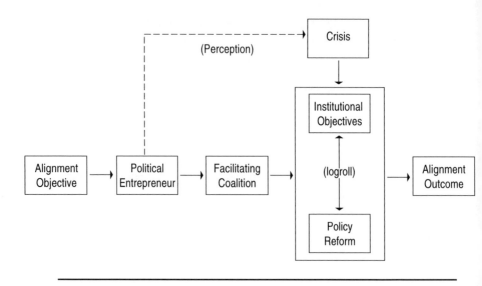

FIGURE 1. The High Risk Model

agenda-setters, establishing priorities for the presentation of issues. Second, they are popularizers, generating and attracting support for the issues presented. Third, they serve as inventors, forging policy options designed to overcome impediments to the bargaining process. Finally, they act as brokers, constructing deals and shoring up support for desired options. In brief, political entrepreneurs engage in what Riker calls heresthetics—the art of political manipulation.[38]

Realignments are sharp, durable transformations in party preference created by attracting the long-term support of groups not previously aligned with the political entrepreneur. Kleppner suggests that "each such transformation can be thought of as having involved the breakdown of one mode of subgroup integration and its replacement by another. What results is an electorally significant and durable change in the composition of party social coalitions and the character of party opposition."[39] Realignments represent opportunities for political parties to expand their bases of support, not just for an election or two, but for a period of a generation or more. What is more, realignments create legacies that ensure a leader's place in history. Thus, not only do realignments in a party's favor provide greater political opportunities for the government of the day, but they serve to ensure the legacy of the government leader or administration that brought about realignment.

In part, realignments are structurally determined, triggered by exogenous forces. One such force—crisis—is described by Burnham as a "sudden, sharp blow [that ignites] a volatilized electoral mixture." The result is a "redefinition of the 'power bloc' at the center of politics, the agenda and chief actors of public policy formation, and a reorientation of primary symbolic codes which sustain and reinforce mass political allegiances and expectations."[40] In part, however, as the American, Canadian, and Mexican cases examined later suggest, realignments may involve agency and may be engineered by skillful political entrepreneurs. In the American case during the interwar period, for example (see chapter 3), President Roosevelt consciously adopted policies that were designed to win over the support of groups—largely the urban and rural underclasses, as well as immigrants and racial minorities—that previously had not identified themselves with the Democratic party. Similarly in Canada (see chapter 4), Prime Minister Mulroney actively sought to attract the long-term electoral support of voters in the critical province of Quebec, who for most of the century had been closely aligned with the Liberal party. Finally, in Mexico (see chapter 5), faced with the prospect of the breakdown of the dominant electoral coalition of his Partido Revolucionario Institucional (PRI), President Salinas sought to construct a new alliance between the popular sector and an emerging entrepreneurial class.

If realignments can be manipulated politically, it stands to reason that manipulation also can prevent realignments. As the British case demonstrates (see chapter 2), an important part of alignment games involves the preservation of existing alignments. In the British case, Prime Minister Peel's overarching concern was to preserve the political alignment of the day against what he perceived to be the threat of potential popular rebellion. (Obviously the term *alignment* is used more loosely in the British case. Victorian Britain did not feature an electoral system based upon universal suffrage, and it is difficult, therefore, to speak of electoral alignments. On the other hand, aristocratic government—featuring institutions such as a limited franchise, an established church, and a powerful House of Lords—may be taken as a proxy for political alignment in pre–universal suffrage Britain.)

A critical means of effecting realignments is to alter the regime-defining characteristics of the polity. Similarly, alignments may be preserved by defending regime-defining characteristics in the face of threat. These regime-defining characteristics may be conceptualized broadly as "institutions," which represent the semipermanent entrenchment of a set of values, interests, and utility streams.[41] Indeed, institutions allocate and redistribute societal resources. Where institutions reflect the values, interests, and utility streams of segments of society, the consequences are analogous to victories in the public policy arena, with the difference being that institutional victories are more permanent. The creation (or retention) of institutions has lasting impact on the bases of a party's electoral support. To take one famous example, President Lincoln's abolition of slavery saw much of the African American vote in the late nineteenth and early twentieth centuries go to the Republican party. It was not until another realignment, entrenched by the creation of the welfare state in the 1930s, that the African American vote switched overwhelmingly to the Democrats.

There is no firm consensus in the social science literature as to what exactly constitutes an institution. For the purpose of this study, domestic institutions are taken to refer to the constitutional order. This comprises the units of the state, as well as the rules—legal and conventional—that structure the jurisdictional boundaries of these units.[42] Further, institutions entail the basic operating rules of the political community. Collectively they are broader than the constitution, encompassing not only society's "rules for making rules," but policies that "give coherence and direction to the country's development for considerable periods ahead."[43] Institutions, therefore, may be as narrow and concrete as the national constitution, or as broad and intangible as, for example, the welfare state. Supranational organizations that structure domestic behavior also may be considered institutions. These supranational organizations, staffed with permanent bureaucracies, may be distinguished from ad hoc agreements because they assign jurisdictional authority and discretion to a supranational set of decision-makers. Examples include the North Atlantic Treaty Organization (NATO), the GATT, and organs of the European Union (EU).

Institutional design (that is, reform or preservation) is not without cost. Institutional change may alienate proponents of the status quo, whereas institutional preservation has the potential to anger powerful advocates of social reform. In seeking to effect institutional innovation or preservation, therefore, the political entrepreneur balances the cost of achieving social consensus with the benefits to be gained in the alignment game. The decision to underwrite potential institutional innovation or preservation will hinge on this calculus.[44]

For political entrepreneurs who engage in alignment games, the most important task is to construct a facilitating coalition. Viability demands that the facilitating coalition be sufficiently broad to incorporate all actors—state or societal—in such a position as to block institutional innovation or to threaten institutional preservation. In order to attract support for the facilitating coalition, the political entrepreneur offers enticements. As noted, enticements take the form of side-payments such as direct subsidies, tax reform, or other compensatory policies; if support is required from within the public sector, side-payments might include enhancement of power or jurisdictional capacities, protection against the loss of material benefits or power, or some combination of the above.[45] The decision to support a particular institutional structure represents an investment of resources in the short term, in order to secure longer-term benefits.[46] To the extent that institutions produce winners and losers, investment in the winning coalition ensures a positive income stream as long as the new institutional structure remains stable.

Within the state, depending on the structure of decision-making and the sources of potential vetoes, coalitions may need to be built among both elected and nonelected officials, or, in other words, in both the legislative and executive branches. In countries that operate according to the principle of responsible government and that feature strong party discipline, support from elected officials for government initiatives can be assumed. Where these conditions do not hold, the political entrepreneur must offer sufficient incentives for elected officials to support the coalition. In systems featuring universal suffrage, the strongest incentive that may be offered to elected officials is societal support. If the political entrepreneur is able to attract the support of enough politically powerful societal interests, the likelihood of support from elected officials is greatly enhanced.

Nonelected state actors will not be enticed into political coalitions by the prospect of institutional design generating increased popular support. Rather, officials within the executive branch will be motivated to support the political entrepreneur by the prospect of gaining power and prestige, or conversely, by fear of losing it.[47] For these officials, institutional design may be conceptualized as jurisdictional imperialism. Decisions to support the political entrepreneur will depend on two factors: the extent to which an official's agency will gain or lose jurisdictional capacity or influence;

and the degree to which a department's societal clientele stands to lose or benefit. In addition, all state officials may be presumed to have an interest in the security of the state. As Lake points out, officials will be motivated by concern for the long-term security of the state—especially in agencies concerned with foreign policy and defence.[48]

Within society, the political entrepreneur must gain significant support from vested interests. Proposed jurisdictional shifts within the state are likely to attract the support of positively affected pressure groups. Clientele groups whose patrons stand to gain increased influence as the result of institutional games can be counted upon to support the political entrepreneur. Groups that have fared badly under the existing institutional structure are likely to support institutional reform; whereas groups that have benefited may be expected to support the political entrepreneur in seeking institutional preservation.

However, where state or societal interests with the ability to thwart a political entrepreneur's institutional initiatives do not support a particular initiative, the entrepreneur will have to take active measures to increase the size of his or her facilitating coalition. Under these circumstances, as mentioned briefly, the political entrepreneur must purchase the support of groups that are opposed—or indifferent—to the entrepreneur's institutional initiatives through the use of side-payments. For present purposes, the most interesting form of side-payment is policy innovation.

Frequently, because of the political risk to governments, the policy objectives of certain groups will be unattainable through regular legislative channels. Free trade policies are an obvious and pertinent example. Construction of facilitating coalitions, therefore, may provide the opportunity for advocates of trade liberalization to commit the government to policy reform in exchange for support for the political entrepreneur's institutional initiatives. In other words, where proponents of trade policy reform are in a position to block the institutional objectives of the political entrepreneur's supporters, trade policy—a natural second-order preference of government leaders—may be logrolled with institutional design in order to satisfy the objectives of both groups.

Members of the facilitating coalition vary across the issues with respect to intensity of preference. Even if some oppose one of the entrepreneur's policies, that will not matter if anticipated benefits from the other initiative outweigh costs. Logrolling may permit a political entrepreneur to achieve realignment even if majorities exist against both proposed changes. Since choice is dichotomous (that is, to approve or obstruct each policy initiative) and utility functions are not, agenda manipulation and other tactics may permit the joint passage of initiatives that almost certainly would be defeated on an individual basis.

Logrolling between advocates of institutional design and policy reform that results in realignment (or alignment preservation) in favor of the political entrepreneur constitutes the core of the high-risk strategy. However, it is important to note that this strategy can be utilized only under certain circumstances. The very term *institution* suggests that these are not ephemeral structures, changeable at the whim of any would-be entrepreneur. Institutional robustness is a function of the costs associated with institutional change. Adjustment costs may be calculated on the basis of the amount of effort required to overcome institutional entrenchment, which is a function of the attachment of vested interests to the institutional status quo. These costs represent a buffer not only against changes in taste, but also against environmental changes. Once created, institutions remain static, often surviving the problem or issue that brought about their creation.[49]

However, institutions are not entirely resistant to change. Over time, institutional stasis and environmental dynamism create tension in the system, which becomes increasingly difficult to contain. When it becomes too great, institutions can no longer cope with the demands brought to bear upon them, and the system is brought into disequilibrium. As a result, the structures that ensured institutional stability weaken, as stable coalitions of interests that had supported the status quo become receptive to alternatives.[50]

The breakdown of institutional equilibrium—or crisis—is of great interest and importance. At the extreme, when institutional equilibrium is lost, the rules of the game stand to be rewritten. Less dramatically, periods of disequilibrium allow for fundamental changes in direction within the polity.[51] As Gourevitch contends:

> it is the crisis years that put the system under stress. Hard times expose strengths and weaknesses to scrutiny, allowing observers to see relationships that are often blurred in prosperous periods, when good times slake the propensity to contest and challenge. The lean years are times when old relationships crumble and new ones have to be constructed. It is then that institutions and patterns are built which will persist long into the next cycle.[52]

Crises represent those points in the alignment game where exogenous forces determine the breakdown of institutional homeostasis. On the other hand, institutional innovation need not be held hostage to structural determinism. Skillful political entrepreneurs may be successful in manufacturing a credible alternative to crisis, by bringing about the perception of crisis. This perception often can be created by exaggerating the extent of an existing problem, obliging interests committed to the status quo to reevaluate that commitment. All crises, real or perceived, are analogous to what the literature on entrepreneurship calls "discoveries," or market opportunities. As Schneider and Teske note, "entrepreneurs engage in the act of 'creative discovery'—they try to take advantage of newly *discovered* or newly *created* possibilities."[53] The danger with such a strategy, however, as the Canadian case shows, is that a full-blown crisis may result in which the political entrepreneur is unable to capitalize on the opportunities created.

Crisis (or the perception of crisis), then, is a necessary condition, where alignment games feature institutional innovation. But crisis is also necessary where the objective is alignment preservation. The reason is obvious: where crisis does not occur, there is no threat to the status quo, and institutional preservation is not required. As in games of institutional innovation, preservation games need not be structurally determined. Where crisis is imminent, political entrepreneurs may be able to escape the potentially disruptive effects by attempting to create the perception of crisis in order to facilitate action designed to preempt threats to the status quo. This strategy was followed by Sir Robert Peel during the repeal of the Corn Laws. In the realm of security policy, a similar strategy was utilized by President Johnson during the Vietnam War with the Tonkin Gulf incident.

In sum, political and economic rationality do not always occur in tandem; and indeed, it is not difficult to find issues where the two are inversely correlated. Certainly one example is trade liberalization. Free trade yields long-term aggregate economic benefits but entails severe political adjustment costs. The result is that few governments in liberal democracies are willing to pay the political price associated with trade liberalization.

· · ·

This study now turns to an examination of four specific instances of trade liberalization. The cases selected for this study reflect a most-different research design. They provide variation in terms of time period; they demonstrate the applicability of the high-risk model to explain trade liberalization in both ascending-hegemonic and non-hegemonic countries; they include both democratic and quasi-democratic cases; finally, they entail games dedicated to both realignment and alignment preservation.

Chapter 2 applies the high-risk model to Britain's historic repeal of the Corn Laws. The argument is that repeal was the price Peel had to pay to ensure that the Anti–Corn Law League did not seek to ally its already powerful organization with groups agitating for greater constitutional inclusion. Chapter 3 concerns the abrupt shift in American trade policy that took the form of the 1934 Reciprocal Trade Agreements Act (RTAA) and its immediate aftermath. The RTAA was enacted as a by-product of President Franklin D. Roosevelt's attempt to create an electoral realignment through the construction of his "Second" New Deal coalition based on the creation of the welfare state. Chapter 3 explores Canada's decision to reverse its century-long policy of bilateral protectionism and enter into a Canada–United States Free Trade Agreement (CUFTA). The suggestion is that in seeking to secure passage of the Meech Lake constitutional amendment package (a move that would attract critical electoral support from the province of Quebec), Prime Minister Brian Mulroney used free trade as an enticement to attract otherwise reticent supporters in western Canada. Chapter 5 examines Mexico's stunning reversal of trade policy in the 1980s. The argument is that President Carlos Salinas de Gortari used free trade as a means to finance his Solidarity package—the means by which he sought to remake the coalition supporting his Partido Revolucionario Institucional. Finally, the implications of the model and the alternative low-risk route to overcoming intractability are discussed in chapter 6.

2

WHY DID PEEL REPEAL THE CORN LAWS?

Although extensively analyzed in studies of international and comparative political economy, Britain's repeal of the Corn Laws remains an enduring puzzle. Many existing explanations turn on international-systemic considerations, economic factors, or pressure group politics, but none fully accounts for Sir Robert Peel's seemingly irrational decision to sacrifice his government for the sake of a policy he long had opposed (Peel's government fell on June 29, 1846, three days after legislation repealing the Corn Laws received royal assent). In seeking to explain his decision, this chapter suggests that the repeal was not a first-order preference for Peel. Instead it was a by-product of his larger objective: to preserve in the face of threat the fundamental political alignment (embodied by the British Constitution), which entailed aristocratic government and a limited franchise. Repeal was necessary to appease the Anti–Corn Law League, which credibly threatened to mobilize the underclasses in rebellion against the existing constitutional structure. Preservation and repeal, therefore, were logrolled within Peel's facilitating coalition to ensure that Peel's first-order objectives were met.

. . .

The English Corn Laws dated from the twelfth century and were enacted to regulate trade in grains.[1] Designed to maintain stable prices of staples such as wheat, oats, and barley, their purpose was threefold. First, they ensured that the price of grains did not rise enough to threaten the subsistence of the poor by permitting the (nearly) free importation of grains after the price reached a critical level. In this way, theoretically, poor harvests would not lead to famine, because imported grain would mitigate the scarcity and allow prices to fall to levels affordable by the poor. Second, they ensured that grain prices remained sufficiently high to induce farmers to continue growing staple crops. This was deemed crucial to state security, due to the perceived importance of self-sufficiency during times of war. Prices were kept high in two ways. Importation of grains was prohibited (or subject to prohibitive duties) as long as prices remained below the pivot price. Thus, abundant harvests abroad could not depress the domestic price of grains. Furthermore, from 1688 to 1765 export bounties were granted to producers. By subsidizing farmers to send their surplus products to foreign markets, grain prices were not driven down by good harvests at home. Third, the Corn Laws were a critical foundation of the agricultural economy and, by extension, the social structure. They were, in short, a pillar of the "aristocratic privilege," because they ensured the economic base of the landed classes.

The debate over appropriate levels of protection became strongly politicized in the aftermath of the Napoleonic Wars (1803–1815), as the postwar period saw a continental backlog of wheat deposited into the British market.[2] The resulting Corn Law of 1815 imposed severe tariffs, which angered the rapidly developing manufacturing interest centered in Manchester. Manufacturers argued that the Corn Law would raise the price of labor and thereby handicap domestic industrialists in competition with foreigners. A slight modification to the Corn Laws in 1828 had little impact, and by the time Peel came to power in 1841, the Corn Laws were a source of intense conflict between rising industrialists and the established agrarian elite.

Thus, early in 1842, despite his party's largely agrarian base of political support (ironically, Peel's Conservatives came to power by defeating Lord Melbourne's Whig government on a motion of nonconfidence inspired by the government's attempt to reduce the agricultural tariff), Peel undertook reform of the Corn Laws with two objectives in mind. First, by significantly lowering agricultural protection, Peel sought to improve the living standards of the poor. This objective, Peel felt, would be to the benefit of all, especially the landed aristocracy. He wrote to J. W. Croker on October 30, 1842: "Rest assured of this, that landed property would not be safe during this next winter with the prices of the last four years, and even if it were safe it would not be profitable very long. Poor rates, rates in aid, diminished consumption, would soon reduce the temporary gain of a nominal high price."[3] Second, Peel attempted, unsuccessfully, to undercut burgeoning reform movements such as the Anti–Corn Law League.

The 1842 Corn Law drove the first wedge into the fragile unity of the Tories under Peel. Conservatives were disillusioned that having defeated the Whigs on the issue of Corn Law reform a year earlier, their own party now had embarked upon a similar course. Nevertheless, Peel recognized that the composition of the House of Commons afforded him a good deal of policy flexibility. Party dynamics made the Whigs far more likely to legislate serious reforms to the Corn Laws (the pro–free trade Radicals were a significant faction within the Whig party), and protectionists felt they had a good deal more to fear from a Whig government than from the Peel ministry. Indeed, the House, as it stood in 1842, defeated a backbench motion to repeal the Corn Laws by a vote of 393 to 90.[4]

The 1842 legislation was unpopular among the Tories' core constituency in the countryside. Agitated and severely reprimanded by their constituents, M.P.s and party members were of different opinions over whether the Peel ministry sought to assail the tradition of agricultural protection, or whether the 1842 law was enacted in final settlement of the Corn Law question. Staunch protectionists like Croker and Disraeli were optimistic.[5] Others such as Broughton, Lord Western, and Malmesbury, long suspicious of what they perceived as Peel's reform-minded tendencies, predicted ominously that total repeal was not far off. Malmesbury's diary of February 7, 1842, for example, states of Peel: "It is clear that he has thrown over the landed interest, as my father always said he would."[6] Such an imputation, if not entirely accurate, was by no means groundless. Peel's closest cabinet colleague, Sir James Graham, was convinced of the need for total repeal as early as December 30, 1842, when he wrote to Peel:

> It is a question of *time*. The next change in the Corn Laws must be to an open trade; and if our population increase for two or three years at the rate of 300,000 per annum, you may throw open the ports, and British agriculture will not suffer. But the next change must be the last; it is not prudent to hurry it; next Session is too soon; and as you cannot make a decisive alteration, it is far wiser to make none.[7]

Peel was unwilling to quell the controversy by committing himself to perpetual preservation of the Corn Laws, but he reiterated consistently his belief that existing agricultural protection did not constitute a burden to the urban poor. Between 1842 and Peel's conversion to repeal in 1845, therefore, agricultural protection ceased to be at issue within the Conservative party.

The rift in the party that would ultimately doom the Peel ministry was far from healed, however, and it widened as a result of events in 1844. Lord Ashley's amendment to the government's factory bill, which would have reduced the maximum workday from twelve to ten hours for women and children, passed with the support of a large number of Conservatives. Only Peel's threat of resignation led to the ultimate defeat of the amendment; but it was clear that in siding with the manufacturing interest, he could henceforth count on only nominal support from many of his backbenchers.

The cohesiveness of the party was severely tested the following year when Peel proposed an increase to the annual grant for the Roman Catholic Maynooth College in Ireland. Maynooth College, a seminary for Roman Catholic priests, had received small annual grants from Parliament since 1795. Peel had long been convinced of the need to improve the lot of the Catholic population in Ireland, in large part to undercut the position of the so-called Irish Repealers who, under the leadership of Daniel O'Connell, wished to sever the union between Britain and Ireland. Peel, ever fearful of agitation in Ireland, felt that the symbolic nature of the Maynooth grant would go some way to soothing Irish resentment toward Britain. His explanation to the House on May 21, 1845, was typical of his propensity to grant preemptive concessions as a means of forestalling popular agitation:

> It was hardly to be expected that the agitation which has been so long going on would cease at once; but by creating a feeling of gratitude and good feeling in the minds of the people, we say we are cutting up the trade of agitation, and we must expect ere long that the agitation will be put an end to altogether. . . . I believe the course the government have taken has greatly diminished the influence of agitation in Ireland generally, and has conciliated—I will not say the confidence of the people towards the government; but at all events, it has diminished the desire of the great body of the Roman Catholics of Ireland to connect themselves with turbulence and agitation.[8]

Peel was aware that the Maynooth Bill would be controversial within his own party. His backbenches held 125 members who, at some point since 1837, had voted against any grant at all to Maynooth.[9] As it was, 149 Tories voted against the bill on third reading, and it only passed with the support of the Whigs. By the time the Maynooth crisis had passed, the party was openly divided. However, disgruntled Tories, despite their obvious antipathy toward the government, were not yet ready for mutiny. It would take Peel's decision to repeal the Corn Laws, announced early in 1846, for the breach to become decisive and permanent.

Conventional Explanations for the Repeal of the Corn Laws

The conceptualization in this book of repeal as a by-product of larger objectives contrasts with existing theories concerning the repeal of the Corn Laws. For example, one widely cited explanation for repeal is that a hegemonic Britain sought to impose a free trade regime on its trading partners.[10] Along these lines James and Lake argue that, by adopting free trade in 1846, Britain hoped to influence the domestic balance of power among pressure groups within its trading partners, thereby achieving reciprocity in free trade and exploiting its own comparative advantage in manufactured goods.[11] They suggest that the United States' Walker Tariff of 1846 resulted directly from the repeal of the Corn Laws. In the 1840s the United States was divided in terms of trade preference between the protectionist North and the free trade South. The balance of power lay with the Western farmers who were uncommitted, but who preferred free trade if it would open up world grain markets. Recognition of this fact and knowledge that free trade would be detrimental to the nascent American industrial sector led Britain to repeal the Corn Laws.

Although the James and Lake thesis appears to explain the U.S. Walker Tariff, the principal difficulty is that there is little evidence that government leaders in Britain allowed foreign policy factors to enter into their decision to repeal the Corn Laws. Granted, Richard Cobden and the Anti–Corn Law League argued that unilateral trade liberalization would be met with reciprocity and would allow Britain to exploit its head start in manufacturing. This line of argument is not surprising, coming from a pressure group dedicated to furthering the interests of industrialists. But such arguments do not appear to have been discussed in cabinet, nor are they found in Peel's correspondence.[12] Upon introducing repeal legislation, Peel noted on January 27, 1846, that: "Our last accounts from the United States give indications of the decline of a hostile spirit [with respect to maintenance of high import duties]." However, this does not appear to have been a decisive factor for Peel. In the same speech he warned that repeal would not guarantee reciprocity and that his government had "had no communication with any foreign government upon the subject of these reductions." James and Lake cite speeches of backbench M.P.s such as Cobden in support of their case. However, these "British officials" can hardly be said to speak for the government. The only speech cited by a government member is by Home Secretary Sir James Graham.[13] However, this speech was made on March 26, 1846, long after the decision to repeal. This is thin evidence indeed that an attempt to influence U.S. tariff policy predominantly motivated the British government.

There was no sound basis to believe that reciprocity would be forthcoming. Indeed, Britain's geographical location meant that transportation costs from North America kept the price of imported grain artificially high for a generation.[14] Finally, the James and Lake thesis raises questions about the timing of Corn Law repeal. If repeal was a function of Britain's seeking to exploit its comparative advantage in manufactured goods, then why did repeal not occur until 1846? Industrialization had been under way in Britain for over half a century.[15] James and Lake offer no compelling arguments to account for this time lag.

Another prominent explanation for Corn Law repeal is that the shifting class balance of power after 1832 weakened the aristocracy's control in the framing of public policy. This argument usually is made in the context of "specific factors" theory, which holds that certain factors (capital and agriculture) are industry-specific, whereas others (labor) are mobile. Factors specific to importing sectors favor protectionism, whereas those specific to exporting sectors pursue free trade. From this perspective, overrepresentation of the landed classes in Parliament prior to 1832 ensured the maintenance of the Corn Laws.[16] However, in the aftermath of the Reform Act, greater representation of the industrial classes caused the composition of Parliament to change. Elimination of agricultural protection became inevitable.

Schonhardt-Bailey is critical of the specific factors explanation on two counts.[17] First, she suggests that the class composition of Parliament did not turn over quickly enough between 1832 and 1846 to justify such a radical shift in trade policy. Indeed, the vast majority of members in the 1841–1846 Parliament were from the landed classes. Second, she questions the specificity of factor holdings in early Victorian Britain. She finds evidence of considerable portfolio diversification during this era, especially after 1825, with the emergence of an active capital market coupled with the expansion of exports in mining and heavy industry. This expansion was aided by the railway boom of the 1830s and 1840s. As a result, by the early Victorian era, many among the landed classes had greatly increased their holdings in nonagricultural stock.[18] The implication is that, by the 1840s, the landed aristocracy no longer relied solely on agriculture for its wealth. As a result, demands for agricultural protection, if not muted, became less vociferous. It is important to note that not all of the landed classes were equally diversified. Tenant farmers and landowners on the verge of insolvency were notably undiversified. Schonhardt-Bailey, therefore, suggests that M.P.s from regions featuring greater proportions of diversified landowners were more likely than those from undiversified regions to support repeal.

Schonhardt-Bailey makes an important contribution to solving the mystery of repeal. Decreasing resistance to agricultural protectionism as a result of portfolio diversification, for example, may help to explain why the repeal bill passed so quickly through the House of Lords in 1846 (there are also other explanations for this, discussed below). There are, however, numerous problems with the hypothesis. Perhaps the most serious is that it constitutes economic reductionism. In the absence of strong opposition to repeal within their constituencies, M.P.s are assumed likely to vote against agricultural protection. But this logic holds only if M.P.s were primarily concerned with fulfilling their representative function. It makes few allowances for ideological considerations, such as the belief that agricultural protection constituted a fundamental component of the social order and that repeal therefore struck a blow against aristocratic supremacy. A more important point is that this logic ignores the role of parties. While parties still meant rather loose coalitions in the 1840s, the Whigs' remarkable cohesiveness on the issue of repeal suggests that partisan considerations played some role. Schonhardt-Bailey does not control for the effects of party.

The absence of ideological and partisan considerations leaves numerous questions unanswered. For example, Schonhardt-Bailey cannot explain why the Peel government (under no illusions as to its fate)[19] committed what amounts to political suicide. Similarly, she cannot explain why the Whigs waited until November 1845 before changing party policy and (almost unanimously) supporting repeal. It is too much of a coincidence to suppose that almost all Whigs came from highly diversified regions and that they recognized the need for repeal at virtually the same moment Peel did. Finally, there is no explanation for why the great shift on repeal occurred so rapidly, between 1841 and 1846, in the absence of a general election and during a period of only moderate economic growth that was unlikely to have encouraged further portfolio diversification.[20]

A final attempted explanation for the repeal of the Corn Laws focuses on the role of pressure groups, most notably the Anti–Corn Law League. The League certainly exerted constant and unrelenting pressure on the government during the early and mid-1840s. However, contrary to pressure group–based arguments, there is little evidence that, in and of itself, the League generated sufficient popular enthusiasm for free trade to compel the government to repeal the Corn Laws.[21] The record of League-sponsored candidates in parliamentary by-elections was mediocre. Moreover, while industrial elites certainly represented the financial foundation of the League, there is little to suggest terribly widespread business support. Petitions to the Board of Trade in the mid-1840s, for example, suggest that businesses were more likely to seek tariff reductions on specific commodities than on imports in general. Indeed, Cobden himself believed that, in the face of continued opposition by Peel, repeal would not have carried, at least not without the creation of a broader-based coalition.[22]

In contrast to existing explanations, this chapter argues that repeal was a rational calculation that served as a preemptive strike against popular agitation for reform. The assumption of political rationality on the part of Peel, whose career was ruined by repeal, is counterintuitive. Yet, understood in the context of Peel's abiding commitment to preservation of the aristocratic order, his actions in repealing the Corn Laws are more readily comprehensible. Thus, in the context of the model set out in chapter 1, Peel represents the political entrepreneur engaged in a game of alignment (and hence institutional) preservation.

Peel as Political Entrepreneur

By 1845, Peel had come to fear for the integrity of aristocratic government in Britain. The extension of the franchise under the 1832 Reform Act had temporarily appeased the middle class but had not altered the fundamental balance of power between the landed and the industrial classes. By the 1840s, however, aristocratic dominance of both polity and economy had become a serious anachronism. The former was still widely acceptable; the latter was not. Indeed, the system of agricultural protection retarded industrial development to an extent that was intolerable to organizations such as the Anti–Corn Law League. Although the League was not powerful enough on its own to change government policy, both Peel and Cobden realized that, by the mid-1840s, the League possessed the resources and organizational capacity to mobilize the urban underclasses to press for democratic reforms, such as the extension of the franchise to the working class and the abolition of the House of Lords. Although the League had no ostensible desire for these ends, it recognized that such an outcome would be disastrous for Peel and others committed to the preservation of the constitutional status quo. The story of Corn Law repeal is, therefore, in large part, the story of Cobden and the Anti–Corn Law League's ability to convince Peel that the aristocracy could not retain control of both the economy and the polity in Britain. If the aristocracy tried to do so, it was likely to lose both—one to the inevitable wave of industrialization, the other to democratic reforms achieved through popular agitation and possible insurrection.

Corn Law repeal threatened more than just political costs for Peel, however. If repeal were mishandled—that is, if it were seen to be in reaction to popular agitation—the result would be disastrous. It would signal that constitutional change was largely an extraparliamentary exercise. The incentive would be for increased popular (and perhaps revolutionary) agitation. Upon recognizing the necessity of reform, Peel was determined to ensure that the process occurred quickly and decisively. Although a proponent of institutional preservation Peel did not oppose reform per se; he regarded it instead as an occasional, necessary evil. However, under conditions where reform was deemed necessary, it was imperative that it be undertaken judiciously. Peel had a clear and consistent philosophy in this regard. He believed that the expansion of democracy should be checked; that conditions that had the potential to give rise to democratic agitation should be ameliorated in order to forestall this agitation; and that concessions dedicated to the prevention of democratic agitation should represent no threat to the Constitution.

To Peel, the great danger with institutional reform was that, once begun, it had the potential to be dictated by popular opinion. Democratic agitation tended to be impulsive, often seeking change for the sake of change. The ruling class had a responsibility, therefore, to temper the passion of the democratic impulse. Moreover, reform tended to feed on itself. As each successive, hastily instituted reform failed to satisfy the masses, the cry for greater and more extensive reform would be raised. Inevitably, badly conceived reforms would create new grievances, often without ameliorating the old. The result would be the steady erosion of faith in the constitutional order. It was for this reason, for example, that Peel had fought a rearguard battle against the 1832 Reform Act, even after its passage was assured. Peel wrote to Lord Harrowby on February 5, 1832:

> Why have we been struggling against the Reform Bill in the House of Commons? Not in the hope of resisting its final success in that House, but because we look beyond the Bill, because we know the nature of popular concessions, their tendency to propagate the necessity for further and more extensive compliances. We want to make the "descensus" as "difficilis" as we can—to teach young inexperienced men charged with the trust of government that, though they may be backed by popular clamour, they shall not override on the first springtide of excitement every barrier and breakwater raised against popular impulses; that the carrying of extensive changes in the Constitution without previous deliberation shall not be a holiday task . . . . Suppose that we had given way, that we had acquiesced in the Bill, and given no trouble to the Ministers. My firm belief is that the country, so far from being satisfied with our concessions, would have lost all reverence and care for remaining institutions, and would have had their appetites whetted for a further feast at the expense of the Church, or the monarchy.[23]

On the other hand, when necessary, Peel considered it imperative that reforms reflect the sober, considered opinions of those most qualified to govern the nation. To entrust reform to the popular impulse was not only foolhardy, but an abdication of responsibility for the most sacred trust of government. As he stated after the Throne Speech of February 24, 1835, he would not be averse to reforming ancient institutions, under necessary circumstances, but would do so only in a climate of consensus and social harmony:

> You may reject my [government's] offers, you may prefer to do the same things by more violent means; but if you do, the time is not distant when you will find that the popular feeling on which you relied has deserted you, and that you will have no alternative but either again to invoke our aid—to replace the government in the hands from which you would now forcibly withdraw it—or to resort to that "pressure from without," to those measures of compulsion and violence which, at the same time that they render your reforms useless and inoperative, will seal the fate of the British Constitution.[24]

At heart Peel was a conservative. He believed that aristocratic rule and respect for the established order served the national interest. The French Revolution (only a generation removed during Peel's politically formative years), as well as the 1830 uprisings in Paris and Brussels, served continuously to underscore the fragility of established constitutions. In Britain, he believed, it was incumbent upon the ruling class to govern firmly and resist the tides of popular passion that ebbed and flowed over the political landscape. But he had little use for the custom of privilege if it came at the expense of undue suffering among the lower classes. Elites who turned a deaf ear to the legitimate complaints of the humbler classes put the security of the realm at risk by inviting popular uprisings and violence. The ruling class had a duty, therefore, to distinguish between passing flights of popular fancy and underlying, pathological faults in the system. The former were to be resisted firmly, the latter ameliorated rapidly. As Peel noted during the Reform Bill debates: "We are here to consult the interests, and not to obey the will, of the people, if we honestly believe that will conflict with those interests." This balanced approach would forestall any mass agitation with the potential to attract proponents of other social grievances, real or imagined, into an unruly confrontation with the defenders of the established order. He noted in his memoirs: "There is a wide distinction . . . between the hasty concession to unprincipled agitation, and provident precautions against the explosion of public feeling gradually acquiring the strength which will make it irresistible."[25]

The economic slump in the aftermath of the Napoleonic Wars was the impetus for a wave of popular demands for constitutional reform. Agitation peaked in 1819, and over the next four years, the majority of the opposition Whig party declared itself to be in favor of reform, including the extension of the franchise, and the disenfranchisement of nomination (or rotten) boroughs. However, by the mid-1820s popular support for reform had abated, and the reform movement was consigned to the margins of the political scene.[26]

The catalyst for the reemergence of the reform issue was the division among the Tories after the passage of the Catholic Emancipation Bill. The resentment ran so deep that many Ultra-Tories, convinced that it was the current system that had allowed the government to defy the popular will in eliminating Catholic disabilities, joined with the Whigs in the resuscitated reform movement. This schism in the antireform party was exploited by the Whigs. The party had a large incentive to change a system that had kept it from power for decades on end. Indeed, Croker estimated that of approximately 275 nomination boroughs, the Tories held over 200.[27]

Reform constituted much of the backdrop to the election of 1830. The election returned the Tories, albeit not overwhelmingly; and the composition of the new Parliament strengthened the position of the Whigs, leaving them poised to strike should the Wellington ministry falter. In November, Wellington—misreading the mood of Parliament—made it clear that his government would take a hard line against reform of any kind. The remark created a furore, and he resigned on November 16, 1830, with Lord Grey being asked to form a government. The Whigs' first attempt to pass a reform bill was defeated in the Lords and led to a dissolution in 1831. Upon being returned, the Whigs passed a second bill through the Commons, only to have that bill defeated in the Lords on October 8, 1831. Riots ensued, and political unions of middle- and working-class reformers began to arm themselves. On the third try, anticipating a sizable minority in the Lords, Grey tried unsuccessfully to commit King William IV to agree to create from fifty to sixty new peers if the bill met trouble in the upper house. William refused, and when the bill encountered difficulties in committee, Grey resigned. After the failure of Wellington to form a government, William, in desperation, acceded to Grey's demands, but the mere threat of creation of more peers was sufficient. On June 4, 1832, the Reform Bill finally passed the third reading in the Lords by a vote of 106 to 22.

For Peel, the Reform Act of 1832 constituted the quintessential example of "hasty concession to unprincipled agitation." He felt that the reformers of 1832 had committed an unforgivable blunder. By extending the franchise in response to what Peel believed to be but a transitory popular outcry, the Reform Act created a dangerous constitutional precedent: the perception that Parliament was susceptible to extraparliamentary agitation. Peel rejected the suggestion, made by leading reformers, that reform would entail a final settlement of the constitutional crisis. Instead, he argued, reform represented merely the thin end of the democratic wedge, and its passage would encourage other groups to press for constitutional reform. On March 24, 1831, he told the House:

> We are told that the chief merit of the scheme is that it is a final settlement. A final settlement!—it cannot be final. If the principles upon which it rests be good,—if the arguments which are its sole vindication be conclusive— they are conclusive against its being a settlement of the question of reform

. . . . When the noble lord [Stanley] says this settlement will be a final one, he is so far right, that probably for a short time, there may be a general wish, at least on the part of the reformers, to acquiesce in its provisions. The expectation of great benefits—gratitude for new privileges—the pleasure of novelty, may secure a short trial for the new Constitution. But these impressions will gradually grow weaker. The classes that are left unrepresented will begin to stir . . . and, with some justice inquire why they should be excluded from its benefits.

Similarly, on December 17, 1831, he stated, "I will continue my opposition to the last, believing as I do, that this is the first step, not directly to revolution, but to a series of changes that will affect the property, and totally change the character of the mixed Constitution of this country."[28]

Peel never believed that the Reform Act effectively preempted constitutional disruption. He felt that the means by which it was enacted—clumsily, with no attempt on the part of the reformers to ensure passage through the legislature before public expectations were raised—was inexcusable. In the end, the act passed as a means of quelling the popular passions its very promise had raised. Moreover, the process set a precedent. The Constitution no longer represented a bedrock, impervious to vicissitudes of popular opinion, flexible only to the point of ensuring good governance. Now it was an open book, waiting to be written by any group strong enough to manipulate the reins of public opinion. To ensure that the precedent would not be repeated, Peel moved to repeal the Corn Laws in 1846.

By 1845 the Anti–Corn Law League had succeeded in portraying the Corn Laws as both a symbol of aristocratic rule and the source of high bread prices.[29] This portrayal—combined with Peel's growing belief that the survival of the agricultural sector did not depend on the Corn Laws, and that the regulations imposed hardships upon the lower classes—convinced him that the status quo could have dangerous consequences. As yet, agitation over the Corn Laws was a middle-class phenomenon. However, despite the relative prosperity of the 1840s, the pitiful condition of the working classes in Britain had not improved appreciably. Moreover, perennial unrest in Ireland served as a reminder of just how volatile that nation remained. Peel recognized that a return to poor economic times could give rise to a new impetus for widespread constitutional reform, with the Corn Laws serving as the rallying point for all disaffected groups. Indeed, as Charles Greville's diary notes, some sentiment already existed within the

League to seek a broad coalition with other disaffected groups. Cobden, however, wisely counseled against such a course of action, preferring to use this tactic as a threat to compel Parliament to repeal.[30]

To grant economic or political concessions under such circumstances would appear too much like another 1832-style capitulation in the face of popular protest. In order to avoid this, Peel decided in the spring or summer of 1845 to launch a preemptive strike against the Corn Laws. Indeed, Peel believed that repeal would eliminate the need for the great engine of social agitation, the Anti–Corn Law League. As he noted on March 2, 1846:

> I cannot help thinking that whatever may be the menaces of continued agitation, that agitation would be of a very different character from that which would prevail if no attempt were made to adjust this question. . . . I think there are a great number of persons who would [upon repeal] withdraw from the Anti-Corn Law League—a great number of persons who would say that this is not an unreasonable settlement.

Graham was of the same opinion. In a letter to Croker of April 2, 1846, he wrote: "One of the great benefits and blessings which I anticipate from Repeal of the Corn Laws, is, that at last there is some hope of surviving the din of this odious and endless topic of democratic agitation." Peel and Graham were no doubt correct in this assessment. McCord quotes from a letter to J. B. Smith, circa February 1846, from the unpublished Cobden papers: "I am doubtful if we could find means to carry on the League if Peel's measures are carried—already people are countermanding their qualifications and talking of not paying further subscriptions."[31]

Peel also worried about the prospect of popular rebellion. He knew, as did the more astute members of Parliament, that a legislative body elected by a mere one-seventh of the male population ran the risk of being out of touch. A regime that considered, or was perceived to consider, only the interests of the voting population risked being overwhelmed by the masses if they ever mobilized politically. And this was the principal threat posed by the League. Unlike either of the great parties in Parliament, the League had the potential to draw political strength from, and stir political passions among, the unmobilized masses. That Peel recognized this threat is clear from his speech in the Commons of May 15, 1846:

> You may say, "Disregard the progress of public opinion; defy the League; enter into a combination against it; determine to fight the battle of protec-

tion, and you will succeed.". . . I will not hesitate to say my firm belief is, that it is most consistent with prudence and good policy, most consistent with the real interests of the landed proprietors themselves, most consistent with the maintenance of a territorial aristocracy, seeing by how precarious a tenure, namely, the vicissitudes of seasons, you hold your present protection system—I say, it is my firm belief that it is for the advantage of all classes, in these times of comparative comfort and comparative calm, to anticipate the angry discussions which might arise, by proposing at once a final adjustment of this question.

Finally, Peel feared the prospect of revolution. In a speech in the Commons on May 4, 1846, he cited Burke's distinction between the aristocracy of England and that of France in consulting public opinion. The English aristocracy, Burke had maintained, knew when to relinquish privilege, while the French did not.[32]

This comparison had clear implications to Parliament. Cobden too made veiled reference to the threat of revolution in a speech on March 13, 1845:

> You, gentlemen of England, the high aristocracy of England, your forefathers led my forefathers; you may lead us again if you choose; but though—longer than any other aristocracy—you have kept your power. . . . This is a new age; the age of social advancement, not of feudal sports; you belong to a mercantile age; you cannot have the advantage of commercial rents and retain your feudal privileges too. If you identify yourselves with the spirit of the age, you may yet do well; for I tell you that the people of this country look to their aristocracy with a deep-rooted prejudice—an hereditary prejudice, I may call it—in their favour; but your power was never got, and you will not keep it by obstructing that progressive spirit which is calculated to knit nations more closely together by commercial intercourse; if you give nothing but opposition to schemes which almost give life and breath to inanimate nature, and which it has been decreed shall go on, then you are no longer a national body.[33]

Peel's reaction to the news of the revolution in Paris of April 1848 illustrates that he had considered the possibility of revolution in the mid-1840s. With heavy irony his memoirs note that, after the poor harvests of 1846 and 1847, many Britons reflected on the fortuity that the Corn Laws had, after all, been repealed:

Many of the men who had been the loudest in the condemnation of the measures of 1846, and the least scrupulous in imputing dishonesty and treachery to the advisers of them, openly rejoiced on the 10th of April, 1848 that provision had been made (by a lucky accident, of course) for the total repeal of the Corn Laws. . . . On the removal of all danger from popular disaffection, or, I should rather say, on the signal proof of general contentment and devotion to the cause of order, the admissions made as to the causal good-fortune of the measures referred to were speedily retracted. They were retracted without due reflection on the causes which had conspired in the hour of danger to promote loyalty to the Throne and confidence in the justice of Parliament.

Similarly, Cobden recounts Peel's response upon being informed of the 1848 revolution: "This comes of trying to govern the country through a narrow representation in Parliament, without regarding the wishes of those outside. It is what this [Conservative] party behind me wanted to do in the matter of the Corn Laws, and I would not do it."[34]

While democratic agitation and its inherent potential for violence or revolution worried him greatly, Peel saw it as imperative that change not be perceived (as it had in 1832) as capitulation by government to the popular will.[35] This was merely akin to the abolition of the existing order by more gradual means. For that reason, when Peel decided to eliminate agricultural protection, he did so on the pretext of an external crisis. The crisis took the form of the Irish potato failure.

The Perception of Crisis

One of the most enduring myths of the era is that the Irish potato crisis necessitated the repeal of the Corn Laws. Peel made this claim in the autumn of 1845, as a means to overcome opposition to Corn Law repeal, and thus to preempt what he saw as a much more serious possibility: the threat of organized mass rebellion. Such an argument, though specious, convinced a number of Peel's allies that repeal was necessary. For example, certain that the Irish crisis doomed the Corn Laws, the Duke of Wellington confided to Greville: "Rotten potatoes have done it all; they put Peel in his damned fright."[36]

With hindsight, however, it is clear that repeal of the Corn Laws did little to alleviate the crop shortage in Ireland. The legislation sought to phase out the Corn Laws over a three-year period. This alone should dispel the notion that a desire to ameliorate the crisis was the sole motivation for repeal. It is not clear how opening the ports would have aided the Irish peasantry. The peasantry relied largely on the potato crop for subsistence and, with the failure of the crop, had limited purchasing power for wheat at any price. Finally, even if the Corn Laws had been suspended, wheat prices would not have fallen immediately. Henry Goulburn, a member of his cabinet, made this point to Peel well before repeal:

> I fairly own that I do not see how the repeal of the Corn Law is to afford relief to the distress with which we are now threatened. I quite understand that if we had never had a Corn Law, it might be argued that we should now have a larger supply in our warehouses, or that from the encouragement given by a free trade in corn to the growth of it in foreign countries, we should have had a larger fund on which to draw for a supply. But I think it next to impossible to show that the abandonment of the law now could materially affect this year's supply, or give us any corn which will not equally reach us as the law stands.

Croker was more blunt in a letter to Graham: "[T]hat Ireland has had anything to do with the grand convulsion that has overturned the edifice that we were all so proud of having erected in 1841, I cannot concede. Ireland has had no more to do with it than Kamschatka."[37]

Peel's use of the Irish crisis as a pretext for repeal becomes obvious from the way he handled the crisis. He informed the cabinet in November of his desire to suspend the Corn Laws and of his doubts that, once suspended, they could be reinstated. (The decision had been reached weeks earlier, as Peel's correspondence with Graham and the Lord-Lieutenant of Ireland, Lord Heytesbury, indicates).[38] However, while it may have been true that suspension of the Corn Laws was tantamount to repeal, it was scarcely incumbent upon him to conflate the issues, as he did in announcing legislation to repeal the Corn Laws in January 1846. Given precedents for suspension of the Corn Laws during times of famine, Peel would have been justified in suspending them for the duration of the crisis and then dealing with the issue of reinstatement at some later point.

As noted, however, the Irish crisis served a purpose for Peel, in that it provided a pretext for emergency debate on the Corn Laws. Peel undoubtedly sought to use the specter of popular agitation in Ireland in order to frighten Parliament into repealing the Corn Laws. But events overtook this strategy. Whig leader Lord John Russell, attempting to spark division within the Tory cabinet, committed his party to repeal. With the support of the Whigs ensured, Peel was free to disregard powerful opposition within his own party and to introduce repeal legislation early in the session of 1846.

The Facilitating Coalition

Peel had at best a fragile facilitating coalition, lasting only long enough to see the Corn Laws repealed before internal contradictions broke it apart. By December 1845, controversy over the possibility of Corn Law repeal had produced outright rebellion in Conservative ranks. Indeed, Peel could count on the continued support of only a small number of "Peelite" Tories. He was forced, therefore, to rely on three principal allies in his endeavors to preserve the British Constitution: the Whig party, the aristocracy in the House of Lords, and the Anti–Corn Law League. The construction of such an unlikely alliance—as he all the while was fighting a rearguard battle within his own party—required tremendous political skill, as Peel maneuvered the components into position over the winter of 1845.

By mid-November 1845, Peel had still not committed to Corn Law repeal. He had made his desire for repeal known within the cabinet but, with the significant opposition among his colleagues, chose not to force the issue. The real catalyst for repeal was an open letter from Russell to his London constituents, openly committing the Whigs to repeal. In Greville's words, the letter "fell like a spark on a barrel of gunpowder." Lord Cottenham's letter to Russell on December 2, 1845, alludes to the troubles he believed Russell's letter caused Peel and is typical of the reaction of certain leading Whigs: "I rejoiced in the opinion it expressed, and in the happy opportunity you had taken of publishing it; neither too soon nor too late, but just at the moment most destructive of the proposals of the one party, and most wanted by the other, and best calculated to forward the course you think ought to be pursued." On the other hand, as a letter of April 5, 1846, from Charles Arbuthnot to Peel suggests, many Whigs were very angry upon the publication of Russell's letter, feeling it represented a foolhardy shift in policy.[39]

In many ways, the Whigs were the natural party to repeal the Corn Laws. Russell's letter made him the first party leader to commit himself publicly to repeal. Traditionally the "progressive" party, the Whigs were aware that, under Peel's premiership, they had been forced to react to a series of Tory initiatives. As Disraeli had joked, Peel "caught the Whigs bathing, and walked away with their clothes. He has left them in the full enjoyment of their liberal position, and he is himself a strict conservative of their garments."[40] However, the motive of the Whigs in supporting repeal seems to have had at least as much to do with electoral politics as with political conviction.

It is not overly cynical to question Russell's timing. Certainly there was pressure to repeal from the Radicals within his party, but this pressure had existed since 1839. The suggestion by the editor of his memoirs that the Irish potato crisis prompted the change is also without basis.[41] As noted, repeal could not have ameliorated the Irish crisis in the short run. Finally, it has been argued that the remarkable consensus on the issue demonstrated by the Whigs indicates that the party recognized the need to make concessions to the masses in order to safeguard the status of the aristocracy.[42] This argument is plausible, but it begs two questions. First, why were Whig backbenchers more perspicacious than the majority of their Tory counterparts on the constitutional issue? Second, what accounts for the coincidence that Russell's conversion to repeal was so closely timed to Peel's?

There is not any one explanation for Russell and the Whigs' conversion to repeal. There is no doubt that to some extent the Whigs were motivated by the desire to safeguard the Constitution. However, the Whigs also recognized that, in taking action to preserve the Constitution, an opportunity arose to split the Tory party, to the electoral advantage of the Whigs. The finer points of political economy were beyond the ken of most backbenchers; the political strategy of divide and conquer was not.

However, Russell nearly overplayed his hand in the fall of 1845. Upon publication of Russell's letter, Peel insisted that the cabinet acquiesce on the issue of repeal. Although most went along reluctantly, Peel, claiming inadequate government support, resigned on December 5, 1845. Peel's resignation put Russell in an untenable position. Although the Whig leader had sought to sow dissension within government, he clearly had no wish to take responsibility for passing repeal legislation. Indeed, given the composition of the House of Lords, he could hardly have succeeded.

Russell agonized for more than two weeks before informing the Queen that he would be unable to accede to her request to undertake an administration. Officially, he failed because Lord Grey refused to sit in a cabinet with Lord Palmerston as foreign secretary. However, that this was sufficient to prevent his forming a government suggests strongly that Russell was not enthusiastic about accepting what Monypenny calls the "poisoned chalice." Peel also rejected Russell's weak excuse to the Queen. In his memoirs he notes: "I need not refer further to this point, because there must be in existence a more full and authentic record of the causes which induced Lord John Russell to abandon the attempt to form a Government than any which I can supply."[43]

The causes about which Peel would not speculate are evident in Russell's correspondence in the aftermath of his decision not to form a government. The Duke of Bedford wrote to Russell on December 19: "I know not when I have felt so happy. The Duchess could not think what had come over me. I was ready to jump out of my skin." Lord Minto wrote to Russell on December 21: "I hope I may now safely congratulate you upon your relief from the most hopeless undertaking to which any man ever devoted himself." Lord Lansdowne wrote to Russell on December 30: "It is good for you and for all to be out of the mess this time on any terms." And finally, Russell himself wrote to his wife: "Power may come some day or other in a less odious form."[44]

With Russell's failure, Peel demonstrated that he alone was capable of forming a government, which gave him enormous leverage in the House of Lords. The aristocracy, despite their loathing the prospect of repeal, had no desire for a general election to be fought over such a divisive issue in the winter of 1846. Moreover, Peel had convinced Wellington that repeal was the only sound course. Despite personal convictions that the Corn Laws should be maintained, Wellington deferred to Peel. The duke's status in the House of Lords made his support for Peel's repeal legislation decisive.[45] Indeed, Wellington piloted repeal through the House of Lords so skillfully that it passed without division.

Peel's actions of December 1845 were those of a cautious, skillful political entrepreneur. Although Whig support after November 22 would probably have permitted repeal, Peel wanted to be certain that cabinet and Parliament realized that there existed no alternative to a Peel government. Peel's memoirs recall that he accepted Queen Victoria's invitation, on December 20, to form a government without even consulting his erstwhile cabinet:

> I informed Her Majesty that, considering that Lord Stanley and those of my colleagues who had differed from me had positively declined to undertake the formation of a Government, and that Lord John Russell, having had the

concurrence and support of all his political friends, with a single exception, had abandoned the attempt to form one, I should feel it my duty, if required to do so by Her Majesty, to resume office. If such were Her Majesty's pleasure, I humbly advised Her Majesty to permit me to decide at once upon the resumption of it, and to be enabled to announce to my late colleagues, on my return to London, that I had not hesitated to re-accept the appointment of First Minister. I thought I should speak with much greater authority if I was to invite them to support me in an effort which I was determined, and which I had positively undertaken to make, than if I were to return to London, apparently undecided, for the purpose of asking their opinion as to the propriety of making that effort.

He sought to ensure, in other words, that the error of 1832, proposing reform with no assurance of success, was avoided. He wrote to Lord Aberdeen in 1847: "In December 1845, I thought repeal indispensable to the public welfare, and to the real interests and security of the Protectionists themselves. Being of that opinion, every consideration became subordinate to the carrying of repeal. I was determined to carry it, for failure after proposing it would have involved this country in most serious evils."[46]

Logrolling: Repeal and Preservation

With the support of the Whigs and the aristocracy in the House of Lords, the final component of Peel's facilitating coalition was the Anti–Corn Law League. Cobden understood Peel better than did most of the prime minister's political allies. He recognized that Peel was frightened by the prospect of popular rebellion; and that such rebellion was not inconceivable. A return to hard economic times and the mobilization of discontented groups such as the working classes or the Irish could, as in 1832, force the government into considerable constitutional concessions. There was only one organization with the resources and organizational capacity to mobilize such discontent, and that was the Anti–Corn Law League.

The increasing strength of the League after 1842 is testimony to its organization and to the futility of Peel's first attempt to mitigate extraparliamentary agitation with his 1842 Corn Law. Even strong harvests in the years from 1842 to 1845 did not prevent the steady expansion of the League's growth and influence. In addition to extraparliamentary agitation, the League recognized the importance of carrying the battle to the parliamentary arena. Its decision in 1841 to seek places for members in the House of

Commons had been important to the League's early success. By 1844, the electoral strategy was extended to take advantage of reforms enacted in 1832, which enfranchised any man who could secure (usually at a cost of between 35 and 60 pounds) a 40-shilling freehold in the countryside. In what became known as its registration campaign, the League actively encouraged its (mostly urban) supporters to qualify as county voters by securing freeholds. (In this way the League sought to take advantage of the so-called Chandos clause in the Reform Act, which was designed to make it easier for tenant farmers to achieve voting requirements and thus prevent too great a shift in the balance of electoral power to the urban classes.) Moreover, the League was diligent in its efforts to raise technical objections to the voting qualifications of protectionists and was able to remove many from the voting rolls. Despite the intensity of the campaign, however, League-sponsored candidates still lost most of the by-elections they contested.

Recognizing the logistical difficulties of securing, in its own right, a free trade majority in the House of Commons, the League focused its efforts in 1845 and 1846 on persuading one of the existing parties to reverse its policy of support for the Corn Laws. For reasons already discussed, the Whigs were the logical party for the League to target. However, the League suspected the Whig leadership of harboring a greater commitment to the love of office than to free trade.[47] Thus, it was Peel to whom the League turned. Indeed, Cobden felt not only that Peel was the most effective vehicle for the advancement of free trade, but that he was increasingly disposed to repeal.[48] From the spring of 1845, the League actively sought first to convert Peel to free trade and then, after his conversion, to support him in Parliament.

The support of the League in convincing Parliament of the consequences of intransigence on the Corn Laws issue—though underplayed by many analysts—was critical to the success of repeal. Once committed to repeal, Peel benefited greatly from the assistance rendered him in Parliament by Cobden. Both Peel and Cobden recognized that the glue holding together the fragile government coalition was the democratic "Sword of Damocles" hanging over the head of Parliament. Although content to maintain the constitutional structure of aristocratic rule, Cobden impressed upon Parliament that he would sacrifice the Constitution if the need arose. In the House of Commons, on February 27, 1846, he issued his starkest warning, threatening to mobilize support for a broad extension of the franchise if Parliament did not acquiesce on the issue of the Corn Laws:

Probably you are not aware on what a very narrow basis this power of yours rests. But I can give you some information on the subject. There are about 150,000 tenants who form the basis of your political power, and who are distributed throughout the counties of this country. Well let it come to the worst; carry on the opposition to this measure for three years more; yet there is a plan in operation much maligned by some hon. Gentlemen opposite, and still more maligned in another place [the House of Lords], but which, the more the shoe pinches, the more we like it out of doors. . . . But you say that the League is purchasing votes and giving away the franchise. No, no; we are not quite so rich as that; but be assured that if you prolong the contest for three or four years (which you cannot do) if, however, it comes to the worst, we have the means in our power to meet the difficulty, and are prepared to use them. Money has been subscribed to prepare our organization in every county, and we are prepared to meet the difficulty, and to overcome it. *You may think that there is something repulsive to your notion of supremacy in all this.*[49]

The menace to Parliament in these words is unmistakable. Cobden understood as well as Peel where the League's true strength lay. In allying his organization informally with the government, Cobden recognized that his role was to demonstrate to Parliament the credible constitutional threat that extraparliamentary agitation embodied. Cobden wrote to a supporter, James Mellor, on March 5, 1846: "I have no reason to doubt that my speech was just what Peel desired. Nay, even in the Commons, it is quite necessary to shake the rod of democracy in their faces, to terrify them from the thoughts of a *compromise.*"[50] Similarly, he wrote to Henry Ashworth on February 19, 1846:

It is the League, and it only, that frightens the Peers. It is the League alone which enables Peel to repeal the law. But for the League the aristocracy would have hunted Peel to a premature grave, or consigned him like Lord Melbourne to a private station at the bare mention of total repeal. We must hold the same rod over the Lords until the measure is safe.[51]

Conclusion

This chapter has focused upon the mystery of Peel's motivations to undertake the seemingly irrational decision to repeal the Corn Laws. Corn Law repeal emerges as a by-product of larger objectives, in particular Peel's desire to preserve the integrity of aristocratic government in the face of potential agitation by groups dissatisfied with the status quo. Corn Law repeal represents an excellent illustration of the high-risk model outlined in chapter 1. Trade liberalization was the most contentious issue of the 1840s in Britain. Indeed, almost the whole of Peel's political power base—the British aristocracy—opposed repeal. It is clear from Peel's memoirs that he understood this point, and that he expected his government to fall over the issue. Thus, trade policy scholars have long struggled with the question, Why did Peel repeal the Corn Laws?

This chapter suggests that repeal emerged as a by-product of Peel's overarching objective in the 1840s—the perceived imperative to maintain the electoral and institutional status quo in the face of anticipated, potentially revolutionary, popular agitation. To achieve this end, Peel constructed a facilitating coalition in Parliament. However, critical to the success of the endeavor was to ensure that the one organization with the logistical capacity to foment and mobilize popular unrest—the Anti–Corn Law League—would not undermine the objective. As Cobden was able to signal to Peel, as well as the more astute members of the House of Commons and the House of Lords, his price for preserving the social peace was Corn Law repeal.

The repeal of the Corn Laws is considered by many to be the harbinger of British hegemony. Certainly the years of prosperity that followed helped secure Britain's position as a world power. But equally important is the point that repeal preserved aristocratic government (as embodied in the British Constitution) both in its content—the franchise was not extended for a generation, and even then without great change to existing institutions—and in its incrementalist nature.

Insofar as it served to expand the franchise in the face of extraparliamentary agitation, the Reform Act of 1832 represented for Peel a dangerous precedent. There was no logical reason, in the aftermath of this settlement, that other groups might not seek to extract similar constitutional demands. By the mid-1840s, Peel had become anxious about the state of the polity. The plight of the working classes remained woeful, despite legislation aimed at ameliorating their living standards; there was still considerable unrest in Ireland; and, most worrying, long years of agitation on the part of the Anti–Corn Law League for repeal of the Corn Laws had transformed that body into a well-organized, well-financed source of pressure. Although unable to generate enough popular support among the electorate to secure free trade, the League (and Peel recognized it) represented a focal point that, in the event of economic crisis, threatened to unite and intensify social disaffection. In order to forestall this apprehended agitation, Peel used the pretext of the potato crop failure in Ireland to construct a facilitating coalition in which preservation of aristocratic government was logrolled with repeal of the Corn Laws.

The Anti–Corn Law League was the most important component of Peel's facilitating coalition. There was no formal arrangement between the government and the League, but each understood the other's position. Peel would enact the policy goals of the League in return for an end to extra-parliamentary agitation. For its part, the League—and especially Cobden—understood that Peel's position would be strengthened by consistent reminders to Parliament (and especially the aristocracy) that the League possessed the wherewithal to organize massive opposition to the constitutional status quo.

The role of the Whigs was almost as important. It was this party, remarkably cohesive on the issue of Corn Law repeal, that supplied Peel with his legislative majority in the House of Commons. It is impossible to say whether apprehension over the crisis in Ireland would have allowed Peel to have repealed the Corn Laws without the support of the Whigs. What is clear, however, is that only after Lord John Russell's public declaration of support for Corn Law repeal on November 22, 1845, did Peel insist in cabinet upon the imperative to suspend and repeal the Corn Laws. Indeed, Greville, with characteristic perceptiveness, noted in his diary as early as December 5 that, contrary to popular belief, Russell's letter had in fact served Peel's interests.[52] Peel's decision on December 5 to resign, ostensibly on the issue of Corn Law suspension, and to return to office upon the failure of the Whigs to form a government underscored to Parliament that he alone could pass repeal legislation. Having demonstrated this, Peel was able to rely on the support of the Whigs in the House of Commons and of the aristocracy in the House of Lords.

3

THE NEW DEAL, THE WELFARE STATE, AND FREE TRADE

The American New Deal produced the country's most significant electoral realignment of the twentieth century. Much analysis of the New Deal realignment, not surprisingly, focuses on the creation of the welfare state. However, an equally important aspect of the New Deal realignment concerns the shift to internationalism, embodied most significantly in the Reciprocal Trade Agreements Act (RTAA) and its immediate aftermath. This chapter explains President Franklin D. Roosevelt's risky decision to abandon economic nationalism during the mid-1930s. As in the other cases examined in this book, trade liberalization was enacted as a means to a larger end. In this case, Roosevelt sought to institutionalize the political support of the agricultural sector, the urban underclasses, and a large segment of the financial and industrial sectors, by logrolling domestic interventionism and international liberalism. In short, Roosevelt's facilitating coalition was a prototype of what Ruggie calls the postwar compromise of "embedded liberalism."[1]

. . .

As early as the Tariff Act of 1816, rent-seekers were active, and usually successful, in lobbying Congress for high barriers to imports. Indeed, most of the nineteenth century was characterized by substantial rates of protection. By the twentieth century, protectionism was well entrenched both institutionally, through congressional tariff-making, and through the orientation of the business community. In fact, the so-called System of '96, an electoral realignment that saw the Republican party dominate from 1896 to 1932, entailed almost universal support from business for the protectionist and tight-money platform of the Republican party.[2]

Prior to American entry into World War I, a slight liberalizing trend, supported by an emerging export-oriented sector, led to the 1913 Underwood Tariff and, three years later, to the establishment of the Tariff Commission. The Underwood Tariff lowered import protection slightly. However, as Goldstein notes, Underwood "was a low-tariff act in a protectionist era."[3] And the trend was short-lived. Instead, the Tariff Commission—the original mandate of which was to provide a counterweight to protectionist special interests in the tariff-making process—became an instrument of protectionists.

The commission was intended as an alternative to (self-interested) producer groups as a source of information for Congress. In addition, after 1922 the commission was responsible for tendering advice to the president on the implementation of the "flexible tariff"—a new presidential power that allowed him to raise or lower tariffs on specific items to appropriate levels. Appropriate levels were taken to be those that equalized production costs between foreign and domestic producers.[4] The Tariff Commission's mandate was problematic on three counts. First and most obvious, the cost-of-production equalization principle was inherently protectionist, in effect serving to institutionalize compensation for comparative and competitive disadvantage. Second, because the determination of production costs at home and abroad for even a single item was so time-intensive, the commission could provide only very specialized information on a narrow range of products. Third, the commission proved little use as a counterweight to special interests, because, although the elected Congress had great incentive to heed the advice of voting constituents, it had relatively little to listen to that of Tariff Commission bureaucrats.

The ineffectiveness of the Tariff Commission was not the only factor leading to increased protectionism during the 1920s.[5] Republican control of the presidency and Congress stimulated a return to higher tariffs and economic nationalism, as did depressed agricultural prices at home and depreciated currencies abroad. Similarly, despite the war's role in increasing the competitiveness of certain American industrial and financial interests globally (which created some pressure to lower tariffs), new infant industries (or "war babies") joined the battle for protectionism. The full force of this rising protectionism was manifested in the Smoot-Hawley Tariff of 1930.

Smoot-Hawley represents the zenith of American protectionism in the twentieth century. Under Smoot-Hawley, tariffs reached an ad valorem average of 54 percent.[6] Originally introduced as a means of compensating farmers for existing levels of industrial protection, the eighteen-month bargaining process deteriorated into a virtual bazaar for state-supplied rents. Congressional tariff-making based on information provided by self-interested economic lobbyists inspired what Cordell Hull described as "a continuous round of political and legislative debauches with graft afore-thought."[7]

Smoot-Hawley accelerated the decline of a world already in the grips of severe economic depression. America's trading partners, deeply in debt due to war loans and tight lending practices in the United States after 1928, had relied on export-led growth as a means of remaining economically solvent. The closing of the U.S. market preempted this strategy and compelled other countries to retaliate in kind. As a result, world exports fell by 50 percent between 1928 and 1932. U.S. exports declined by 66 percent over the same period. In the domestic realm, U.S. Gross National Product (GNP) fell from $104 billion in 1929 to $58 billion three years later. Unemployment increased thirtyfold.

In 1934 Roosevelt formally requested an amendment to Smoot-Hawley known as the Reciprocal Trade Agreements Act.[8] Although its effects were not felt immediately (in part because Roosevelt, in the spring of 1934, was not fully committed to internationalism), the RTAA and its aftermath constitute a watershed in American trade policy, marking the start of a free trade era in the United States that continues to the present.[9] The RTAA sought to redress the negative effects of excessive protectionism, representing a significant departure from a number of past practices. Under the terms of the legislation, tariffs could be reduced by no more than 50 percent. In addition, a "peril point" clause obliged the Tariff Commission to determine the point below which tariff reductions would cause undue harm, and therefore must not be allowed to fall. Finally, an "escape clause" allowed the government to withdraw trade concessions if domestic interests could show that liberalization had caused (or threatened to cause) serious injury.

Of these changes to past practices, two especially are worthy of note.

First, while the flexible tariff provision of 1916 was retained, the RTAA abrogated the aforementioned cost-equalization principle in the determination of tariff rates. Henceforth, tariffs could be reduced on grounds of economic efficiency, with tariff reductions serving to stimulate international trade. Second, tariff-making authority passed from the legislative to the executive branch. In this way the pernicious consequences of congressional logrolling could be avoided in the setting of tariff rates, and the role of interest groups was severely curtailed. Under the old system of congressional tariff-making, interest groups played two crucial roles: first, applying pressure and, second, providing what amounted to a virtual monopoly on information concerning the effects of trade within each sector.

Both roles were mitigated with the RTAA. Under the new law, decisionmakers were far less susceptible to pressure from interest groups. Tariff-making authority was transferred from Congress, a vulnerable institution, to the more insulated executive branch. Moreover, the administrative arm of the RTAA—the Trade Agreements Committee (TAC)—operated its own information-gathering network, which provided a counterweight to testimony of less-than-partial producer groups in the determination of tariff rates. The TAC consisted of representatives of the departments of State, Agriculture, Commerce, and the Treasury, as well as the Tariff Commission. It was supported by a series of subcommittees. Whenever a trade agreement was proposed, a subcommittee was struck to examine trade between that country and the United States. In preparing reports for the TAC, each country subcommittee could draw on the resources of various commodity-specific subcommittees in order to determine the impact of commodity exchange.

Societal interests, however, were not completely shut out of the trade agreement process. Interested parties had the opportunity to testify before the president or a body designated by the president. It was for this reason that the Committee for Reciprocity Information was created. Before the formal negotiation of any trade agreement (although after the conclusion of preliminary negotiations), a notice of hearings by the Committee for Reciprocity Information was announced. The committee, consisting of high-ranking officials (most of them also sitting on the TAC), prepared a report for the TAC that reflected the opinions and concerns of affected societal interests. On the other hand, because public hearings were not conducted by the Committee for Reciprocity Information until after preliminary negotiations had taken place, the relevant subcommittee would have already undertaken comprehensive research on concessions to be granted and sought. As a result, testimony from societal interests could be evaluated in the light of existing information and knowledge. In addition, the RTAA contained a three-year sunset clause. Because the RTAA was subject to triennial renewals, interest groups had the opportunity to influence, and possibly overturn, the new trade policy process.

The RTAA was designed, as Haggard suggests, to increase "the costs of protectionist lobbying while decreasing the likelihood of success." However, opposition to the bill (as well as to passage of triennial renewal legislation) was fierce.[10] It is to explain the president's decision to risk the wrath not only of vested societal interests but also of actors within Congress and the administration that this analysis now turns.

Conventional Explanations for the RTAA

Existing explanations for the passage of the RTAA can be classified according to two broad groups. Statist and systemic-level explanations assume a proactive role for the American state, whereas societally based explanations conceptualize government as largely reactive.

Statist and systemic-level theorists alike seek to explain the RTAA in terms of state preferences. Analysts such as Tasca, Sayre, and Kindleberger, for example, suggest that the moral imperative of leading the international economy had become evident to U.S. policy-makers by the mid-1930s and had precipitated the enactment of internationally oriented policies such as the RTAA. Kindleberger condemns the United States for not taking the initiative to lead the world economy to recovery sooner than it did. Although he applauds the RTAA as being significant, he suggests that it was the exception to a sorry rule of economic isolationism during the 1930s.[11] Others such as Goldstein and Lake, less inclined to subscribe to the benevolence of the United States, suggest that the RTAA was an attempt to ameliorate the crisis triggered by the Smoot-Hawley tariffs, which had invited foreign retaliation and had therefore closed off export markets.

Similarly, Conybeare argues that the RTAA was a rational, albeit predatory, trade policy for the United States to undertake.[12] Export markets were opened, but imports were limited by extending concessions narrowly, and principally to small countries from which the United States could extract the optimal terms of trade. This is a contentious point. Although it is true that no reciprocal trade pacts were signed with a number of large countries (such as Germany, Italy, Spain, and the USSR), the limiting factor, it could be argued, was the political orientation of these governments, rather than optimal tariff calculations. Moreover, significant trade pacts were signed with Britain, Canada, and France. Finally, if the United States was truly concerned with limiting the scope of trade agreements, it would have been unlikely to include unconditional most-favored-nation clauses into the agreements that it signed.

Such explanations tend toward excessive reductionism. There are significant problems with "state-interest" theories (see chapter 1). The most important is that they lack a theory of domestic politics. The state is conceived as a single, rational actor, which acts in the "national interest." However, such analytical parsimony masks significant conceptual problems. States do not always act rationally in the national interest. If they did, free trade (for example) would be the rule and not the exception. Indeed, "states" rarely can act rationally because they must balance and aggregate narrow domestic interests. Moreover, the concept of the state itself is merely the reification of a number of often competing actors, who, given the opportunity, may choose to act in ways widely divorced from the national interest. In short, while rational-state theories may go part of the way toward explaining the international politics of trade liberalization, they ignore significant dimensions of the issue.

A second group of arguments holds that the RTAA was a function of shifts in the interests of significant societal actors. Ferguson and Frieden, for example, portray the RTAA as a victory of internationalist interests over nationalist ones.[13] Ferguson suggests that the New Deal represented the final breakdown of the System of '96. After World War I, a rift within the business community emerged between a protectionist, labor-intensive, nationalist bloc and a free-trading, capital-intensive, internationalist one. Ferguson argues that the internationalist bloc ultimately prevailed, by virtue of winning over the Democratic party and thereby realizing its policy objectives through policies such as the RTAA.

Frieden is more sensitive to the interaction between state and societal interests. He, too, documents the emergence of a nationalist bloc and an internationalist bloc after World War I. During the interwar era, each bloc aligned itself with a portion of the state apparatus: the internationalists with the State Department and the Federal Reserve System; the nationalists with the majority of the Congress and the Commerce Department. It was not until the national and international crises of the 1930s altered the relative influence of societal actors that the internationalist bloc emerged triumphant with the passage of such initiatives as the RTAA and the Tripartite Monetary Agreement (TMA)—a monetary stabilization accord between the United States, Britain, and France that tied the dollar to gold.

Frieden's analysis, though more sensitive to the interaction of state and societal forces than Ferguson's, still focuses too narrowly. The shift to internationalism by the Roosevelt administration is not explicable merely by the shifting balance of power among societal interests and, hence, among their respective allies within the state apparatus. Such an interpretation ignores a crucial component of the story: the proactive role played by Roosevelt in the construction of a New Deal coalition, which undertook considerable domestic reforms in the creation of a nascent welfare state. Indeed, the shift to internationalism coincided with a dramatic shift in Roosevelt's domestic policy—a shift marking the transition from the First to the Second New Deal.

In sum, the principal problem with much of the existing literature seeking to explain the RTAA is not that it provides an inaccurate portrayal but that it provides an incomplete one. Existing explanations provide important insights into the sources of the RTAA as a movement toward international liberalism in the United States during the New Deal era, but, in focusing only on the policy of international liberalism, such explanations fail to take into account concomitant, larger objectives of actors within the state. (Not all analysts of the RTAA are guilty of this. Haggard's argument is similar to that provided below, except that his "institutional game" involves the creation of international institutions in the postwar era.)[14] To be specific, existing explanations do not take into adequate consideration the role played by trade liberalization in assisting Roosevelt to realize his institutional objective: creation of the welfare state.

Roosevelt as Political Entrepreneur

Two principal objectives motivated Roosevelt upon assuming power in 1933. First, he sought to ensure national economic recovery. In addition to the normal concerns that every president experiences during times of economic distress, Roosevelt feared for the future of liberal democracy itself in the United States. Events elsewhere had convinced him that intensifying social and economic forces constituted a threat to capitalism and democracy.[15] Second, Roosevelt had a political agenda. He recognized that the Depression afforded the Democratic party an opportunity to overcome the minority party status it had endured since 1896. For the first three decades of the twentieth century, the Democratic coalition of northern urban bosses and southern agricultural elites rarely had attracted sufficient support to challenge Republican dominance in Congress. Nevertheless in 1932, Hoover's inability to deal effectively with the Depression produced a Democratic landslide in both congressional and presidential elections. Roosevelt took this opportunity to construct a new electoral alliance, which he sought to institutionalize into a full-scale realignment.

During the "First" New Deal, Roosevelt constructed a corporatist institutional structure, which was designed to secure the electoral support of the agricultural sector and much of the business community. Upon the failure of this coalition, Roosevelt changed tack dramatically. His "Second" New Deal involved two significant shifts. First, the Second New Deal featured a move to the left in order to capture the support of the urban poor. This involved altering Roosevelt's institutional priorities to entail the construction of the welfare state. Second, the New Deal moved away from economic nationalism—a move intended to attract the support of internationally oriented industry and finance.

Throughout the New Deal era, Roosevelt demonstrated ample skill as a political entrepreneur. His natural charm was of incalculable benefit in generating popular—and hence congressional—support. Nevertheless, Roosevelt also had a Machiavellian side and could utilize strong-arm tactics when the need arose. He was adept at logrolling issues within Congress. Roosevelt had relied on such a strategy when seeking to pass his Economy Bill of March 1933, for example, when he coupled this legislation with the prospect of the widely popular prohibition repeal. Indeed, as Brenner notes: "If Congressmen had doubts about some particular measure, they would vote for it anyway because they optimistically expected to be compensated, if necessary, by side payments to be received sometime in the future in some yet undetermined form."[16]

The heterogeneity of his facilitating coalitions meant that Roosevelt had to be cognizant of the necessity of balancing interests. This was accomplished through the passage of legislation designed to compensate one group for the negative consequences arising from satisfying the demands of another group.[17] Roosevelt's abilities as a political entrepreneur are perhaps best illustrated by the fact that, during the New Deal era, he was able to forge not one but two distinct coalitions in pursuit of his institutional objectives. Aimed at the construction of corporatist institutional structures, the First New Deal embodied two distinct philosophies: economic planning and economic nationalism.

To many of the president's closest advisers, the Depression seemed to indicate an abiding pathology within the domestic economy, and many within the administration believed that the government was obliged to become more proactive in resolving immanent economic problems. As one presidential adviser recalled, the movement to economic planning was "based on the assumption that the nation was not suffering a hangover from a single speculative orgy in 1932, but that it had chronic dyspepsia of its economic system." Economic planners felt that the causes of the Depression were domestic in origin, and the solutions would be found at home as well. To this end, Schlesinger notes, "they desired a nation where external controls could render internal planning safe from the economic tempests of the world outside."[18]

Two acts in particular—the National Industrial Recovery Act (NIRA) and the Agricultural Adjustment Act—typified the movement toward central planning under the First New Deal. These acts laid the groundwork for the reorganization of the American economy based upon corporatist accommodation of competing interests within the agricultural and industrial sectors. The National Recovery Administration (NRA) was set up to administer the NIRA, which passed into law on June 16, 1933. Its mandate was to ensure recovery through government-sanctioned and -supervised codes of fair competition for each industry. These codes (which were really little more than legally sanctioned industrial collusion) had the full force of law. Each was administered by a separate code authority and was designed to eliminate destructive competition, while introducing orderly regulation of production.

The NRA was faced with the enormous, and often ill-defined, task of replacing market forces in regulating the operation of industry; it came to have a staff of over three thousand and presided over the drawing up of over five hundred codes representing roughly 96 percent of U.S. industry.[19] Such a mandate ultimately led to conflict and confusion. As might be expected of an institution that relied heavily on the premise of voluntary cooperation, the NRA was ultimately doomed to collapse under the weight of its own internal conflicts. Many business leaders came to resent the intrusive role of government, especially as the economy began to recover slightly in early 1934. The NRA was weakened similarly by the growing rift between conservative, labor-intensive (nationalist) business and more progressive, capital-intensive (internationalist) industries. The latter sided with financial interests, already alienated by the nationalist thrust of the New Deal, to press for greater international economic cooperation. Thus it was long before the Supreme Court's Schechter decision of 1935, which found the NIRA unconstitutional, that most businesspersons had abandoned the NRA, thereby making that institution the most visible failure of the First New Deal.[20]

The Agricultural Adjustment Administration (AAA) was far more successful and remained an integral part of the Second New Deal coalition. The Agricultural Adjustment Act was designed to deal with the crippling crisis that had brought financial ruin to numerous farmers, and it proposed a means for farmers to return to a standard of living more in line with the standard they had enjoyed prior to World War I. (Farm incomes fell throughout the 1920s. In 1929, even before the onset of the Depression, the purchasing power of farmers was 91 percent of its pre–World War I level.)[21] The AAA was among the most successful of Roosevelt's innovations during the First New Deal. As farm incomes grew during the New Deal era, the expanded role of both the AAA and the Farm Bureau (the primary organization representing farmers) solidified the corporatist relationship. The agricultural sector remained firmly committed to Roosevelt even after the failure of the First New Deal and the creation of the Second.

That the AAA succeeded where the NRA failed is largely attributable to two important considerations. First, in spite of bureaucratic squabbles within the AAA, the organization enjoyed a secure administrative base. Unlike the NRA, it was not set up as an independent agency but, rather, was made a part of the Department of Agriculture. This provided a foundation from which the AAA could draw its expertise.[22] Second, the AAA and its major clientele group, the American Farm Bureau Federation, did not experience the same antagonism that characterized relations between the NRA and big business.

As the Depression deepened in the early 1930s, two schools of thought emerged on how best to salvage the domestic economy. Internationalists, largely in the financial sector but increasingly within industry as well, believed that economic recovery was retarded by the fragmentation of the world economy. Beggar-thy-neighbour monetary and trade practices kept the international economy locked in a downward spiral. The key to recovery, from this perspective, was to reverse the decline by fostering international cooperation by stabilizing currencies and reducing trade barriers. Nationalists, on the other hand, felt that currency controls and high tariffs could insulate the domestic market, thereby allowing the government to work for recovery at home without being captive to decision-makers abroad.[23] Roosevelt turned to nationalism during the First New Deal, largely because the nationalist course constituted the path of least (political) resistance, and because the majority of the business community was wedded to economic nationalism. Indeed, much American business was inward-looking during the New Deal era. The domestic market had absorbed 90 percent of manufactured output during the 1920s, and for most of the business community the temptation had not yet arisen to explore new markets.[24]

Roosevelt came to power just months before the scheduled World Economic Conference in London, which was designed to overcome the effects of the Depression by fostering international economic cooperation. The agenda included a return to the gold standard (Britain had gone off gold in 1931, while the United States did the same in April 1933), tariff reduction, and other means of international cooperation. However, the timing of the conference was poor and Roosevelt's domestic priorities doomed it almost from the start. The first blow fell on the eve of the conference, when Roosevelt sent word to Secretary of State Cordell Hull that he had decided against sending a trade reciprocity bill to Congress during the spring session for fear of endangering his domestic legislative program. The fate of the conference was sealed, later in the spring, when the dollar began to fall against the pound. This depreciation appeared to stimulate the domestic economy. As a result, Roosevelt, already reluctant to engage in monetary stabilization, grew even less inclined to strike a deal.[25]

The nationalist course followed at London had been charted well before and would be followed for the remainder of the year. The decision to abandon strict adherence to the gold standard had struck the first blow for nationalism and had alienated many within the financial community. However, tight-money policies were unpopular in the politically important agricultural sector. Moreover, within Congress a strong inflationist bloc had emerged. Unwilling to risk a battle in Congress and keen to secure the support of agriculture, Roosevelt supported an inflationary amendment to the Agricultural Adjustment Act. The so-called Thomas Amendment contained three principal components. It allowed the president to issue up to $3 billion in greenbacks—money not backed by precious metals. It allowed

AUGUSTANA UNIVERSITY COLLEGE
LIBRARY

him to remonetize silver by setting its price in terms of gold. Finally, it permitted the president to fix the gold content of the dollar by executive order.

With the failure of the London conference, the United States continued to pursue an inflationary monetary policy, abandoning any pretense of monetary cooperation. In the fall, Roosevelt devalued the dollar and began a controversial policy of purchasing gold in large quantities. The gold-purchasing plan had a stimulating effect on the U.S. economy but put extreme pressure on gold-backed currencies such as the French franc. Predatory U.S. monetary policy continued unabated until 1934. In January of that year the United States finally made minor concessions to international monetary stability with the passage of the Gold Reserve Act. Under the terms of the legislation, Roosevelt strengthened the link between the dollar and gold by fixing the value of the dollar at 59.06 percent of its last official gold value. The profits generated by devaluation of the currency were to go into a stabilization fund, which could then be used (albeit unilaterally) to stabilize foreign currencies.[26]

The Gold Reserve Act, although by no means a great concession, was the first glimmer of the internationalism that was to characterize the Second New Deal. By the early months of 1934, other harbingers of change appeared. The most significant were the growing disaffection of the business community toward the First New Deal, pressure from the left for Roosevelt to address the issue of social welfare, and the Reciprocal Trade Agreements Act.

The Requisite Crisis

Much as it had served as the catalyst for construction of the First New Deal coalition, the Great Depression stimulated the creation of the Second. It is dangerous to point to any single cause of something as complex as the Depression. However, it is safe to suggest that the Depression owed much of its severity to one colossal blunder—the Smoot-Hawley Tariff. War debts and reckless U.S. lending practices during the 1920s had led to a liquidity crisis for debtor-nations. Debt repayment required either the extension of new loans or the possibility of repayment in goods and services. As money markets grew tight after the crash of 1929, few nations could cope with higher interest rates, which thus precluded the feasibility of taking on greater debt (even if the option were available to them). In desperation, countries turned to their only viable option and sought to expand their export sectors.[27] The Smoot-Hawley Tariff, however, threw the international economy into disarray, and America's trading partners had no alternative but to retaliate.

Immediately following Roosevelt's inauguration in March 1933, the near collapse of the banking structure necessitated a special session of Congress. This session—the celebrated Hundred Days—witnessed the passage of substantial emergency legislation. Indeed, the severity of the crisis provided Roosevelt with a great degree of political maneuverability, which he sought to exploit from the start. In his inauguration speech, he announced that he intended to request from Congress "broad executive power to wage a war against the emergency as great as the power that would be given if we were in fact invaded by a foreign foe." For its part, Congress was eager to cooperate. Paralyzed by the magnitude of the crisis, Congress rarely demurred in delegating authority to newly created executive agencies. So severe was the Depression that any form of action was seen as being preferable to inertia.[28]

Roosevelt was astute enough to recognize, however, that congressional accommodation would not last indefinitely, especially in the absence of significant results. Indeed, maximum maneuverability was possible only as long as the system remained in crisis and Roosevelt was able to command the confidence of Congress. As cracks appeared in his First New Deal coalition during 1934 and 1935, therefore, Roosevelt took steps toward the construction of a Second New Deal coalition.

The Facilitating Coalition

By 1934, the brief artificial recovery brought about by the devaluation of the dollar caused much of the business community to desire a return to the orthodoxy of the pre-Depression era. Despite the attractiveness of the NRA in terms of relief from antitrust laws, state regulation of the economy had led to severe tensions between government and business. Over the summer of 1934, the defection of conservative business interests moved Roosevelt to solidify support from groups opposed to business orthodoxy. In August, industrial giants Alfred P. Sloan, John Jacob Raskob, and Pierre S. Dupont resigned from the administration's Business Advisory Council and formed an anti–New Deal lobby group, the American Liberty League, which was opposed to what it saw as the principal threats to the American way of life, including communism, trade unionism, liberal Democrats in Congress, social welfare policies, and especially Roosevelt himself.[29]

As the First New Deal gave way to the Second, opposition to Roosevelt intensified. The Liberty League came increasingly to perceive its role as safeguarding the Constitution against the institutional tinkering of the Second New Deal.[30] Although loath to align publicly with the League, congressional conservatives drew strength from its stance. Similarly, important business associations such as the National Association of Manufacturers turned against the New Deal following the creation of the League.[31]

It is ironic that although the Liberty League emerged as a powerful voice against the New Deal, it actually played a significant role in furthering the forces it opposed. It was the defection of conservative business organizations that forced Roosevelt's hand in 1934. Indeed, that spring, although close friend and adviser Felix Frankfurter was insistent that orthodox business interests would never support progressive social change, Roosevelt was far more equivocal.[32] This equivocation was almost certainly because he was uncertain as to which interests he was willing to sacrifice at that time.

Many point to Roosevelt's speech in Green Bay, Wisconsin, on August 9, 1934, as the turning point in his relations with conservative big business. Roosevelt responded to business leaders' criticisms that the New Deal was undermining confidence by noting: "There is no lack of confidence on the part of those business men, farmers and workers who clearly read the signs of the times. Sound economic improvement comes from the improved conditions of the whole population and not a small fraction thereof." On the other hand, Moley contends that Roosevelt was under intense pressure to turn against conservative big business in the autumn of 1934, but that it was not until the following spring that the president began his "crusade" against conservative business interests.[33]

Roosevelt's shift toward internationalism was an important feature of the transition period between the First and Second New Deals. Although he introduced the RTAA early in 1934, he clearly was not committed to internationalism at this time. However, as it became more apparent that conservatives within the business sector could not be reconciled to the New Deal, Roosevelt moved away from economic nationalism and began cultivating new political relationships. As Ferguson suggests:

> With the pressure beginning to tell on Roosevelt, he looked around for new allies. He sponsored an inquiry into foreign economic policy . . . which recommended freer trade. Simultaneously he allowed Secretary of State Cordell Hull to promote reciprocal trade treaties in a series of speeches. The

prospect of a change in U.S. tariff policy drew applause from segments of
the business community that had mostly been hostile to Roosevelt. . . . As
the first New Deal coalition disintegrated under the impact of interindus-
trial and class conflicts, Roosevelt turned more definitively toward free
trade.[34]

By the spring of 1935, the apparent failure of the First New Deal compelled Roosevelt to shift his domestic priorities to the left. The continuing
Depression was providing opportunities for other would-be reformers on
the left to construct power bases within the constituencies most affected by
the economic crisis.[35] Perhaps the most famous of the Depression dema-
gogues was Senator Huey Long of Louisiana, whose "Share Our Wealth" tax
reform proposals enjoyed strong support among the urban underclasses. In
a similar way, Father Charles Coughlin, a Detroit radio preacher, built up a
large and loyal following for his National Union for Social Justice and his
crusade against plutocratic government. Finally, Dr. Francis Townsend's
old-age-pension movement, built on the plan that would see every senior
citizen given $200 per month on the condition the money be spent within
thirty days, sparked the creation of thousands of Townsend Clubs nationwide.

Having already lost the conservative elements of the First New Deal
coalition, Roosevelt could not afford to lose the progressive elements as
well. Thus, by 1935, with mounting pressures from both the left and the
right, he moved to consolidate support in creating what Wolfskill calls "the
most far-reaching program of economic and social legislation ever undertaken in the history of the Republic"—the welfare state.[36]

The Second New Deal, like the First, was an attempt to marry diverse interests for political gain. Like the First, the objective was to consolidate the
coalition by creating a set of institutions to privilege and entrench these interests, this time in the form of the welfare state. The coalition had three
principal elements: agricultural interests (whose corporatist institutional
structure and support carried over from the First New Deal); the urban
underclasses, including immigrants, the aged, the unemployed, blacks,
women, and organized labor; and internationally oriented business and financial interests.

At the heart of the Second New Deal coalition was the large constituency of Americans who were poor. The Depression had overwhelmed
the capacity of existing structures such as family, charitable organizations,

and urban political machines to deal with the disadvantaged, whose ranks were swollen by the large number of able-bodied unemployed. It was for this reason that the First New Deal had entailed a large volume of emergency legislation to mitigate the worst effects of the Depression. Scores of ad hoc relief organizations funded by the federal government emerged. Some—such as the Civilian Conservation Corps (ccc), the Public Works Administration (pwa), the Tennessee Valley Authority (tva), and the Federal Emergency Relief Administration (fera)—had significant palliative effects. However, with few exceptions, the "alphabet agencies" were designed to provide short-term recovery, not long-term reform.

The Second New Deal embodied a commitment toward long-term reform in order to ensure that the American poor would never again be subjected to the misery wrought by economic depression. This reform project entailed a series of laws, enacted in 1935, that have been characterized as the "Second Hundred Days."[37] In addition to the Social Security Act and the Wagner National Labor Relations Act (discussed below), this period saw the extension and entrenchment of existing progressive legislation in banking, housing, and rural electrification. The tax structure was overhauled, increasing the tax load of the wealthy. The so-called Soak-the-Rich Tax was passed in June 1935, which taxed excessive corporate surpluses, greatly increased inheritance and gift taxes as well as taxes on incomes over $50,000. And increased regulation of utility holding companies was imposed to ensure fairer utility rates.[38]

At the heart of the Second New Deal, the Social Security Act contained four major provisions. First, it created nationwide unemployment insurance. Although this is a state responsibility, the federal government instituted an employment tax, 90 percent of which could be offset if the employer contributed to a state unemployment fund. Second, it provided for the transfer of federal money so that states could administer welfare to the needy. Third, it granted the states matching funds for a wide range of programs, including vocational rehabilitation, infant and maternal health, and assistance to crippled children. Fourth, the act created a comprehensive federal old age security program.[39]

The new political importance of labor was felt not only with the passage of the Social Security Act but also with the Wagner Act, which enforced the right of workers to unionize by majority vote, while at the same time prohibiting company-run unions. Moreover, the Wagner Act transformed the government's role in labor relations from the passive (seeking to mitigate industrial violence and disruptions) to the active (mediating between the interests of organized labor and capital). This shift in government emphasis was crucial to the survival of unionism and collective bargaining. Given the economic climate of the time, unionism in the free market would not have survived the excess supply and limited demand for labor. With the active support of the government, however, the power of organized labor grew dramatically. From less than 4 million members in 1935, unions came to represent 8 million by 1939, and this number had doubled again by the end of World War II.[40] The government's commitment to labor was maintained during the remainder of the Depression, most significantly through the passage of the Fair Labor Standards Act (1938), which made provisions for maximum-length workweeks and minimum wages.

With the Second Hundred Days, Roosevelt attracted new sources of political support to the Democratic party, especially in urban areas. In addition to solidifying the support of workers, the 1936 election marked the first time that a majority of blacks voted for a Democratic presidential candidate, with almost 75 percent of those casting ballots supporting Roosevelt.[41] Such impressive numbers, however, were not merely fortuitous externalities of the shift to the Second New Deal. Democratic party strategists were well aware that changing demographics made the urban vote critical to any permanent realignment. As party strategist Ed Flynn told Moley:

> There are two or three million more dedicated Republicans in the United States than there are Democrats. The population, however, is drifting into the urban areas. The election of 1932 was not normal. To remain in power we must attract some millions, perhaps seven, who are hostile or indifferent to both parties. They believe the Republican Party to be controlled by big business and the Democratic Party by the conservative South. These millions are mostly in the cities. They include racial and religious minorities and labor people. We must attract them by radical programs of social and economic reform.[42]

With the support of agriculture already assured from the initiatives of the First New Deal, the other major societal component of the Second New Deal coalition—internationally oriented business—was also secured by the election of 1936. This support was attracted by the international orientation of the Second New Deal.

Logrolling: Forging the Compromise of Embedded Liberalism

The success of the facilitating coalition turned on the ability of its three principal elements—agriculture, progressive (internationally oriented) business, and the urban underclasses—to accept the necessity of making concessions in order to realize their separate objectives. Each element recognized that none could attain its goals in isolation. For example, the urban underclasses, led by organized labor, suppressed traditional demands for lower food prices in exchange for support from the agricultural sector for the new system of industrial relations under the Social Security and Wagner Acts. In turn, farmers supported legislation aimed at assisting the urban poor in return for the broad range of price supports under the AAA, and for initiatives such as rural electrification.

Even more crucial to the success of the Second New Deal coalition and the institutionalization of the New Deal realignment in 1936, however, were progressive business and financial interests. Forming an important economic and political counterweight to the American Liberty League, in particular, and to conservative business, in general, roughly one-third of U.S. business executives were onside for the Second New Deal.[43] Progressive business interests tended to be capital-intensive (thus facilitating the alliance with labor), and export-oriented. They had two principal reasons for aligning with Roosevelt's Second New Deal coalition. First, they saw interfactoral warfare among business, labor, and agriculture as being economically inefficient and a threat to the existence of the capitalist system. Second, they saw international cooperation as being both vital to economic recovery and a vast opportunity for growth. Thus, sectors as diverse as banking, shipping, high-technology industries, crop-exporting agribusiness, and oil, as well as organizations such as the U.S. Chamber of Commerce, the National Automobile Chamber of Commerce, the American Manufacturers' Export Association, and the Committee on Commercial Policy, all supported Roosevelt, while pressuring his administration to abandon economic nationalism.[44]

During the critical transition period between the First and Second New Deals, internationally oriented business actively supported the president's Second Hundred Days legislative program. In return, almost at the same instant, in the spring of 1935, Roosevelt moved away from plans to increase regulations on the banking sector and away from the inflationary policies of the previous two years. Further, Roosevelt committed himself to two critical initiatives designed to curry favor with business progressives: international monetary cooperation and cooperation in trade policies.[45]

As noted, Roosevelt had taken tentative steps toward internationalism in 1934. For example, the Gold Reserve Act was enacted to stabilize all major currencies, while on the other hand significant movement toward international monetary cooperation was limited. Foreign currencies (principally the British pound and the French franc) were supported by a fund created by the depreciation of the dollar, a move designed to stimulate the U.S. economy at the expense of America's trading partners. The decision in the spring of 1934 to remonetize silver (which created a run on silver-backed currencies) undermined international monetary cooperation. By spring 1935, however, as legislation critical to the construction of the welfare state was being framed, Roosevelt embarked upon serious monetary reform, which culminated in the Tripartite Monetary Agreement (TMA) between the United States, Britain, and France. The TMA restored all three countries' currencies to gold convertibility and committed each to mutual consultations prior to currency devaluation. The TMA was soon joined by Belgium, the Netherlands, and Switzerland and laid the foundations for the international dollar standard that followed World War II.[46]

Trade liberalization also began in the spring of 1934 with the passage of the RTAA, which, although politically risky in its own right, was merely enabling legislation, allowing for the possibility of significant tariff reductions. Even so, the act was resisted strongly in Congress and by special interest groups.[47] Triennial renewals in 1937 and 1940 attracted even stronger opposition because of the demonstrated effectiveness of the RTAA in reducing the tariff rate.[48]

Like the Gold Reserve Act, the RTAA initially was more show than substance. Roosevelt was still undecided in 1934 over whether to break with orthodox business. He introduced the RTAA partially as a means of hedging his bets, and partially to satisfy Hull, who had pushed hard for free trade even before joining the Roosevelt administration in 1933. Roosevelt's ambivalence toward internationalism is clear in how vague the legislation was with respect to a crucial consideration: whether most-favored-nation (MFN) treatment was to be bestowed conditionally or unconditionally. (Conditional MFN treatment entails ensuring that each concession is met with a specific quid pro quo. Unconditional MFN treatment means that any concession offered to one country with MFN status must be extended to all such countries. In this way, there is a ratchet effect toward international liberalization of trade. Each time a country within the trading system lowers import barriers on a particular commodity, all countries in the system reap the benefits.)

Although the United States had extended unconditional MFN treatment since 1922, there was no agreement within the administration over whether it was to be extended under the RTAA. Hull was a powerful advocate of unconditionality, whereas another important figure within the Roosevelt administration, George Peek, insisted upon conditionality. Roosevelt made no attempt to resolve this debate in 1934. Indeed, he apparently cultivated the controversy by naming Peek foreign trade adviser to the president in March 1934, before the RTAA was even enacted. The appointment of Peek came as a shock to Hull, who noted in his memoirs: "If Mr. Roosevelt had hit me between the eyes with a sledge hammer he could not have stunned me more."[49]

Hull was a driving force for free trade. He was convinced that it was only by shifting tariff-making authority to the executive branch that the United States would be able to utilize its unique position in the world economy to institute an international free trade regime. Although he may not have conceived of anything so regimented as the GATT, Hull clearly believed that the bilateralism embodied in the RTAA was merely a first step toward multilateral cooperation in trade. It was for this reason, for example, that he insisted that reciprocal trade agreements negotiated by the United States contain unconditional MFN clauses. In this way the ratchet effect of tariff increases brought about by predatory trade practices would be reversed. Each bilateral accord would not just increase trade flows between the signatories but would benefit third-party exporters as well.[50]

It was not until 1935, when it had become clear that internationally oriented business would support his proposed welfare legislation, that Roosevelt sided with Hull, and Peek was eased out of the administration. Roosevelt's commitment to internationalism subsequently paid off in the election of 1936, which institutionalized the New Deal realignment. Republican presidential candidate Alfred Landon lost the support of many business leaders when he came out against the RTAA. Landon's attacks on social security were rebutted, not just by labor and the urban underclasses but by the heads of organizations such as Standard Oil of New Jersey, General Electric, the Pennsylvania Retailers Association, the American Retail Federation, and the Lorillard tobacco company. In fact, the Chase National

Bank loaned the Democratic National Committee the then significant sum of a hundred thousand dollars.[51]

As is well known, Roosevelt defeated Landon in one of the most lopsided elections in American history. Although much of the business sector eventually would defect to the Republican party after World War II, the rest of the facilitating coalition has remained with the Democratic party. Indeed, not only has the System of '36 survived for almost sixty years, but the compromise of embedded liberalism still prevails.[52]

Conclusion

This chapter has sought to explain Roosevelt's decision to enact the Reciprocal Trade Agreements Act. Although controversy surrounding the passage of the RTAA was mitigated because the act was merely enabling legislation, in Congress the legislation was the most contentious of the early New Deal. It also aroused a good deal of societal opposition, and because it required congressional renewal every three years, its passage and successful administration entailed a good deal of political risk. Roosevelt undertook that risk because it helped him realize his larger political objectives: partisan realignment in favor of the Democratic party.

Roosevelt realized early in the Depression that the extent of the crisis, combined with his predecessor Herbert Hoover's inability to ameliorate its effects, represented a chance to undertake massive policy and institutional reforms in order to realize two wholly compatible objectives. First, he wished to return the country to economic prosperity. This was to be achieved while preserving the system of capitalism and liberal democracy that were under severe threat elsewhere, and that were by no means secure in the United States during the Depression. Second, he sought to construct a new base of electoral support for the Democratic party.

The interwar period is characterized by two distinct New Deals. The First constituted an alliance among elements within industry and agriculture. Although there was a parallel concern with economic recovery, the institutional initiatives were corporatist and entailed the creation of the National Recovery Administration and the Agricultural Adjustment Administration. The Second New Deal sought a broader alliance, among agriculture, the urban underclasses, and progressive export-oriented business and finance. More important, the Second New Deal sought to institutionalize recovery through the creation of a set of institutions designed to protect society's most vulnerable elements from the vicissitudes of the economy. It was the shift toward the Second New Deal—precipitated largely by the defection of conservative business interests from the First New Deal coalition—that saw the revival of internationalism within the Roosevelt administration. Pressure from internationally oriented industrial and financial interests ensured that the Second New Deal also featured a logroll among advocates of domestic interventionism and international liberalism. This specific prototype of the postwar compromise of embedded liberalism entailed the creation of the welfare state, the Tripartite Monetary Agreement, and the Reciprocal Trade Agreements Act.

4

THE TWO-LEVEL GAMBLE

Why Canada Enacted Free Trade

Constitutional reform and free trade preoccupied the Canadian polity during the era of Conservative prime minister Brian Mulroney. This chapter attempts to explain the superficially puzzling Canada–United States Free Trade Agreement (CUFTA) as a by-product of political entrepreneurship in pursuit of electoral realignment. The argument is that Mulroney's desire to preserve his anomalous position as leader of a Conservative majority government accounts for the divisive free trade initiative. Mulroney attempted to create a strong electoral base in Quebec and thereby effect a permanent realignment by undertaking constitutional reform designed to meet Quebec's demands. This objective required the construction of a facilitating coalition that bridged the trade and constitutional issues. The politically risky CUFTA therefore progressed in tandem with the Meech Lake Accord (a controversial constitutional reform package, discussed below), as a means to realizing Mulroney's larger objectives of electoral realignment.

· · ·

The lure of protectionism is manifest throughout Canadian economic history. Events many years ago established a disposition against free trade, most notably with regard to the United States. Canada's economic history for the century preceding the passage of CUFTA was conditioned largely by the National Policy of 1879, the government of the day's blueprint for nationalist economic development.[1] The first real challenge to the National Policy came in 1911, when Canada's incumbent Liberal government went to the polls, largely over the issue of free trade with the United States. The reciprocity agreement reached earlier that year would have dismantled the system of protective tariffs created under the National Policy. However, the agreement proved extremely unpopular. Financial and manufacturing interests, along with much of the Central Canadian electorate, joined the opposition Conservatives to hand the Liberals a resounding defeat.

Although Canada eventually signed significant bilateral accords with the United States (most notably in 1935 and 1938 under the auspices of the RTAA and in 1965 with the Auto Pact), these agreements were relatively modest in scope and did not obviate the National Policy tariff structure. Even participation in the GATT allowed Canada to maintain fairly substantial restrictions on import penetration.[2] It is clear that the specter of 1911 dissuaded Canadian prime ministers from enacting a comprehensive free trade agreement with the United States. Prime Minister Mackenzie King negotiated an agreement in secret with the United States in 1947, only to lose his resolve before the accord was made public. In 1953, the Eisenhower administration proposed a bilateral free trade accord, but the idea was rejected as too politically risky by the government of Louis St. Laurent.[3]

Political risks associated with free trade explain the reluctance of Canadian prime ministers to consider its potential net benefits. It was surprising, therefore, that in the mid-1980s, the Mulroney government approached the United States to begin negotiations on a comprehensive free trade agreement. What makes this bold stroke even more remarkable is that Mulroney was an unlikely candidate to introduce free trade. Far from being a lifelong free trader, Mulroney went on record—only two years prior to the decision to negotiate a free trade agreement—in opposition to the suggestion that Canada seek bilateral free trade with the United States. Mulroney's style and reputation as a brokerage politician meant that he was not given to taking a strong stance on substantive issues, especially those fraught with considerable political risk.[4]

Although early polls showed substantial support for the free trade initiative, a leaked document from the Prime Minister's Office (PMO) in the autumn of 1985 shows that the government recognized numerous sources of potential danger. The memo suggested, in part, that

A number of significant risks to the strategy will have to be faced. The major risks can be summarized in one word: fear. Fear will be manifest in intense lobbies by those concerned with sovereignty, cultural issues and job losses. It will be the strongest unifying force in what might be called "the bottom up" lobbies from communities that feel threatened. Plant managers, local union leaders, mayors, chambers of commerce, etc. may join forces with similar groups across the country. Intense pressure on caucus members may threaten government's solidarity.

Moreover, the PMO was clearly skeptical about the validity of polling on hypothetical issues. As the leaked communication notes: "Sampling Canadian public opinion on the issue of free trade is not unlike canvassing children for their views on world peace." Indeed, over time, as the issue shifted from "free trade" in the abstract to the concrete CUFTA, support fell dramatically. This was especially true if questions were phrased to suggest alternatives to free trade.[5]

As predicted by the memo, numerous cultural and economic groups opposed the agreement. Prominent critics included unions, academics, artists, many industrial and agricultural interests, along with women's, church, and charitable organizations.[6] Lobbies such as the Pro-Canada Network and Canadians Concerned About Free Trade also helped to generate considerable popular opposition. Extremely controversial, CUFTA was opposed by more Canadians than supported it, as can be seen in the results of the 1988 general election, which was widely interpreted as a referendum on free trade. The controversy surrounding CUFTA in Canada was no doubt a function of the fact that the U.S. economy is so critical to Canada. By 1986, for example, 77.6 percent of Canada's exports were absorbed by the U.S. market, whereas 69.5 percent of Canada's imports were from the United States. It is Mulroney's conversion to free trade, with full knowledge of the political risks involved, that makes Canada's decision to enter into CUFTA an interesting and important example of trade liberalization.[7]

Conventional Explanations for CUFTA

Despite the importance of free trade to the Canadian polity, economy, and society, the literature about its passage remains relatively sparse. This is in part because neither comparative nor international political economy focuses on CUFTA as a watershed policy. The absence of such treatments is not surprising, given that Canada is a small economy that traditionally commands little international attention.

Since Canada's trade policy conversion lacked implications for hegemonic leadership, the case is not relevant to standard systemic-level explanations. It is possible that the impending threat of U.S. protectionism forced Canada to comply with the wishes of the United States. However, this begs the question of why the United States would wait until the 1980s, fifty years after laying the groundwork for a liberal trade regime, to coerce Canada into liberalization.

An initially more promising line of enquiry emerges from the neo-Marxist or left-nationalist tradition within political economy. Cameron, Langille, Rocher, and Richardson, among others, note that the Canadian government's decision to abandon protectionism coincided with the reversal of big business's long-standing opposition to bilateral trade liberalization.[8] This reduces the matter to an instrumentalist argument: the government responded to the policy demands of the bourgeoisie. This inference that bourgeois preferences translate directly into outcomes is unsupported, although there is no doubt that the reversal on trade policy among the most significant members of the business community influenced the government.[9] Neo-Marxist or left-nationalist theorists provide no evidence that business preferences decided the issue of free trade for the Conservatives. The argument depends instead on structural economic factors. Aside from the assumption that the state merely serves the interests of the dominant classes, the entire line of reasoning is devoid of any theorizing about politics.

Watson is more comprehensive and less reductionist in seeking explanations for CUFTA.[10] His list of government priorities provides an excellent organizing principle for discussing state- and societal-level accounts of the agreement. Governments, Watson argues, do not merely respond to the imperatives of a capitalist economic structure but are motivated by one or more of three factors. First, they may do what is best for society at large. Thus a government might conduct a cost-benefit analysis of a particular course of action. Second, leaders may be motivated by self-preservation. From this perspective, governments seek to develop support coalitions and to satisfy dominant interests within such creations. Third, governments may be influenced by ideology, most notably changes in underlying societal beliefs and opinions. For any government, these priorities are expected to vary in importance, depending upon the electoral cycle and a wide range of other considerations.

However, Watson argues, none of these factors can explain Canada's decision to liberalize cross-border trade during the 1980s. Whereas the government may have hoped to increase national welfare, that consideration cannot explain the actual timing of the decision. For decades, numerous large-scale studies have concluded that Canada would benefit greatly from free trade with the United States.[11] These findings had no decisive impact until the Mulroney era. Moreover, Watson observes, the Canadian and U.S. economies have become more similar in recent years, so the benefits to be derived from a free trade agreement are actually less now than they would have been in the past.

Based on Watson's second priority for governments, the decision about free trade might be explained from a statist perspective. He suggests that the Mulroney government could have perceived free trade as a means to build and maintain popular support. This argument assumes the existence of more than one potentially winning electoral coalition and that Mulroney merely opted for a different base of popular support than did previous Liberal governments. While Watson concedes that there is some evidence of this (the Tories typically have done better among business groups and in the West than have the Liberals), the electoral system traditionally has featured two parties that alternate regularly between government and official opposition. Thus, he argues, the median-voter hypothesis dictates that both competitors will adopt similar platforms.[12]

Cairns, however, points out that Canada's electoral system has contributed to the regionalization of the major national parties.[13] The Liberals, for example, have been loath to commit scarce resources to regions such as western Canada, where they are unlikely to win seats. Similarly, the Conservatives have underallocated resources in Quebec. The policy orientations of the major parties have reflected these regional biases. If Cairns is correct (and there is plenty of evidence to support his claim), the median-voter hypothesis need not prevail in Canada.[14] Parties may adopt diverse positions on the issues, in competition for minimal winning coalitions.[15]

Change in a government's ideology, the third potential explanation noted above, is also dismissed by Watson. Free trade lacked consistency with other Conservative government policies, although it was consistent with the neoconservative agenda of the Anglo-American community during the early 1980s.[16] Indeed, the Mulroney agenda was sufficiently centrist to inspire the neoconservative Reform party to form as an alternative.

Watson appears to close this line of inquiry prematurely. Although he is correct to exclude the Mulroney government from the neoconservative camp, he overlooks the possibility that government ideology changed along a different dimension. Smiley, for example, argues that Mulroney's policies, including free trade, represented a shift from the nationalist political centralization that characterized previous Liberal governments (most notably under Pierre Trudeau) to a continentalist and decentralized vision of the Canadian polity.[17]

Smiley's argument—that the Mulroney era represented a fundamental ideological shift—provides an important piece in the puzzle as to why Canada enacted its watershed trade policy during the mid-1980s. In a comprehensive treatment of CUFTA, Doern and Tomlin go one step further.[18] They suggest that Mulroney used policies such as free trade to construct a new, winning electoral coalition based on support from Quebec and western Canada. These regions, despite their many differences, were united in antipathy toward Trudeau's centralist agenda.

Mulroney as Political Entrepreneur

Mulroney came to power in 1984, determined to effect a partisan realignment that would make the Conservatives the new dominant party. Through a series of policy initiatives, he attempted to create a Quebec/western axis, while taking advantage of underlying philosophical differences and policy-related conflicts within Confederation. As Doern and Tomlin note, electoral arithmetic played a considerable role in the decision to target Quebec and the West. There are only three electorally significant regions: Quebec, Ontario, and the West. The Atlantic provinces are sufficiently small to have been ignored, in deed if not in word. Thus, to construct a winning electoral coalition, Mulroney attempted to secure the lasting support of two out of three regions.[19]

Prior to 1984, the Conservative party served primarily in opposition. Between 1935 and 1983, the Tories managed to form a majority government only once. Although fairly strong in western Canada, and competitive in Ontario and the Atlantic region, the Conservatives barely existed in Quebec. By contrast, the Liberal party—dubbed Canada's "Natural Governing Party"—has owed most of its electoral success to its dominance in Quebec.

Quebec's consistent support for the Liberal party, as well as its penchant for voting en bloc in federal elections, ensured that the Liberals were able to form the government after seventeen of twenty-four federal elections from the turn of the century through 1980.

A majority government following the 1958 election provided the lone exception to the rule of Conservative futility in Quebec. However, it is clear in retrospect that 1958 represented an aberration. Quebec voters merely registered a protest against the long years of Liberal government in Canada. In the election of 1962 and for a generation thereafter, the Liberals again dominated Quebec, and by extension, federal politics in Canada.

Mulroney recognized that lack of organization in Canada's only francophone province created an insurmountable obstacle to Conservative status as a majority party. He noted in 1980:

> With few if any exceptions, the Conservative Party has been consigned to the Opposition benches for one reason alone—its failure to win seats in the French-speaking areas of the nation. From northern and eastern Ontario and into northern New Brunswick, the electorate has rejected the Conservative party with a consistency that is at once staggering and overwhelming.

Permanent transformation of the Quebec vote to the Conservatives became Mulroney's overarching political objective. In 1983 he campaigned for the Conservative party leadership on the strength of his ability, as a fluently bilingual Quebecker, to deliver the francophone vote. The 1984 general election offered Mulroney the opportunity to make good on this promise. Campaigning on the theme of constitutional reconciliation, he pledged to address the constitutional aspirations of Quebec and vowed to alter the recently repatriated Constitution to allow Quebec to endorse it "with honour and enthusiasm."[20]

Although the Conservatives took fifty-eight of Quebec's seventy-five seats in the 1984 election, Mulroney recognized the need to convert antipathy toward the Liberals into active and permanent support for the Conservatives. To achieve this goal, Mulroney sought to establish a network of grassroots support in a province where none had existed for almost a century. Constitutional renewal served this purpose. Reform had powerful appeal to supporters of both major provincial parties in Quebec—the federalist Parti Libéral du Québec (PLQ) and the nationalist Parti Québécois (PQ). With constitutional reconciliation, Mulroney hit upon a popular theme in Quebec. It was both the glue with which to cement his Quebec "coalition of '84" and the wedge to drive between Quebeckers and their traditional Liberal representatives in Ottawa.

On the other hand, given Canada's regionalized political divisions, acceding to Quebec's constitutional demands posed a problem for Mulroney. It had the potential to alienate voters in the Tories' traditional support base in western Canada and to reinforce the long-standing perception that the interests of central Canada (Quebec and Ontario) took precedence over those of the West. To avoid such perceptions, Mulroney sought to provide side-payments to western Canada. These included the deregulation of energy and foreign investment, the creation of a Western Development Fund to help diversify the western economy, and the free trade agreement.

Quebec and the West represent opposite poles in a country noted for its political, cultural, and economic diversity. Quebec is a francophone province, whereas the western provinces are anglophone. Quebec's economy traditionally has depended on industry and finance (like Ontario), the West's on agriculture and resource development, especially petroleum and forestry. In terms of population, Quebec is large and the western provinces are much smaller (although the gap is declining). Quebec has long sought to protect its identity and culture by demanding powers broader than those available to the other provinces, largely on the grounds that the province is home to one of the country's two great "nations." Hence, Quebec's constitutional worldview has been grounded in collective rights and "asymmetric federalism."[21] By contrast, the western provinces—especially Alberta and British Columbia (bc)—traditionally have been ardent defenders of the classical Liberal notions of political and economic individualism. Moreover, especially since 1980, the West has demanded provincial equality. With at least implicit attention to the federal system in the United States, these provinces argued strongly that none should have greater constitutional powers or influence than the others.[22]

Given the economic, demographic, and philosophical differences between them, it is not surprising that Quebec and the West have locked horns on numerous constitutional and public policy issues. Yet Mulroney's strategy of constructing a Quebec/western axis to effect partisan realignment in the mid-1980s made good political sense. Within both Quebec and the West, a powerful antipathy has arisen to what Smiley calls Canada's "Third National Policy."[23]

The Third National Policy resulted from the Trudeau government's effort to redefine what it meant to be Canadian. It sought to create overarching symbols of nationhood, which would foster commitment to common values and undermine the regional differences that had characterized the country. The cornerstones of this national blueprint were the Official Languages Act (1969), which served to advance bilingualism throughout Canada; the nationalist Foreign Investment Review Agency (FIRA), set up in 1974, which allowed the government to block foreign investment that it felt was not in the best interests of Canada; the National Energy Program (NEP) of 1980; and the Charter of Rights and Freedoms, a major component of the Constitution Act [1982]. Taken together, these policies guaranteed that all Canadians could claim a unified set of rights and values and ensured that ownership of strategic sectors, such as petroleum, remained largely in the hands of Canadians. Moreover, the NEP ensured that oil revenues would be distributed nationally, rather than being concentrated only in the oil-producing regions.

The Third National Policy promoted Canadian nationalism and the centralization of political and economic authority. In the language of Canadian federalism, it was an exercise in nation-building that confronted the postwar growth of province-building, manifested in the extreme by Quebec separatism. However, in fostering a "new Canadianism," this nationalist vision clashed violently with regional values and politics. This conflict is illustrated most vividly in the NEP and the 1982 Constitution Act. The analysis now turns to a discussion of the NEP and the Constitution Act, respectively.

The NEP was introduced in October 1980 as a means of regulating the country's petroleum sector, located largely in Alberta.[24] Regulation of natural resources is a sensitive issue in Canadian politics. The Constitution gives the provinces ownership of natural resources. However, regulation of these resources is the prerogative of the central government.

The NEP unilaterally imposed a price schedule that called for only marginal increments in the domestic prices of oil and natural gas. This schedule kept the domestic price well below predicted market prices and therefore constituted a huge subsidization of domestic petroleum consumption. At the outset of the energy crisis in 1973–1974, the federal government had used its taxation powers to force the producer provinces to maintain a dual pricing system, with domestic prices below world (that is, market) prices. In 1978, the domestic price was over 85 percent of the market price, but by 1980, under the NEP, it had fallen below 45 percent of the world price. The unilateral nature of the NEP price schedule represented a breach of the convention that domestic prices were set by negotiation between the producer provinces and the federal government.

In addition, the NEP introduced a series of new federal taxation measures on petroleum producers. Excise taxes were raised to pay for subsidization of imported petroleum, and to increase Canadian public ownership in the oil patch. By the federal government's own estimates, such measures raised its share of petroleum revenues from 10 to 24 percent. In dollar terms, former Alberta premier Peter Lougheed estimated in 1988 that the NEP had cost his province $60 billion in federal taxation and consumption subsidies.[25]

The increased federal presence in the energy sector had predictable consequences for foreign investors. The Canadianization of the oil patch was achieved, in great measure, by regulating American producers out of the market. American investors abandoned the Alberta oil fields in favor of more attractive opportunities in the United States. The result was the loss of thousands of jobs in the petroleum sector.

The NEP enraged western Canadians. For them this was merely the most recent, and most blatant, manifestation of one of the great evils of Confederation—the ability of central governments to make economic policy designed to represent the interests of only the two most populous provinces. From the National Policy to the NEP, the economic interests of western Canada were consistently forsaken. The aftermath of the NEP witnessed palpable changes in western attitudes toward Confederation. Western alienation manifested itself first in a spurt of enthusiasm for western separatism. Soon, however, the provincial governments—led by Alberta—began to press for constitutional changes within Canada. The most important demand was for an elected, effective, and equal (Triple E) Senate.[26] A strong provincial presence in the upper house of Parliament, it was felt, would prevent central Canadian majorities in the House of Commons from repeating the treachery of the NEP. In addition, by the mid-1980s, and again as a reaction against the NEP, the western premiers began to press for economic decentralization. The most obvious manifestation of this was support for free trade with the United States.[27]

The Constitution Act [1982] also created a good deal of political instability in Canada. Although Canada's history has never been entirely free of constitutional wrangling, the antecedents of the constitutional quagmire of the late 1980s and early 1990s can be traced to the May 1980 referendum

on separatism. In that referendum campaign, the Trudeau government offered Quebeckers a new constitutional settlement in return for a rejection
of separatism. Familiar with the sclerosis typically produced by interprovincial constitutional bargaining in Canada, Trudeau took the unprecedented step of declaring that the federal government would patriate
the Constitution unilaterally.

Patriation is a novel concept for those not familiar with Canadian politics. Because Canada's initial constitutional document—the British North
America Act (now Constitution Act [1867])—was an act of the British Parliament, no amending formula was included. Amendments were merely
acts of the imperial legislature. However, upon achieving full independence in 1931, Canada was unable to decide upon an amending formula
that was suitable to all provinces. The Constitution therefore remained an
act of the British Parliament and could only be amended as such. It was
this anachronism that patriation ultimately rectified.[28]

On this initiative Trudeau was supported by only two provinces—Ontario and New Brunswick. The rest formed the infamous Gang of Eight,
which opposed the precedent Trudeau threatened to set. During negotiations that took place throughout most of 1981, the Gang of Eight carried on
a parallel constitutional dialogue among themselves. They countered the
comprehensive federal constitutional package, which included a Charter of
Rights and Freedoms, with a much more modest proposal. In November
1981, in an attempt to reach a compromise, the first ministers met in Ottawa. Late on the night of November 5, 1981, representatives of the federal
government and the Gang of Eight informally (and allegedly in the hotel
kitchen) forged an agreement. Quebec representatives, however, were not
included in the process because (it was later claimed) the Quebec delegation was not available, being quartered for political reasons across the river
in Hull, Quebec. On the other hand, Quebec's geographic isolation was not
inconvenient. Quebec has traditionally resisted any centralization of political power and would have been unlikely to accede to the Charter—a document that greatly empowered the Supreme Court of Canada. So Quebec
premier René Lévesque awoke the next morning to find that Quebec was
isolated in opposing the package, which had nominally been that province's reward for rejecting separatism in 1980.[29]

The legacy of Quebec's isolation in November 1981 was a lasting one. Although legally bound by the Constitution, Quebec is not yet a signatory to
it. Moreover, in protest, Quebec has boycotted constitutional conferences

since 1981. (With the prospect of success, Quebec did participate in the Meech Lake talks and did attend the final negotiations of the 1992 Charlottetown Accord—a constitutional amendment package defeated in a nationwide referendum in October 1992.) In all, the process created a good deal of bitterness in the province of Quebec. If not a spur to separatism, the outcome of the Patriation Round stimulated Québécois nationalism. Traditional antipathy toward political centralization ultimately extended into the economic sphere, as in the early 1980s political and economic leaders in Quebec began to renounce economic centralization as well.[30]

With CUFTA and Meech Lake, Mulroney sought to reverse the effects of the Third National Policy. Meech Lake was designed to address Quebec's objections to the Constitution Act [1982]. Free trade offered the most effective means of preventing further federal incursions into the energy sector. The federal minister of international trade during the CUFTA negotiations, Patricia Carney, stated in Calgary: "Critics say the problem with the Free Trade Agreement is that under its terms Canada can never impose another National Energy Program on the country. The critics are right. That was our objective in these negotiations." Similarly, in a submission to the House of Commons Standing Committee on External Affairs and International Relations, former Alberta Premier Lougheed asserted that "the biggest plus of this agreement is that it could preclude a federal government from bringing in a National Energy Program ever again."[31]

In short, Mulroney hoped to solidify political support in Quebec and thereby achieve electoral realignment. In the quest for a sustained Conservative majority, Mulroney used institutional reform, in the guise of the Meech Lake Accord, as a means to ending Quebec's constitutional isolation. Free trade, by contrast, attracted much needed political support from the western premiers, unlikely to be enthusiastic about Mulroney's institutional initiative. With agricultural and resource-based economies, the western provinces had long resented the National Policy tariff structure as a subsidization of the manufacturing sector, located almost entirely in Quebec and Ontario. Equally important, free trade meant that further NEP-style interventions in the petroleum sector would be prevented. Finally, free trade held the promise of economic diversification.[32] Needing the support of the western premiers for constitutional reconciliation, and knowing that the western population harbored a long-standing antipathy toward what it perceived to be Quebec's preferential treatment within

Confederation, Mulroney was willing to gamble that free trade would ensure western support for his constitutional initiative.

The Perception of Crisis

A critical impediment to Mulroney's blueprint for electoral realignment in
Canada, however, was that constitutional reform was not widely considered necessary in the mid-1980s. Canadians were weary of constitutional
wrangling, having just endured a round of significant reform in 1980–1981.
Moreover, the mid-1980s was a period of relative political calm in Canada.
For the first time in over a decade, Quebec separatism was in abeyance, as
the Parti Québécois reevaluated its commitment to Quebec independence.
In short, the mid-1980s was strategically a suboptimal period to engage in
constitutional reform. Because the system was perceived by few to be in a
state of crisis, there was little incentive to deviate from the status quo, if
this threatened to yield another round of destabilizing constitutional conflict. (This is not to say that there were no sources of constitutional friction, of course. Quebec's symbolic isolation was problematic to those who
sought to heal the nation after the fractious debates of the early 1980s.
More concretely, talks on constitutional entrenchment of aboriginal rights,
postponed from 1981, were stalled because of Quebec's boycott of constitutional conferences. Substantial reform on the aboriginal issue, therefore,
was not possible.)

Given structural limitations to his constitutional initiatives, Mulroney
formulated a three-part strategy to facilitate movement on the Constitution.[33] First, the Mulroney government sought to limit the constitutional
agenda. It was made clear to the provincial premiers (the principal players
of the day, because each had constitutional veto power) that any constitutional negotiations would be designed to address only Quebec's grievances. No proposals emanating from other provinces would be enter-
tained. Because all premiers had at least a marginal preference to have the
Quebec issue settled, once and for all, this demand was not considered unreasonable. The Edmonton Declaration of August 1986—a unanimous
agreement to limit the constitutional agenda—permitted the process to
move ahead.

The second prong in the Mulroney strategy was to ensure that formal
negotiations did not begin until the chances of success were ascertained to
be high. Mulroney felt that formal (semipublic) negotiations would limit
the flexibility of the premiers. Once committed to a public stance on con-

stitutional issues, none would risk losing face by compromising, and sub-stantive negotiations would be rendered almost impossible. In order not to place the premiers in a position where they would be forced to precommit, much of the negotiating for the Meech Lake Accord was undertaken bilat-erally, between individual provinces and members of the Quebec or federal government. Indeed, even the first ministers' meeting of April 30, 1987, which produced the Meech Lake Accord, was billed publicly merely as a preliminary meeting at which it would be determined whether future progress on the Constitution was possible.[34]

The third and final part of the Mulroney strategy was to create the per-ception of crisis. A multilateral meeting of senior federal and provincial of-ficials on March 5 and 6, 1987, exposed serious gulfs in the constitutional objectives of many provinces. According to a member of the Ontario con-stitutional delegation, Patrick Monahan, Mulroney wrote to the premiers on April 10, 1987, suggesting that failure to reconcile Quebec's constitu-tional demands would jeopardize "the capacity of Canada to adapt its con-stitutional and institutional framework to meet new challenges," and that if steps were not taken to resolve the issue soon, the problem might have to be addressed "in more difficult circumstances and less tranquil times."[35]

By April 17, 1987, reports that the April 30 meeting would entail substan-tive negotiations were leaked to the press. As government after government issued public "clarifications," it became clear that wholly secret negotia-tions would not be possible. In fact, the negotiation process appeared to have begun, as many premiers made public statements regarding their dis-satisfaction with Quebec's demands. As the process threatened to unravel, Mulroney stepped into the fray and suggested publicly that constitutional innovation was critical to the financial well-being, and possibly even sur-vival, of the country.[36]

After the Meech Lake Accord was reached on April 30, the crisis theme was revived to help ensure ratification in the provincial legislatures. Under the rules of the Constitution, all agreements must be ratified by the appro-priate legislatures (usually this entails the ten provincial legislatures and the federal Parliament) within three years of the date the first legislature ratifies. Quebec's National Assembly ratified on June 23, 1987, making June 23, 1990, the deadline for the unanimous ratification of the accord. Over the next three years, as opposition to the accord grew—and the likelihood of its ratification diminished—Mulroney attempted increasingly to rally support for the accord by raising fears of national disintegration. On May 31, 1990, for example, he stated in the House of Commons:

> While I do not want to underestimate the divergences on the remaining issues [with respect to Meech], what is in dispute is modest when compared to what is really at stake. What is really at stake is Canada. Failure would compromise our capacity for living together in unity and diminish the kinds of prosperity that Canadians have enjoyed over so many decades . . . it would curtail opportunities for constitutional change, in such important areas as Senate reform and aboriginal rights, for the foreseeable future. I believe it would send a very damaging signal about Canada to the international community with consequences for our national well-being.[37]

The crisis strategy was utilized most obviously as the final deadline for unanimous ratification approached. At the first ministers' conference of June 3–9, 1990, which was dedicated to overcoming opposition to the Meech Lake Accord in three provinces, Mulroney cast the discussion in the terms of Canada's survival as a nation.[38] By the end of the conference, all three recalcitrant premiers had agreed to seek ratification of the accord. Indeed, Newfoundland Premier Clyde Wells, the staunchest opponent of the accord in its final days, was extremely bitter about Mulroney's pressure tactics. He capitulated, he said, because he did not want "any responsibility for doing irreparable harm to this nation."[39]

The Facilitating Coalition

Mulroney's facilitating coalition consisted of the ten provincial premiers, and the business community. Mulroney's skillful interest-brokering meant that supporters of constitutional reform and trade liberalization became allies. Although few within the coalition actively opposed either initiative, Quebec clearly had greater commitment to constitutional reform. Business leaders and the western premiers, leery of popular reaction to the entrenchment of Quebec's constitutional demands, were more enthusiastic about free trade.

For at least two reasons, the provincial premiers collectively occupied a central position in Mulroney's scheme. First, the Meech Lake Accord required unanimous consent, each premier possessing potential veto power over proposed institutional reforms. Second, the premiers typically aggregate and articulate the demands of societal actors within their provinces.

Sensitivity to the agenda of provincial premiers was perceived as a cost-effective means of satisfying regional interests.

Fairly widespread support-in-principle existed among all the provinces for a trade initiative by early 1985. The resource-based Atlantic provinces, like the West, saw free trade as a means to diversify their economies. Ontario showed ambivalence, and (somewhat surprisingly) Quebec, still led by the PQ government, favored liberalization. The PQ had supported free trade since the defeat of the 1980 referendum on sovereignty. What Courchene calls "market nationalism" is the PQ's strategy to lessen its economic dependence on the rest of Canada as a first step toward the ultimate goal of political separation.[40]

However, the western premiers were clearly the most committed. Premiers William Vander Zalm of British Columbia, Grant Devine of Saskatchewan, and Peter Lougheed (later Donald Getty) of Alberta were effusive in their support for free trade in numerous speeches over the period from 1985 to 1988. They explicitly asserted that consequences for national unity would be negative if the central Canadian provinces blocked free trade.[41] Manitoba remained apart from the other three western provinces on both the free trade and the Meech Lake initiatives, for at least two reasons. First, during this period and until the spring of 1988, the social democratic New Democratic party (NDP) formed the government. Much of the NDP's natural constituency was made up of anti–free trade groups, so Manitoba muted its traditional support for trade liberalization. Second, Howard Pawley's successor as premier, Conservative Gary Filmon, led a precarious minority government from 1988 until after the failure of Meech. Thus the politics of maintaining opposition party support for Filmon's government drove much of Manitoba's strategy during this period.

The other western provinces, especially Alberta under the premiership of Lougheed, were instrumental in persuading Mulroney to seek free trade. Lougheed's involvement in the free trade process started early in 1984. Even before the election of that year, he had pressured Mulroney to abolish the NEP and FIRA as well as to commit to free trade.[42] In February 1985, seven months before Mulroney announced his intention to pursue trade liberalization, the government of Alberta publicly declared its support for free trade and actively solicited reinforcement from the other premiers.

Lougheed exercised a great deal of influence over Mulroney. His stature, both on the national stage and as a representative of western interests, made Lougheed an important factor in Mulroney's decision to begin free trade negotiations in 1985. Lougheed succeeded in limiting opposition to free trade among the ranks of the premiers, making it clear that the West would not accept any intransigence from the central provinces on an issue of such vital importance.[43] Even after stepping down as premier in November 1985, Lougheed continued to play a significant role behind the scenes, and his influence was felt through his successor and close political ally, Donald Getty.

Big business also proved an invaluable ally in the fight for free trade. If the major financial and industrial interests had thrown their weight against the government, it is likely that free trade would not even have been proposed. Since the National Policy, business had been at the forefront of the fight to maintain protectionism. In the early 1980s, business effected a remarkable volte-face on the issue of trade. Led by the Business Council on National Issues, allied with pro–free trade forces in the federal bureaucracy under the leadership of Derek Burney, groups such as the Canadian Chamber of Commerce, the Canadian Manufacturers' Association, and the Canadian Federation of Independent Business formed a powerful united front in support of free trade.[44]

There are numerous reasons why the business community changed its stance on free trade. Business disliked the interventionist policies of the Trudeau era, which had limited its influence and culminated in the NEP. Fear of U.S. protectionism and the relatively weak performance of the Canadian economy reinforced new ways of thinking; free trade now seemed beneficial because it would force the government out of the marketplace. Moreover, the undervalued Canadian dollar had increased Canada's balance of trade, and business felt confident about its ability to compete at the international level. Finally, the Tokyo Round tariff cuts had weakened industrial protectionism, making production for the domestic market less attractive than before. Tariffs no longer provided sufficient rents to make industrial protectionism the optimal policy for big business.[45]

Logrolling: CUFTA and the Meech Lake Accord

Meech Lake and free trade constituted a classic public policy logroll. Although government actors took pains not to connect the two initiatives publicly, there is plenty of evidence that major players within the facilitating coalition signaled their preferences and threats. The lack of public links on the trade and constitutional initiatives is not difficult to explain. Logrolling among elected officials is always facilitated by secrecy, which relieves politicians of the necessity of retreating from publicly stated positions. As noted, Mulroney strived to ensure that the initiatives were negotiated—with discretion—at the elite level.

Although the CUFTA and Meech Lake Accord involved regional trade-offs between Quebec and the West, three important qualifications must be made before we proceed with this analysis. First, the other major regions—Ontario and the Atlantic provinces—each played a role in these ventures. However, it is reasonable to suggest (at a considerable risk of oversimplification) that Mulroney did not perceive these regions as presenting great obstacles to the success of either initiative. With the exception of tiny Prince Edward Island, the Atlantic provinces offered fairly strong support to free trade. Whereas Ontario officially opposed free trade, this was interpreted as posturing, at least to some degree. On the constitutional front, unlike the West, neither Ontario nor the Atlantic provinces brought significant constitutional agendas of their own to Meech Lake.[46] The second qualification is that, all things being equal, the western premiers wanted to achieve constitutional reconciliation. Third, and finally, Quebec was not opposed to free trade. Robert Bourassa's Liberal government was not as enthusiastic as the previous PQ regime had been, however. Although Bourassa's initial resistance to free trade lessened after discussions with Quebec civil servants and business leaders, it was not until after the Meech Lake Accord that Bourassa became an unqualified and ardent supporter of that initiative.[47] These qualifications notwithstanding, there is sufficient evidence to conclude that a regional trade-off took place.

Meech Lake had its genesis in Mulroney's attempt to campaign during the 1984 election, on an issue that would unite federalist and separatist Quebeckers. Movement on the Constitution began soon after Mulroney's stunning victory. Representatives of the PQ government approached the new prime minister in the autumn of 1984 with a series of twenty-two demands for constitutional reconciliation. Although tempted to begin negotiations, Mulroney heeded his advisers' suggestion that, given the tension within the PQ government, he await the outcome of the impending provincial election. The separatist PQ had governed Quebec since 1976. After its referendum defeat in 1980, the party gradually moved away from outright separatism and by 1984 had softened its position dramatically. This shift, however, led to tension between hard- and soft-liners on the issue of separatism, and many of the former left the party in the early and mid-1980s. In

December 1985, the PLQ returned to power, setting the stage for the constitutional bargaining that culminated in the Meech Lake Accord.

Two months earlier, the government had committed to free trade. A deadline was set for October 4, 1987, for fast-track approval (mandated by Congress), which meant that an agreement in principle had to be worked out by the summer of 1987. Meanwhile, Quebec's intergovernmental affairs minister, Gil Rémillard, announced his government's constitutional demands in May 1986. These demands, ultimately incorporated into the Meech Lake Accord, consisted of (1) a Quebec veto on all constitutional amendments; (2) a greater role for Quebec in selecting that province's three members of the Supreme Court of Canada; (3) constitutional entrenchment of an existing arrangement between Quebec and Canada, whereby Quebec had the option of admitting and selecting immigrants above and beyond federal quotas; (4) the right, with full financial compensation, to opt out of federal spending initiatives within areas of provincial jurisdiction; and (5) recognition of Quebec as a distinct society within Canada. The Meech Lake Accord extended the first four demands to the other provinces. In addition, Meech contained provisions for a new method of selecting senators and for annual first ministers' conferences on the Constitution.[48]

Mulroney reacted cautiously to Quebec's demands. He knew the dangers of opening another round of interprovincial constitutional bargaining. Although the Tories hoped to capitalize on the Liberal party's constitutional blunder of 1981, they recognized that a misstep of their own might lead instead to divisiveness and resentment if the process stalled. In July, Mulroney wrote confidentially to the premiers asking them to accommodate Quebec's demands and not to link other issues to them.[49] The next month, the premiers met in Edmonton and in a joint communiqué—the Edmonton Declaration—agreed to shelve their own constitutional agendas in order to deal with that of Quebec.

The Edmonton Declaration provided the basis from which to launch negotiations. It was hoped that the emerging constitutional settlement would not generate much public interest or enthusiasm anywhere outside the province of Quebec. And it was in this hope that the Mulroney government sought both to limit the constitutional agenda and to ensure that the process did not become politicized. Cohen notes of the mood of the country during the fall of 1986:

Everyone knew that the whole exercise, this Quebec Round, was not terribly popular in some parts of the country, particularly the West. Of course, that assumed that people knew and cared. Canadians were talking about free trade and [the bilateral dispute over] softwood lumber that November. The constitution was far from the public mind and the premiers and prime minister were content to keep it that way.[50]

Cautious, informal negotiations followed the Edmonton Declaration. At the same time, to guarantee a degree of quid pro quo, the free trade negotiations continued under the shadow of Congress's deadline. Throughout the fall of 1986, Senator Lowell Murray (federal minister of state for federal-provincial relations) and Quebec's Rémillard quietly toured the country, laying the groundwork for a constitutional settlement. While there were reasons for optimism (the other provinces appeared willing to cooperate), ominous signs also appeared on the horizon. The downturn in the western economy, based on falling energy and grain prices, brought rumblings of discontent. There were renewed calls to ensure that a Triple-E Senate would be part of any constitutional initiative. As the contours of a constitutional deal were taking shape early in 1987, therefore, the spirit of cooperation faded.

During the run-up to the first ministers' conference at Meech Lake, the press began to warn about very limited potential for success. Graham Fraser noted in the *Globe and Mail* on April 25 that "the risks are high that any premier, either because he does not want to be seen to be catering to Quebec or because of objections to one or another proposal, will scuttle the process." Similarly, the *Toronto Star* on the same day noted that "the Western provinces have suffered over a year of low oil prices and plummeting grain payments since [May 1986], and are feeling ill-disposed toward Ottawa and Central Canada."[51]

During the early months of 1987, with the success of the free trade talks by no means assured, Alberta Premier Getty's position hardened. Despite the agreement in Edmonton, Getty insisted that any new constitutional settlement would have to include Senate reform. In March he went further, "irrevocably" tying himself to the Triple-E proposal. With the constitutional conference set to open the following month, the prospects for a settlement looked bleak. All four western provinces announced disapproval of a Quebec-only constitutional veto. Saskatchewan opposed the spending power opt-out and immigration proposals, and British Columbia and Alberta denounced the idea of any one province receiving special constitutional status.[52]

In the midst of such pessimism, it is more than a coincidence that Bourassa chose the last week of April to signal his ambivalence about free trade, and his willingness to derail the trade talks if Quebec's constitutional demands were not met. He stated, for example, that the provinces needed time to study the free trade proposals and also to work out a provincial ratification process.[53] As Bourassa and his colleagues knew, such a process—effectively introducing ten new (provincial) actors into difficult bilateral negotiations—was tantamount to scuttling the project. Similarly, the next day the *Globe and Mail* reported another implicit threat from the Quebec premier: Bourassa indicated that Canada could not reasonably expect to sacrifice the sovereignty necessary to consummate free trade without first having "its socio-cultural identity well established." An astute editorial in the *Toronto Star* on April 28 noted the link between the constitutional and free trade initiatives:

> Unfortunately, in its eagerness to win favor in Quebec—and perhaps relying on the public's lack of interest in this topic elsewhere—the Mulroney government has indicated its willingness to go along with Bourassa.... It is not beyond the realm of possibility that Mulroney would scratch Bourassa's back on this question in return for the Quebec Premier's support for his free trade initiative.

Bourassa's actions after the agreement at Meech Lake on April 30 also suggest links between the trade and constitutional initiatives. Although recently declassified briefing papers from the government of British Columbia suggest only a moderate commitment to free trade by Quebec in the spring of 1987, in the aftermath of the accord Bourassa became one of the strongest supporters of CUFTA, even going so far as to extol its virtues during a tour of western Canada in the weeks prior to the 1988 election.[54]

When the first ministers' conference got under way at Meech Lake on April 30, it is obvious in retrospect that the principals understood each others' positions. Indeed, given the constitutional change of heart experienced by the western premiers, it is apparent that Bourassa's threat to scuttle free trade had credibility. Despite his commitment to Senate reform and his strong stance against Quebec's constitutional proposals in late April, it became evident when the dust had cleared after Meech that Alberta's Getty had settled for much less than he had promised to accept.

Not only did the Meech Lake Accord recognize Quebec's constitutional distinctness, but Senate reform actually had been made even more difficult. Under the existing formula, Senate reform would have required the support of seven provinces, which collectively constitute 50 percent of the Canadian population. With Meech, however, such changes would require unanimous approval. Although an interim agreement on the Senate had been reached whereby provincial governments received a greater say in the appointment of senators, western observers noted discrepancies between what Getty promised and what he delivered.[55] Similarly, British Columbia's Vander Zalm and Saskatchewan's Devine also muted their opposition to the Quebec proposals.

Mulroney tried to ensure the success of Meech Lake by publicly underplaying the importance of the negotiations in the months between the Edmonton Declaration and Meech Lake, while privately applying maximum pressure on the premiers to strike a deal. He underscored the link between Meech and western objectives such as free trade by embarking on a three-day tour of western Canada in the first week of May. The prime minister spoke effusively on free trade and sparingly about the recently concluded and not terribly popular constitutional negotiations. Moreover, he chose this post-Meech tour to announce plans to unveil the new Western Diversification Initiative, whereby federal funds would be used to assist in the diversification of the western economies.[56] By deflecting attention from the constitutional issue and concentrating instead on the concurrent economic gains made by the West, Mulroney maintained his public stance that the two initiatives were discrete. He simultaneously bought off potential opposition in western Canada through the implicit bargain—free trade for constitutional reconciliation—that had been struck at Meech Lake.

Mulroney's tactics—of brokering interests and buying off potential opposition with his prowestern initiatives, secretive elite bargaining, and the skillful creation of a facilitating coalition—almost succeeded, at least on the surface. With ratification in the provincial and federal legislatures apparently at hand, constitutional entrenchment seemed likely within the three-year limit.[57] In the end, however, Mulroney's institutional reform efforts did not come to fruition. Delays in the ratification of Meech caused the facilitating coalition to crumble. Changes of government at the provincial level and growing mass opposition to Meech increasingly politicized the constitutional process and compromised elite accommodation.[58]

Much of the opposition to Meech Lake came from western Canada and occurred after passage of the Free Trade Implementation Act. Although the westernmost premiers maintained their commitment to the accord, those in Manitoba, New Brunswick, and Newfoundland drew on mass opposition in their refusal to seek ratification. The fragile agreement reached at the first ministers' conference of June 1990 unraveled in two legislatures, through outright opposition in Manitoba and passive resistance in Newfoundland.

Mulroney's clearly was a failed initiative. His attempt to create the perception of crisis in the passage of the Meech Lake Accord, actually led to a full-blown constitutional crisis in the aftermath of the doomed accord. A new constitutional initiative, designed to meet that crisis, also ended in failure.[59] Indeed, the result was another referendum on Quebec sovereignty held on October 30, 1995. In that referendum, Quebec independence was narrowly averted by a vote of 59.56 percent to 49.44 percent. Moreover, although passage of CUFTA in 1988 satisfied western voters, the politics of constitutional renewal did not. When the passage of CUFTA was ensured after the 1988 election, western voters abandoned the Conservatives in favor of the prowestern Reform party.[60] Finally, Mulroney's electoral strategy in Quebec proved unsuccessful. As the general election of October 1993 suggests, the two failed constitutional rounds led Quebec voters to turn away from the Conservatives and toward a new nationalist party—the Bloc Québécois. In short, while the result of Mulroney's twin initiatives was electoral realignment, change did not favor the Conservatives. The Tories won only two seats nationally in the 1993 election. The Reform party in the West and the Bloc Québécois in Quebec appear to have divided between them the spoils that were to have gone to Mulroney and the Conservative party.

Conclusion

This chapter attempts to explain Mulroney's superficially puzzling decision to enter into a comprehensive free trade agreement with the United States. Bilateral free trade had long been considered a risky proposition for government leaders in Canada. When the decision was made to negotiate the CUFTA in 1985, virtually no one believed the initiative would be popular. The results of the 1988 (free trade) election confirm that point. Pro–free trade parties received less than 50 percent of the popular vote in that election. However, Mulroney saw the opportunity to retain support in western Canada and simultaneously to break new electoral ground for his Conservatives in Quebec through free trade and the Meech Lake constitutional initiative. Mulroney attempted to use free trade and Meech Lake to effect a partisan realignment in Canada through the construction of a Quebec/western electoral axis.

Canada's passage of the Free Trade Implementation Act can best be explained in terms of the model advanced in chapter 1. Free trade constituted a by-product in the larger game of institutional design. Mulroney represents the political entrepreneur engaged in a game of institutional reform. His facilitating coalition consisted of the ten provincial premiers (most critically those from Quebec and the westernmost provinces of British Columbia, Alberta, and Saskatchewan) and the business community. This constituted a natural alliance of forces opposed to the nationalist, interventionist, and centralizing ventures of the Trudeau era. Two of these initiatives in particular—the NEP in western Canada and the Constitution Act in Quebec—mobilized considerable political opposition. Mulroney's twin initiatives of economic and constitutional decentralization were designed to appeal to these disaffected regions.

Mulroney relied on a three-pronged strategy in order to minimize the potential for popular (and largely western) opposition. He sought to limit the constitutional agenda. He attempted to keep negotiations as secretive as possible. Finally, he relied on the perception of crisis to facilitate movement on the Constitution. Mulroney's strategy entailed considerable danger. By acceding to Quebec's constitutional demands in the Meech Lake Accord, Mulroney risked alienating his party's traditional support base in western Canada. Western alienation did follow largely from the belief that federal initiatives reflected bias toward central Canada. Subordination of the western constitutional agenda to that of Quebec did nothing to diminish this perception.

In retrospect, Mulroney's strategy of linked initiatives proved disastrous. The Conservative party was all but obliterated in the 1993 general election. Moreover, the perception of crisis that Mulroney sought to foster in the constitutional arena emerged as a prophecy. Not only has the separatist Bloc Québécois dominated federally in Quebec since the failure of the 1992 Charlottetown Accord, but in 1995 a hard-line separatist PQ government held yet another popular referendum on Quebec independence. In sum, while the Mulroney legacy did yield the CUFTA, the political price paid by Mulroney and his party was high. Moreover, the worst may be still to come. In the constitutional arena the legacy of Mulroney's high stakes gamble ultimately may be the breakup of Canada.

5

NAFTA AND SOLIDARITY

Institutional Design in Mexico

The six-year term, or *sexenio,* of President Carlos Salinas de Gortari (1988–1994) will long be remembered as a turning point in Mexican economic and political development. Coming to power in the midst of intense economic turmoil, and with his hegemonic Partido Revolucionario Institucional (PRI) in danger of political annihilation, Salinas seemed to revitalize both the Mexican economy and the electoral fortunes of the PRI. This chapter explains Mexico's reversal of long-standing antipathy toward closer economic relations with the United States through the NAFTA initiative. It suggests that with the apparent breakdown of the electoral alignment that traditionally had supported the PRI, Salinas was obliged to effect fundamental realignment. This was to be achieved by regaining the support of the peasantry and the urban poor through the comprehensive Programa Nacional de Solidaridad (PRONASOL). In order to attract the foreign investment necessary to fund PRONASOL, as well as to entice the much needed support of private investors in Mexico, Salinas constructed a facilitating coalition in which the North American Free Trade Agreement (NAFTA) and PRONASOL initiatives were logrolled.

. . .

A critical component of Mexico's corporatist and authoritarian political tradition has been a powerful commitment to Mexican nationalism, traditionally an important element binding the diverse sectors that have supported the PRI.[1] Nationalism still touches a responsive chord in Mexico, based largely on sentiments that range from distrust to active dislike of the United States. The 1990 World Values Survey, for example, shows that only 20 percent of Mexicans "trust" Americans, compared to 52 percent who "distrust" them.[2] The roots of this sentiment are not difficult to comprehend, considering how much American territory once belonged to Mexico. Mexican elites regularly have relied on expressions of nationalism as a means of generating political support during times of unrest. The classic example was the nationalization of the energy sector in 1938 following a protracted struggle between Mexican oil workers and their foreign employers. Less successfully, President José López Portillo nationalized the banks in direct response to the external debt crisis of 1982.

In the economic sphere, nationalism manifested itself in economic protectionism. Between the 1940s (when import controls were introduced) and the 1980s, Mexico maintained one of the highest levels of trade protection in Latin America. This protectionism originally took the form of high tariffs and import licensing, although the latter gradually became the main weapon of import protection. By 1970, almost 80 percent of Mexican imports were covered by licenses.[3]

Moreover, the use of "official pricing" in the setting of tariffs—whereby the Mexican government determined the market value of a commodity before tariff duties were added—made import protection even more substantial. Protectionism initially benefited all sectors of the economy. The agricultural sector expanded and generated large surpluses. Economic prosperity brought fiscal and monetary stability, which in turn attracted foreign investors who contributed to the construction of a solid industrial infrastructure. Finally, economic growth stimulated the expansion of a vigorous service sector, a major component of which—tourism—was an important source of foreign currency.[4]

The engine that powered the economic prosperity of the postwar years was import-substituting industrialization (ISI), an economic development strategy employed by very late industrializers (largely in Latin America). ISI leaves a decidedly mixed legacy. The short-term benefits are substantial. The initial phase is characterized by the emergence of industries dedicated to production of consumer goods for the domestic market. These industries flourish in the absence of effective foreign competition. In addition to import protection, ISI involves a variety of credit and fiscal policy tools, including subsidies, the creation of state-owned development banks and other credit institutions, and pressure on foreign importers to set up manufacturing operations in the host countries to assist in the creation of backward and forward linkages.[5] Rapid industrial growth stimulates the economy, creating incentives for expansion in the industrial sector. Indeed, the Mexican economy grew at an average rate of 6 percent between 1940 and 1980.[6] However, the potential for growth beyond the domestic market is limited. Because ISI involves the importation of technology from abroad, domestic production tends to follow existing trends rather than develop new products. As a result, exports are rarely able to penetrate world markets.[7]

When domestic growth potential slows, ISI becomes problematic. Firms that expanded rapidly during the exuberant phase discover that they have overestimated demand. Profits and investment decline, and plants are left with aging and obsolete equipment. This final phase of ISI is characterized by slow economic growth, unemployment, and a deteriorating balance of payments. However, perhaps the most serious problem associated with ISI is that it renders domestic industry dependent on continued import protection. As a result, despite the evident exhaustion of ISI in Mexico by the early 1970s, over the next decade domestic manufacturers strongly resisted policies that would have liberalized Mexico's structure of import controls. Fundamental economic reform actually was attempted during the *sexenio* of President Luis Echeverría (1970–1976). However, as Rubio notes:

> The first attempts at reform . . . met the intransigence of various vested interests. Echeverría thus equated reform with instability. He abandoned all attempts to introduce the kind of reform that was needed. . . . Echeverría could not afford reform because the economy kept growing at about 6 percent, albeit ominously fuelled largely by increasing foreign borrowing after the first oil shock in 1973. In that context, inducing a recession for the sake of reform was logically considered to be political suicide.[8]

Nevertheless, severe economic problems in the 1980s obliged the Mexican government, under President Miguel de la Madrid (1982–1988), to reevaluate the statist policies that had prevailed for decades. Under pressure from the International Monetary Fund (IMF), the de la Madrid administration rejected comprehensive statism in favor of privatization of numerous state enterprises, reduction of public spending, and emphasis on promoting growth through exports.[9] In 1983 Mexico doubled the number of products to be imported free of tariffs, while by 1985 import licensing requirements were removed from over 60 percent of imports.[10]

More significant liberalization followed Mexico's decision to enter the GATT in 1986. Since that time, import licensing requirements have virtually been eliminated, while by 1987 tariff levels fell to an average of 20 percent and continued to decline.[11] During this period, Mexico's export profile shifted from reliance on oil to dependence on manufactured goods. In 1982, manufactured goods constituted only 14 percent of Mexican exports. By 1989, on the other hand, 55 percent of Mexico's exports were in manufactures, and the average annual rate of growth in manufacturing exports since the opening of the Mexican economy in the mid-1980s was a staggering 22.4 percent.[12]

However, despite encouraging signs, the de la Madrid economic stabilization package was largely unsuccessful. Not only were the reforms politically unpopular, they resulted in limited improvement to the Mexican economy. Although de la Madrid introduced important economic reforms, the most notable changes were effected by his successor. Indeed, within two years of taking office, Salinas had extended initiatives to control inflation, renegotiated the foreign debt, privatized the banks, and (most dramatically) announced that his government planned to reverse Mexico's historical antipathy toward closer ties to the United States and take the risk of seeking continental integration of the Mexican economy through NAFTA.

Conventional Explanations for NAFTA

Insofar as NAFTA was initiated and ratified only recently, there is relatively little literature regarding its passage. As is typical of much of the comparative and international political economy literature explaining shifts to free trade, both systemic- and societal-level explanations of NAFTA rely largely on deterministic arguments.

At the systemic level, some analysts explain NAFTA in terms of dependency theory. For example, Alarcón and McKinley—along with Béjar and Pichardo—portray NAFTA as a product of declining U.S. hegemony and the subsequent imperative of consolidating a U.S.-led and controlled hemispheric trading bloc.[13] From this perspective, as U.S. influence elsewhere in the world has declined, the United States has sought to impose its hegemony regionally, at the expense of its continental neighbors. The implication is that NAFTA was imposed on both Mexico and Canada in order to institutionalize the unequal division of labor and distribution of resources between the two countries. Béjar and Pichardo maintain:

> U.S. economic power has seriously declined in the past decade. As the recession has deepened, first in Canada and then in the United States, it has become obvious that the formation of a North American commercial bloc tends to formalize Mexico's role as *maquiladora*, with an abundant supply of cheap labor to ensure its place in the economic restructuring of the great North American industrial, agricultural, and banking enterprises.[14]

There are numerous logical problems associated with such *dependencia*-derived explanations for the causes of NAFTA. It is unclear, for example, how the United States was able to exercise its influence so decisively. Although the United States admittedly had made its interest in free trade with Mexico clear over the years, Mexico's successful rejection of these overtures suggests that American influence was less than compelling. Indeed, it was Mexico that approached the United States about the prospect of a North American free trade agreement, a point belying the notion that continental free trade was imposed by the United States.[15] It is also not clear that the relative gains to be derived from NAFTA will favor the United States. Mexico is not a rich country with a large and prosperous internal market. In fact, optimal tariff theory suggests that the short-term benefits from free trade with Mexico would be minimal for a large country such as the United States.[16] Although the United States admittedly does benefit from cheap labor in Mexico (a point emphasized particularly by Béjar and Pichardo), the importance of this issue should not be exaggerated. Not only is Mexico far from being the world's exclusive source of cheap labor, but free trade actually may be expected to create wage convergence between the two countries. In other words, wages in Mexico almost certainly will rise because of NAFTA. Indeed, this appears to be the crux of U.S. interest in Mexico: as that country grows richer through free trade, it will become an important market for U.S. exports. However, in order for this to occur, the relative gains that accrue to Mexico almost by definition must outpace those to the United States.

More promising explanations for NAFTA focus on shifting societal demands within Mexico. Davis argues that internal politics within the PRI led to the empowerment of pro–free trade forces and to the weakening of protectionists. Davis suggests that the most protectionist elements in the PRI's electoral alliance were weakened because of internal changes in the PRI. As a result, Salinas was not compelled to be as mindful of protectionist demands as previous leaders had been.

> When inflation and economic restructuring after 1981 debilitated the labor movement, drove middle classes away from the ruling party, and eliminated some business activities while stimulating others, the traditional foundations of one-party rule weakened. Pro-protectionist elements within the party lost bargaining power with government policymakers, while new domestic forces openly supportive of trade gained clout.[17]

Hellman enhances this argument, suggesting that shifting societal demands over the NAFTA issue were a function, in part, of asymmetrical access to information. She maintains that potential winners under NAFTA were more likely to understand the benefits than were potential losers to understand the costs. Pastor and Wise maintain that by the time the losers in the process might have realized the true costs of NAFTA, they would have been too weak to extract political revenge.[18] Still others portray free trade as an economic imperative, suggesting that NAFTA was necessary for the revival of the Mexican economy. Indeed, Baer holds that NAFTA was the logical culmination of the trend toward an expansion of Mexico's manufacturing sector after the collapse of oil prices in the 1980s.[19]

Arguments that turn on shifting domestic politics and on economic necessity can be compelling. These factors clearly influenced Mexico's decision in 1990 to initiate NAFTA. But such explanations are incomplete. Not only are they entirely deterministic, allowing little possibility for entrepreneurial ability within the Mexican government, but they do not account for the timing of the NAFTA decision. The economic crisis in Mexico began in 1982 and the imperative for reform was apparent even earlier, yet even as late as 1989, NAFTA was not even considered a serious option. Thus, without rejecting contentions that economic crisis and shifts in domestic politics were important factors in the decision to pursue NAFTA, we still have not found the answer to the puzzle of why Mexico shifted its trade policy so radically in 1990.

From the statist perspective, Poitras and Robinson suggest that NAFTA was the overarching objective of Salinas and his close circle of presidential advisers.[20] They maintain that the principal obstacle to free trade in Mexico was predicted opposition from within Mexico's "popular sector"—the lower urban and rural classes that traditionally supported the PRI. Thus, in order to achieve economic liberalization without losing the political support of the masses, Salinas bought off potential opposition through his PRONASOL reforms. In short, free trade was made politically feasible, in large part, by virtue of a logroll over policy reform and institutional innovation.

Poitras and Robinson's argument is similar to the one advanced in this book. The critical difference, however, lies in the perception of which initiative—PRONASOL or NAFTA—constituted the first-order preference of the Salinas administration. Poitras and Robinson's contention that NAFTA was the overarching objective of the Salinas government, with PRONASOL as a by-product, makes intuitive sense. Indeed, many of Salinas's closest advisers, trained at prestigious American universities, were ideologically committed to trade liberalization. On the other hand, Poitras and Robinson's theory suffers from a potential timing problem. Salinas introduced his PRONASOL initiative shortly after taking office in the summer of 1988, and by the spring of 1990, when the Salinas government changed its position on continental free trade, PRONASOL was an established and promising program. Given that PRONASOL preceded what Poitras and Robinson call Salinas's "stunning redirection of the nation's foreign economic policy," there is reason to question if PRONASOL was a by-product of NAFTA, or rather (as suggested here), if NAFTA was a by-product of PRONASOL.[21]

Salinas as Political Entrepreneur

Upon coming to power in July 1988, Salinas took over a party that seemed on the verge of collapse. The PRI long had represented a formal alliance of labor, peasantry, and the popular sector, held together by nationalist populism, clientelism, and repression.[22] In addition, economic protectionism ensured the support of much of the private sector. However, the 1988 election witnessed significant defections from the PRI's traditional electoral alliance. (Between 1929 and 1988, the PRI and its predecessors won every presidential, gubernatorial, and senatorial election in the country.) Indeed, in the election of 1988, the once unchallenged PRI faced considerable threats from both the right and the left. It is probable that the PRI actually lost the election, and that Salinas was returned only because of massive electoral fraud. As it was, official results gave the ruling party only the slimmest possible margin of victory. It was against this backdrop of political instability that Salinas sought to reconstruct his party's electoral alliance. While an electoral realignment favoring the PRI was of fundamental importance to Salinas, it is important to note that he was equally concerned with turning around the economic fortunes of Mexico.[23] Because Mexico's Constitution does not make allowance for presidential reelection, a president's legacy is measured in terms of both what he accomplishes for the party and his accomplishments for the country.

The PRI began in 1929 as the Partido Nacional Revolucionario (PNR). The founding of the PNR signaled the end of the violent struggle for control of the state, which had characterized the early postrevolutionary years, and cleared the way for the ascension to power in 1933 of the architect of the PRI's electoral alliance, Lazaro Cárdenas. Cárdenas sought to construct an indomitable electoral alignment in Mexico based on the support of the peasantry, organized labor, the popular sector, and the military.[24] In addition, close links were established between the dominant alliance and the private sector.

Land reform was an integral part of Cárdenas's program. In all, Cárdenas turned over 18 million hectares of land to 800,000 peasants.[25] The cornerstone of this policy was the Expropriation Law (1936), which permitted the state to seize property if such action was deemed in the national interest. Insofar as previous land expropriations had affected mostly inferior or unutilized land, the quality of land redistributed, as much as its quantity, distinguished Cárdenas's land reforms from those preceding them. Another key agrarian reform that contributed to the PRI's success in securing and maintaining the support of the rural underclasses was the creation of numerous agrarian collectives, or *ejidos*. The *ejidos* provided not only land (which was government owned and could not be sold), but accessible credit as well. Equally important for the Mexican economy, these collectives were large enough to maintain efficient economies of scale, thereby allowing the countryside to remain productive.[26] The peasantry was organized through the Confederación de Campesinos Mexicanos (CCM) and the Confederación Nacional Campesina (CNC), and for the next fifty years remained a powerful source of support for the dominant alliance.

Cárdenas also undertook significant reform of the labor movement. A 1936 strike at the Vidriera Monterrey glass factory stimulated the creation of a comprehensive labor program that institutionalized the pro-labor orientation of the PRI and inextricably bound the labor movement to the party. One of the most significant results was the creation of the Confederación de Trabajadores de México (CTM). Other peak organizations for labor included the Confederación General de Trabajo (CGT), and the Confederación Regional Obrera Mexicana (CROM). Until 1988, these organizations were consistently able to deliver the vote of organized labor to the PRI.

The popular sector—consisting of civil servants, teachers, small landowners, students, professionals, and other members of the middle class—was organized formally in 1943 as the Confederación Nacional de Organizaciónes Populares (CNOP). Over time the bureaucrats within the CNOP gained considerable influence, becoming arguably the most powerful visible group within the PRI.[27]

Although officially hostile to the private sector, the PRI alliance maintained important ties to business. Decades of economic growth stimulated by rapid industrialization helped solidify ties between the private sector and the PRI. ISI brought the private sector firmly under the control of the state. As firms became increasingly reliant on protectionism, they also became more dependent on the government. Indeed, because import licenses and tariffs could be imposed, altered, or removed at the whim of the state, the government could demand the compliance of the private sector across a variety of issues. Moreover, the state owned most of the key strategic sectors of the economy including the railroad, telegraph, telephone, electrical power, steel, aviation, petroleum, natural gas, and (most important) much of the financial sector. Thus, in addition to exercising tight political control over the central Banco Nacional de México, the state was involved directly in more than thirty public credit institutions, which effectively allowed it to control the supply and direction of credit.[28] Finally, state control of the private sector was facilitated by the 1941 Chambers Law, which required all but the smallest enterprises to be members of one of Mexico's business confederations: the Confederación de Cámaras Industriales (CONCAMIN), the Confederación de Cámaras Nacionales de Comercio (CONCANACO), the Confederación Patronal de la República Mexicana (COPARMEX), or the Cámara Nacional de la Industria de Transformación (CANACINTRA). These peak associations constituted the channels through which much of the interaction between state and private sector took place.[29]

The PRI alliance was constructed as a series of patron-client relationships. The primary function of elites within the alliance was to maintain popular support. So inviolable was the principle of regime stability that the government often resorted to such extralegal activities as electoral fraud, kidnapping, murder, and other forms of brutal repression in response to perceived forms of political countermobilization.[30] However, despite the potential for authoritarian responses to political threat, the alliance operated largely on institutionalized rules of corruption, patronage, nationalist populism, and co-optation.

Co-optation was facilitated by the structure of the representative sectors, organized into peak associations. The heads of these associations were among the most powerful elites within the alliance. Groups within peak associations were mobilized along regional and functional lines. For example, such mobilization prevented tobacco workers in one state from allying either with tobacco workers from other states or with other rural laborers in their own region.[31] Because sectors were fragmented regionally and functionally, and because class- or sector-wide solidarity was discouraged, grassroots unrest tended to be directed at specific issues of local concern and could therefore be easily contained.

One of the keys to regime stability was the minimization of competition among elites. In the interest of maintaining regime stability, there were two fundamental operational rules among elites: they were expected to control the demands of their clientele; and they were not permitted to expand their respective power bases at the expense of other elites within the alliance, or to make unreasonable demands on the alliance. As long as there were adequate resources to distribute to all within the dominant alliance, elites placed a higher premium on regime stability than on competition for marginal rents. In this sense the PRI alliance resembled an Olsonian inclusive group.[32] However, when the supply of national resources contracted in the early 1980s, the dominant alliance began to break apart.

The disintegration of the existing electoral alignment occurred gradually. The nationalization of the banks in 1982, under López Portillo, sparked the defection of many in the business community to the conservative Partido Acción Nacional (PAN). Heredia notes:

> In spite of the [de la Madrid] administration's clear attempts to regain the confidence of the private sector . . . business government relations did not return to their pre-1982 patterns and molds. Relations between the president and the new business leadership . . . remained tense up to the very end. The participation of major business figures as PAN candidates in important electoral contests, including the 1988 presidential one, also steadily increased.[33]

On the left, stabilization measures alienated core constituencies of the PRI. It is ironic that, while the party's rightward shift under de la Madrid did not appease conservative business, it alienated the rural and urban under-classes. Popular opposition to the government manifested itself in support for the new Partido Revolucionario Democrático (PRD), originally a rump within the PRI known as the Corriente Democrática (CD), which broke away from the party in 1987. As the PRD, it contested the 1988 presidential election, calling for a return to the original objectives of the alliance—redistribution of wealth and the maintenance of economic protection.

By the end of the de la Madrid administration, the dominant alliance had splintered. On the right, the PAN had capitalized on support from northerners, much of the business community, the middle classes, and the church. The PRD, in turn, was supported by disaffected labor, the peasantry, and public employees.[34] While enough residual support remained to make the PRI competitive (if not the honest victor) in the 1988 presidential election, the survival of the party was in grave doubt. Reynolds suggests: "The long-standing pact between the government and the private sector, including labor unions, peasant agriculture, and popular organizations, was bankrupt both literally and figuratively. What was clearly an economic crisis proved to be a political crisis as well." In short, Mexico clearly was in a state of electoral dealignment during the late 1980s. As late as 1991 when respondents were asked if they sympathized with any party, 56 percent stated that they had no party preference. Similarly, while support for the PRI in 1982 was about 55 percent, it declined steadily throughout the 1980s (except for a slight recovery in 1988) and reached its nadir in 1990 at 25 percent.[35]

The NAFTA decision was a bold and unexpected move. Prior to March 1990, the Salinas government officially opposed North American free trade.[36] Although the opening of the economy under de la Madrid had forced much of the business community to adapt to—and ultimately support—free trade, there remained powerful opponents. For example, most of the labor movement, a traditional pillar of support for the PRI, was opposed strongly to free trade. The support of the peasantry, yet another historical source of PRI electoral dominance, was steadily defecting to the anti–free trade PRD. Indeed, early in 1994, Indian peasants in the impoverished state of Chiapas undertook armed insurrection against free market initiatives in Mexico.[37]

In short, the introduction of NAFTA threatened to precipitate the permanent loss of much of the PRI's traditional constituency on the political left. Salinas himself predicted that liberalizing the economy through NAFTA entailed "a political cost, no doubt, but I am convinced that the social and economic benefits will compensate." Baer commented: "The decision to pursue a [continental] free-trade agreement was a stunning political act—heretical in some Mexican intellectual and political circles—and it defies Mexico's long history of defensive nationalism." On the other hand, opinion poll data from 1991 suggest that over 60 percent of Mexicans approved of a proposed free trade agreement. The salience of this figure, however, must not be exaggerated. As the Canadian case illustrates, public opinion data on hypothetical issues are not a good predictor of how people will react to concrete issues. Indeed, as Basáñez notes, the same opinion poll indicated that 44 percent believed that free trade would be of greater benefit to the United States than to Mexico, and 66 percent believed that free trade would make Mexico even more dependent upon the United States.[38]

In seeking to prevent the ultimate breakup of the PRI alliance, while at the same time maintaining political stability in Mexico, Salinas assumed office with a two-part strategy. First, it was necessary to stabilize the economy. Second, he sought to rebuild his dominant alliance by constructing a logroll among supporters of his institutional initiative—PRONASOL—and proponents of free trade with the United States and Canada.

The Necessary Crisis

As noted, the 1980s were crisis years for Mexico. During the 1970s, difficult decisions regarding economic restructuring were avoided by the López Portillo administration due to the discovery of important oil and gas reserves. Industrial production was stimulated by increased government spending and heavy foreign borrowing. However, declining oil prices brought severe economic consequences.[39] Between 1978 and 1982, the public sector deficit rose from 7.4 to 17.9 percent of the Gross Domestic Product (GDP), while the foreign public debt expanded from 29 to 61 percent of GDP. At the same time, the peso fell drastically against the dollar, as inflation went from 20.3 percent in 1979, to 98.2 percent three years later. Capital flight amounted to $84 billion during the de la Madrid administration. Despite dedicated attempts at economic stabilization, largely undertaken in the second half of his administration, the economy continued to decline under de la Madrid. In the last quarter of 1987, with the inflation rate at 160 percent, the Mexico City stock market finally collapsed under the weight of declining investor confidence.[40]

Upon taking office, Salinas's first objective was to continue efforts begun under de la Madrid to bring down Mexico's inflation rate. In the last months of the de la Madrid administration, the government enacted the Pacto de Solidaridad Económica (PSE)—an incomes policy designed to ensure wage and price cooperation between business and labor. Under Salinas, the PSE was reorganized into the Pacto para la Establidad y el Crecimiento Económico (PECE). The PSE and PECE were agreements to freeze prices and to index wages to the rate of inflation. Government spending was reduced and services were made more costly in an attempt to reduce the fiscal deficit. Finally, the peso was pegged to the American dollar. The results were encouraging. By 1993, Mexico's inflation rate had fallen to 9.5 percent, while real economic growth and levels of private investment increased. Equally important was successful renegotiation of the foreign debt crisis. Under the so-called Brady Plan, almost five hundred participating creditor banks (which collectively held about one-half of Mexico's foreign debt), agreed to forgive the principal owed, to reduce interest owed, or to lend new money. The result was the reduction of foreign debt from about $48.5 billion to approximately $20.5 billion.[41]

In some ways, the timing of the crisis benefited Salinas politically. Although associated with de la Madrid by virtue of partisan ties (he was the outgoing president's handpicked successor), Salinas was able to take credit for economic amelioration, while avoiding much of the political flak for the more difficult decisions taken by de la Madrid. Indeed, because bureaucratic inability to respond effectively to crisis is an effective means of initiating institutional reform, the crisis was critical to the success of Salinas's plan to effect electoral realignment within Mexico.[42] Bureaucratic opposition to the PRONASOL initiative was overcome in large part because traditional corporatist responses to the economic crisis failed.

The Facilitating Coalition

By the middle of 1990, building on efforts initiated by his predecessor, Salinas had succeeded in temporarily stabilizing the Mexican economy. (Economic troubles began anew in late 1994 and 1995, when a staggering balance of payments deficit coupled with inadequate U.S. dollar reserves forced devaluation of the peso and a new round of high inflation.) Salinas's primary focus shifted, therefore, toward effecting electoral realignment through the reconstruction of much of the old PRI alliance, and to institutionalizing the economic progress achieved in Mexico.

Salinas recognized politically that the continuation of PRI hegemony entailed eliminating threats on both the left and the right. In practice this meant recapturing the support of the peasantry, urban poor, indigenous peoples, and residents of impoverished regions, on the one hand, while regaining the allegiance of the business community on the other. In the process, the PRI has sought to reform itself, eliminating the clientelistic structure of party support and appealing instead directly to the Mexican electorate. In sum, realignment has entailed three critical tasks: "fortification of the PRI, dehibilitation of the PRD, and cooptation of the PAN." Similarly, as Dresser notes for the PRI: "Political survival involves calculating the costs of attracting new supporters and maintaining old ones." The first two objectives, undertaken simultaneously, involved institutional design in Mexico through the introduction of PRONASOL.[43]

Salinas's Solidarity program radically reorients state-society relations in Mexico. Bureaucratic inefficiency associated with the traditional corporatist structure of the PRI has been replaced by direct interaction between the government and the target constituencies. Put differently, PRONASOL bypasses the bloated Mexican bureaucracy, providing funds directly to local communities to provide basic social services. The genesis of PRONASOL is found in Salinas's early academic work.[44] Salinas found that support for the political system in Mexican communities was not correlated positively with the amount of public spending in those communities. Indeed, in many cases the relationship was negative. Salinas drew two conclusions from this finding. First, public resources often were wasted, misappropriated, or absorbed through bureaucratic overhead. As a result, although a good deal of public money was dedicated to local projects, relatively little was allocated productively. Second, top-down decision-making in Mexico City often resulted in spending initiatives that did not address issues of local concern. Indeed, Salinas found that where projects were initiated locally and reflected local needs (rather than what Mexico City bureaucrats perceived as necessary), the granting of public resources was rewarded with increased community support for the PRI. It was this theory, put into practice, that resulted in PRONASOL.

Solidarity is the Mexican equivalent of the American New Deal. It creates numerous programs for the creation of sewage, potable water, health, education, food distribution, electrification, street paving, housing, and affordable credit.[45] At the same time, reform has been undertaken to semi-privatize agricultural collectives. The *ejido* system was overhauled to afford *ejidatarios* rights akin to private ownership. These rights include security of tenure, the right to sell their land to other *ejidatarios* (but not to outsiders), and the right to enter into joint ventures with the private sector.[46] In this way, not only is the countryside projected to become more productive, but living standards of the *ejidatarios* are expected to increase.

PRONASOL represents an enormous commitment of scarce resources in Mexico. In 1991 Solidarity accounted for 44 percent of the programmable federal investment budget. By the midterm elections of August 1991, PRONASOL had funded projects in over 1,500 municipalities, including the introduction of electricity into the homes of 5 million Mexicans, and running water into the homes of 3 million.[47] PRONASOL funds have been targeted at selective communities. Resources have been allocated disproportionately toward areas of strong PRD electoral support. In 1992, for example, 12 percent of the annual PRONASOL budget was allocated to the state of Michoacan, a relatively small state but the region most sympathetic to the PRD. The bulk of the funds were allocated immediately prior to the gubernatorial elections of that year. The PRI has been forthright about the political dimension of PRONASOL. A former member of the Salinas Programming and Budget team notes: "The intention behind PRONASOL is to create, through public works and services, a new urban base for the Mexican state. By the end of the '80s the social bases of the Mexican state were unravelling. We were confronted with an urban scenario that we didn't know, and that we had to organize politically."[48]

The Solidarity program has been a political success in Mexico. The results of the August 1991 midterm elections confirm the point. The PRI won back most of the votes (13 percent) it had lost between the 1985 and 1988 elections, with one party official estimating that PRONASOL had accounted for roughly one-quarter of the PRI vote in 1991. Indeed, in the aftermath of the midterm elections, 62.2 percent of Mexicans claimed to be in favor of the government's Solidarity initiative.[49] The success of the PRI's PRONASOL strategy has seriously undercut support for the PRD. Whereas the new party passively sought a natural progression from social movement to established party, the PRI actively worked to reinstitutionalize its support on the political left. On the right, the PRI strategy was more delicate. Not only was the support of the business community politically necessary, but recapturing that support was an economic imperative for the future of the government's institutional initiative.

Logrolling: PRONASOL and NAFTA

As in the other cases examined in this book, logrolling took place within the facilitating coalition. The Mexican right, led by the PAN, was an early and potent opponent of PRONASOL, condemning the initiative as "paternalistic waste."[50] Such conservative opposition to PRONASOL represented a dangerous problem for Salinas. Indeed, the active support of the business community was critical to PRONASOL's success, and this was by no means assured in the early years of the Salinas administration. Collectively, the business community possessed an effective veto over the Solidarity initiative. In the absence of the support of Mexican investors (many of whom had expatriated a good deal of capital during the 1980s), economic growth certainly would falter, rendering the Solidarity program fiscally unfeasible. It was to regain the support of the business community (as well as the confidence of foreign investors), and to benefit from the repatriation of capital necessary to fund the government's institutional initiative, that Salinas undertook the NAFTA gamble. Smith argues: "At bottom, the *salinistra* strategy entails a high-risk gamble: that liberalization will generate and sustain sufficient economic growth to forestall social unrest."[51]

The transformation of the Mexican business community over the course of the 1980s and 1990s was remarkable. Until the early 1980s, business enjoyed a mutually profitable relationship with the state. Not only did the government supply generous subsidies to industry, but labor was tightly regulated, allowing for the maximization of profits. Tight government regulation of society-at-large provided a stable environment in which to conduct business. Under these optimal conditions, economic nationalism "became the banner under which Mexican entrepreneurs extracted unearned rents from the general public."[52]

As the economic climate deteriorated during the 1980s, Mexico began to suffer less autonomy in terms of fiscal and foreign economic policy. The government could no longer afford to provide economic rents at the same rate as in the past. Subsidies such as cheap energy and support for research and development, for example, all but stopped after 1982. At the same time, the government began to allow market forces to rationalize the least efficient Mexican industries.[53] For the business sector, the impact of the state's inability to provide sufficient rents was felt early. In addition to the nationalization of the country's banks, the destabilizing effects of the crisis meant that the government could no longer provide a social climate conducive to productive enterprise. Thus, even before the government petitioned for membership in the GATT, part of the big business community—faced with a dramatic decrease in state-supplied rents—had begun to mobilize for the introduction of free market policies and an end to economic statism.[54]

The GATT decision of 1985–1986 was divisive and controversial within the business community. Small- and medium-sized businesses especially were opposed, while certain big business organizations such as CONCAMIN also disliked the idea of opening the economy.[55] By the late 1980s, however, although still in a state of transition, trade preferences within the business community had shifted overwhelmingly toward active support for free trade. The reduction of import protection after the decision to enter the GATT in 1985–1986 helped shift the trade policy preferences of many in Mexican business. Businesses that had prospered by producing for the protected domestic market were forced to reorganize in order to become internationally competitive. Businesses that were successful subsequently pressed the government for the opening of export markets abroad through trade initiatives. Many of those that were unsuccessful did not survive to press for increased protectionism.[56] Poitras and Robinson point out:

> With only minor reservations, most state-recognized business associations were strong supporters of free trade. The Mexican Employers Federation (COPARMEX), known as the conservative conscience of [the] business community, endorsed free trade with the United States along with other "pro-business" measures. So too did the CONCAMIN, the national confederation of industry, which stressed the benefits of economic growth while warning of the potential harm to small business. The CONCANACO, the national association of chambers of commerce, took its support one step further, not only staunchly defending the free trade agreement but also advocating that it be extended to petroleum as well. . . . The consensus and unity within the organized business community extended even to small and medium-sized companies, which marked a major shift on this issue.

Indeed, Poitras and Robinson further maintain: "Since its creation in 1941, CANACINTRA has been one of the largest business associations in Mexico because all small and medium size businesses are required by law to belong. Thus, CANACINTRA's stand on NAFTA served as a bellwether of how far the business community was willing to go in its embrace of free trade."[57] With the stabilization initiatives of the 1980s, the traditionally laissez-faire PAN became even more supportive of free-market and antistatist policies. Thus, the PRI moved rightward during the 1980s, and the PAN did likewise, bringing much of the business sector along with it. Salinas's task was to recapture the right of the political spectrum without compromising the support of the left. The task was made trickier because the very statism that had alienated much of the right lay at the heart of the Solidarity initiative.

In part, Salinas relied on supply-side economics to regain the support and confidence of the business community. By 1991, the top tax rate had been reduced to 35 percent, down from 50 percent five years previously. The top corporate rates fell from 56 to 35 percent over the same period. Of perhaps greater significance, in May 1990 Salinas reprivatized the banks. It was the nationalization of the banking structure in 1982 that had precipitated the rift between the PRI and the business community. This was one of many privatization initiatives. Indeed, by 1992, there were roughly 200 state-owned enterprises in Mexico, down from over 1,100 in 1983.[58]

However, the most effective initiative in regaining business support and investor confidence was NAFTA. Between 1988 and 1992, Mexico's exports increased by 32 percent. Because the preponderance of Mexico's trade is with the United States, business leaders considered the signing of NAFTA to be indispensable to their survival and prosperity.[59] Business leaders, especially in the industrial center of Monterrey, worked closely with the Salinas administration, urging it to press for guaranteed access to the lucrative U.S. market.

The NAFTA initiative was Salinas's masterstroke. Not only did it appeal politically to the business community by institutionalizing free-market economic policies in Mexico (thus undercutting the role of the PAN),[60] it also helped create sufficient domestic investment economic growth to fund the PRONASOL project. (In a sense the tradeoff was classic welfare economics. The profits from liberalization of trade are redistributed to compensate those injured by liberalization—and, in this case, other economic stabilization measures. The outcome is Pareto-preferred.)[61]

Both foreign and domestic investment increased in Mexico after the announcement of NAFTA. In 1990, Japanese investment in Mexico doubled, to roughly $4 billion. In total, the flow of private capital into Mexico went from $1 billion in 1987 to $14 billion in 1991. Even more telling is that, in the aftermath of the stockmarket crash of 1987, the Bolsa Mexicana de Valores was among the fastest-growing stockmarkets in the world (this growth was interrupted severely by the monetary and fiscal crisis of late 1994 and early

1995). By the end of 1993, capitalization was at $200.6 billion. In 1993 alone, capitalization increased by 43.9 percent (this progress was also seriously undermined by the crisis of 1994–1995).[62]

Increased investment in Mexico permitted PRONASOL to flourish. Between 1989 and 1993, annual PRONASOL spending increased from $500 million to $2.4 billion. In sum, the NAFTA and PRONASOL initiatives combined to create a "compromise of embedded liberalism" in Mexico.[63] Economic liberalization was coupled with comprehensive state intervention in the construction of a Mexican welfare state. Between them the initiatives attracted critical political support from the left and the right. Economically, NAFTA ensured the investor confidence necessary to fund PRONASOL and provided sufficient deregulation of the economy to appease the business community, even as the government moved ahead with the institutional reform designed to ensure political stability among the poorest within Mexican society.

Conclusion

The objective of this chapter has been to explain Salinas's decision to overturn more than a century of anti-American sentiment in Mexico and undertake comprehensive continental free trade. It argues that Salinas, the political entrepreneur, sought NAFTA in large part as a means to reconstruct his party's electoral alliance. Although a risky policy, NAFTA helped secure the support and confidence of the Mexican business class within his facilitating coalition, a fundamental prerequisite for his institutional initiative.

The severe economic crisis of the 1980s permitted Salinas to undertake comprehensive institutional reform with his Solidarity program. PRONASOL, the Mexican equivalent of the New Deal, provided basic social services to the most impoverished Mexicans. Not only was this a means of forestalling political instability, but the program was designed to replace the corporatist structure of the PRI with a more direct link between state and society. In this way, many of the core supporters of the old PRI electoral alliance were enticed back to the party.

The crisis also obligated the Mexican government to undertake radical economic stabilization measures. Building on reforms initiated by his predecessor, Salinas moved toward a free-market approach for the Mexican economy. However, the economic reforms of the 1980s failed to win back the support of a business class that had been alienated by the 1982 nationalization of the banking sector. Indeed, businesses that survived the turmoil of the decade increasingly moved to support the PAN platform, which was even less statist than that of the reformed PRI. In order to regain the political support and confidence of the business class, thereby stimulating the private investment and economic growth necessary to fund the PRONASOL plan, Salinas initiated NAFTA negotiations in 1990.

By undertaking his twin initiatives of NAFTA and PRONASOL, Salinas appears to have regained substantial electoral support on both the right and the left. Although the March 23, 1994, assassination of PRI presidential candidate Luis Donaldo Colosio was a serious blow, the party managed to emerge victorious from the 1994 presidential elections. Indeed, from the dealignment of the late 1980s to the apparent realignment of the 1990s, Salinas appears to have restructured the Mexican electoral system without the PRI relinquishing power. The "silent regime change" of the early 1990s undoubtedly will result in the opening of the Mexican political process.[64] For this reason alone, another sixty-five years of PRI hegemony is not to be expected. On the other hand, the party has constructed a solid political base from which to compete in the new era of Mexican electoral politics.

The success of Salinas's two initiatives will ultimately have to be analyzed in the fullness of time. The devastating effects of the peso crisis of 1994–1995 is an illustration that Salinas's gamble was not without its dangers. Indeed, Salinas's legacy in Mexico—and abroad (Salinas was a major candidate to lead the World Trade Organization, successor to the GATT, prior to the crisis)—has been badly damaged, at least in the short term, by the perception that he was the unwitting architect of the crisis. Whether he is vindicated with time, as Peel was, or destined to suffer the same legacy as Mulroney will become apparent over the coming years.

6

CONCLUSION

High Risks, Low Risks

Free trade represents an enigma for students of comparative politics and international political economy. It is economically beneficial for society at large but alienates vested interests without attracting a concomitant degree of political support. For this reason free trade is less common than its relative economic merit might lead one to expect.

This book has developed a model to explain one route to overcoming the political intractability associated with policies of trade liberalization. The high-risk model holds that political entrepreneurs will be enticed to accept the risks associated with free trade only if doing so assists them to realize objectives of a higher order. These objectives typically involve effecting electoral realignments or, alternatively, preserving the existing electoral alignment. Alignment games entail attracting or preserving the semipermanent support of electorally significant groups within society. The most effective means of attracting or preserving this support is through reform or preservation of the regime-defining characteristics of the polity—conceptualized as institutions. Because institutions may be taken to represent an entrenched set of values or interests, altering or preserving the institutional structure of the polity has implications for the bases of a party's long-term electoral support. Critical to the task of the political entrepreneur is the construction of a facilitating coalition that consists of all groups or individuals with the power to veto the entrepreneur's institutional initiative. Many within the coalition will support the political entrepreneur. However, those who do not will have to be brought onside with incentives and side-payments.

In some cases (such as those examined in this book), those opposed or indifferent to the entrepreneur's institutional initiative will demand policy reform as compensation for agreeing not to block the institutional initiative. The most interesting example of such policy reform is trade liberalization. In such cases, trade liberalization comes about merely as a by-product of the political entrepreneur's attempt to realize higher-order objectives.

The conceptualization of free trade as a by-product of larger objectives places this theory in sharp contrast to prevailing literature in comparative and international political economy. In none of the four cases examined was trade liberalization a first-order preference of the political entrepreneur. Indeed, the British, Canadian, and Mexican leaders went on public record as opposing free trade, whereas in the U.S. case, Roosevelt actively pursued policies of economic nationalism before changing tack and deciding to embrace trade liberalization.

In the American case, Roosevelt sought to effect an electoral realignment, first through the construction of corporatist institutions to regulate the industrial and agricultural sectors and, upon the failure of this initiative, through the construction of the welfare state. Creating a welfare state in America promised to secure for the Democratic party the lasting support of such groups as the African Americans, immigrants, labor, and urban poor. With the support of the agricultural class already ensured through the continuance of the AAA, Roosevelt sought to win over the political support of the third critical component of his Second New Deal alliance, internationally oriented industry and finance. By liberalizing trade under the terms of the RTAA, not only did Roosevelt attract the much needed political support of internationally oriented business, but he deepened the rift within the American business community, thereby isolating the Second New Deal's most prominent enemy, nationalist big business.

In Canada, with less success, Mulroney sought to build an entrenched electoral axis between Quebec and the West with his Meech Lake Accord. Mulroney envisioned constitutional reform as a means of wresting electoral support in the province of Quebec from the Liberal party. However, because constitutional reform favoring Quebec was not popular in the Conservative party's traditional support base in the West, and because the western premiers were in a position to scuttle the institutional initiative, Mulroney moved to satisfy long-standing western demands for continental free trade. Although the logroll among supporters of the institutional and free trade initiatives was successful, the Meech Lake Accord was doomed by other, unforeseen forces. Instead of a successful realignment, therefore, Mulroney precipitated a shift that saw his Conservative party all but shut out in the 1993 general election.

In Mexico, Salinas was in the unusual position of seeking to effect re-alignment while his party was still in power. Despite winning the (tainted) 1988 election, the PRI found itself in grave danger of political annihilation. Powerful opposition on both the left and the right created significant de-fection from the PRI's traditional electoral alliance. In order to regain sup-port on the left, the Salinas government embarked on an ambitious project to construct a comprehensive, New Deal–style welfare state in Mexico. However, severe economic turmoil threatened the scope, and indeed the very existence, of Salinas's Solidarity initiative. Thus it was with the twin intentions of recapturing the support of the business community and of restoring the private investment necessary for economic growth that Sali-nas radically altered Mexican trade practices by initiating a free trade agreement with the United States, and later with Canada.

It is important to note that alignment games under the high-risk model need not necessarily feature attempts at realignment. In the British case, Peel was motivated to preserve the existing alignment. Despite fairly con-sistent agitation for constitutional reform since the Reform Act of 1832, Britain's regime in the 1840s seemed a stable one. The greatest clamor came from the Anti–Corn Law League, which sought to end aristocratic privi-lege in the form of agricultural protection. Although prominent, the mid-dle-class agitators were but marginal actors politically. On the other hand, Peel was sufficiently astute to recognize that, if the Anti–Corn Law League were to seek to mobilize the discontented underclasses in England or Ire-land, the result might well be widescale reform of the British Constitution. Using the pretext of a potato crop failure in Ireland, Peel repealed the Corn Laws in order to forestall a credible and powerful threat to the existing in-stitutional and electoral order.

Each of the four political entrepreneurs studied here undertook consid-erable political risk when he radically shifted his position on free trade. In-deed, Peel and Mulroney were sanctioned severely for their efforts, and Salinas's reputation has been badly tarnished by the peso crisis of 1994–

1995. At the analytical core of this study has been the attempt not only to explain the actions of these political entrepreneurs but also to provide clues toward an answer to the larger question of why governments accept the risk of free trade.

The high-risk model set forward in this book is grounded in rational choice theory. However, unlike other explanations based on the assumption of rationality, it does not rely on structural, deterministic factors to explain apparently suboptimal behavior on the part of those accepting the risk of trade liberalization. Instead, in the tradition of Putnam and Tsebelis, this study emphasizes the importance of conceptualizing politics as a game that takes place in multiple arenas, and of understanding that political entrepreneurs often look in multiple directions simultaneously, linking seemingly disparate events into a cohesive, rational strategy.[1]

From the Specific to the General: Policy Innovation in the 1990s

Identifiable within the field of comparative public policy is a set of policies that might be termed politically intractable. Like free trade, these policies benefit the population as a whole, but they also generate sufficient political opposition to dissuade governments from seeking to enact them. The universe of such politically intractable policies (PIP) is broad. Although the classification axiomatically is subjective, it includes all policies that benefit a narrow range of rent-seeking interests within society, while imposing deadweight costs onto society as a whole. Examples of particular importance to policy analysts and political economists include policies dedicated to the retrenchment of public spending; fiscal and monetary discipline as a means to limit inflation; elimination of subsidies to interest groups (such as transfer payments, industrial regulation, tariffs, quotas, and so on); and the provision of public goods such as safe cities and clean natural environments.[2]

The affluence of the postwar era in Western liberal democracies provided unprecedented opportunities to expand the scope of state-supplied rents. The growth of the welfare state led to the proliferation of clientelistic relationships between societal interests and government, while steady economic growth yielded sufficient surplus resources to distribute. By the 1970s, however, demands for rents began to outstrip the supply of resources, which was limited severely by the coincidental pressures of economic stagnation and hyperinflation. The economic problems of the 1970s and early 1980s prompted analysts to reevaluate the effects of the postwar settlement.

Critics claim that Western economies reaped what they had sowed during the boom years of the 1950s and 1960s. Under the terms of the postwar settlement, the state replaced the marketplace as the ultimate arbiter of redistribution, and citizens and pressure groups came to regard the government's role as that of a provider of goods and services. As the economic slowdown of the 1970s hampered states' abilities to generate new resources, it stimulated increased demands on existing resources. The resulting "demand-overload" or "post-pluralist malaise" led some to predict a crisis of ungovernability in the Western democracies.[3] The pernicious effects of what Bell generally refers to as the "revolution of rising expectations" was exacerbated by the breakdown of the international monetary regime created at Bretton Woods. The end of the dollar standard provided democratic governments with increased discretion over monetary policy. Governments found that in the short term, pressure group demands could be satisfied by increasing the domestic money supply.[4]

In the long term, the resultant inflationary effect only increased demands on the state as the economic malaise intensified. In addition, inflation led to increased wage demands and heightened industrial conflict, which further hampered economic performance. So pervasive were the political and economic ailments of the 1970s and early 1980s that in some quarters there was fear for the future of democracy itself. Indeed, Brittan suggests that democracy may be inherently self-defeating. The problem is that although voters are able to manage their private resources to the extent that they do not spend beyond their means, and to the extent that they realize that each spending decision represents an opportunity cost, they are not cognizant of similar constraints on the public purse. As a result, voters demand low taxes and low inflation but high levels of government spending. Similarly, the democratic process encourages politicians to make promises that they cannot possibly fulfill. Election campaigns create incentives for politicians to outbid one another in making spending or tax-cutting commitments, or both. Politicians thus are motivated to promise whatever it takes to gain office, and then seek to repair the damage created by these unrealizable promises once in power. The result, not surprisingly, is alienation and disaffection on the part of the electorate, which simply compounds the problem of ungovernability.[5]

Whether stimulated by the supply-side economic policies of Great Britain and the United States or by mere force of the business cycle, the world economy improved throughout the 1980s. However, the extended slump of the early 1990s has led to a renewed round of concern among economic analysts. As early as the mid-1980s, it had become clear that most member states of Organization for Economic Cooperation and Development (OECD) were experiencing unhealthy levels of public debt, large budget deficits, and ratios of government spending to GNP that were far higher than they had been during the 1960s.[6]

With the end of the 1980s' economic boom, governments in industrialized states once again must come to terms with the prospect that the continued prosperity of the postwar order is by no means assured. The anticipated problems of the 1990s—including slow growth rates, unemployment, mounting deficits fueled by high debt ratios, and increased demands for entitlement spending—threaten to emerge as a serious economic crisis.[7]

The threat is underscored by the slow recovery of the world economy from the recession of 1990–1991. Slow growth rates since 1990 have seen unemployment rise to over 10 percent in Canada and Europe and to over 7 percent in the United States. The recession of the early 1990s is a cyclical phenomenon, but this should not obscure the fact that it is part of a larger trend in economic decline. In the United States, annual growth of GDP fell from an average of 2 percent in the period 1955–1973, to an average of 1.3 percent in the period 1973–1986. For Japan, the drop over the same two eras was from 8.8 to 3.3 percent. In West Germany it fell from 4.2 to 2 percent; while the combined rate of decline for Britain, Canada, France, and Italy was from 3.8 to 1.7 percent.[8] Governments seeking to restore investor confidence will be compelled to exercise greater self-restraint and discipline in fiscal, monetary, and trade policies.

Outside the developed world, the economic stakes are even greater. The transition to democracy in the former communist states of Eastern Europe, for example, also underscores the need for governments to utilize scarce resources efficiently. Because rent-seeking has been so pervasive in these countries (thus raising the expectations of beneficiaries) and because resources are now so limited, the future of democracy and economic prosperity will depend on how effective governments are at balancing political stability with the passage of PIP.[9] It is ominous that governments unable to maintain popularity risk not merely electoral punishment, but the prospect of full-scale revolution. Elsewhere (in China and to some extent Mexico, to take two prominent examples), governments have delayed transitions to democracy in order to avoid the problems associated with maintaining political stability while undertaking politically difficult economic reforms.[10]

In sum, the coming decades promise to compel governments, both democratic and predemocratic, to make politically unpopular economic decisions. Governments must seek to overcome intractability if prosperity, and in some cases political liberty and stability, is to continue. To put this a different way, passage of politically intractable policies seems poised to go from being a policy option to a virtual policy imperative.

The high-risk model developed in this book provides an important means of explaining why state actors have risked the passage of one type of PIP, liberalization of trade. Moreover, the model enjoys some portability. Its logic may be extended to other realms of public policy in which rent-seeking special interests consistently prevail. Much as groups seeking free trade may be in a position to extract policy concessions from political entrepreneurs engaged in alignment games, given the appropriate circumstances, advocates of other politically intractable policies should be in a position to advance their policy demands in a similar fashion.

On the other hand, the general applicability of the model must be qualified somewhat. Although a useful explanatory device, the high-risk model is not prescriptive. It provides no guidance, for example, for actors whose first-order objective is the passage of politically intractable policies. For this reason, it would be helpful at this stage to broaden slightly the analytical perspective of this book.

It is possible to conceptualize a corollary, a low-risk strategy for policy innovators whose first-order preferences involve the passage of politically intractable policies. The low-risk strategy entails comparatively little political hazard, but also a marginal political payoff. Essentially defensive in nature, it involves the insulation of policy-makers from the pressures of societal rent-seeking. The low-risk strategy is not necessarily analytically distinctive from the model articulated in this book. As the American case demonstrates, the liberalization of trade during the interwar period was facilitated because the RTAA was enabling legislation that transferred tariff-setting authority away from Congress and toward the more politically insulated executive branch. This two-step process in the liberalization of American trade policy somewhat mitigated the political risk involved.[11]

There are a number of ways policy-makers can be insulated from rent-seekers. Perhaps the most common is to transfer policy-making authority from vulnerable institutions to more insulated ones. This may be done horizontally or vertically. Provision for the autonomy of central banks from the political control of elected officials is an example of such horizontal devolution. The autonomy of the German Bundesbank (along with its success in controlling inflation) is testimony to the efficacy of such an approach.

Policy jurisdiction may also be transferred vertically. In federal states, authority may be shifted downward to subnational governments. One way for the United States to control spending, for example, might be to grant a wider range of constitutional authority—and hence spending responsibility—to the states. (Obviously this would have to be accompanied by some kind of financial compensation, which might take the form of federal income tax abatement providing additional tax room for the state governments.) The primary advantage is that state budgets are far easier to balance than the federal budget. There are several reasons for this: states cannot print money; credit ratings in most states are more volatile than federal credit ratings, making it more difficult for states to float government bonds, and serving as a deterrent to excessive government borrowing; tax levels are effectively regulated at the state level because interstate capital is more mobile. Relatively low dislocation costs would contribute to capital flight from states that rely on excessive taxation to finance high levels of government spending.

Similarly, policy-making authority may be transferred upward to supranational institutions. In the area of trade policy, the devolution of power to a supranational institution—the GATT—has worked effectively in tying the hands of the institutions that administer trade within the various member governments. The European Single Market works in much the same way. An even better example, perhaps, is European Monetary Union (EMU). Sandholtz suggests that EMU is a direct result of European states' desire for (and in most cases inability to achieve) monetary discipline. Although it entails the sacrifice of a good deal of national autonomy, monetary union promises an effective means of controlling inflation, and hence of promoting economic growth. Even ad hoc international agreements can work to shield domestic policy-makers, as Putnam's discussion of the 1978 Bonn economic summit suggests.[12]

A second method is to insulate vulnerable existing institutions. Rogowski suggests that legislatures, for example, can be made less politically vulnerable by creating large electoral districts, and by adopting electoral systems based upon proportional representation (PR).[13] Large electoral districts help diffuse the political impact of geographically concentrated, policy-specific interests. Similarly, PR politically insulates legislatures in two important ways. First, because candidates' electoral fortunes are entirely in the hands of the party leadership, PR imposes strict party discipline on members of the legislature. Members exercise relatively little policy discretion, and as a result there are fewer access points for groups seeking to apply political pressure. (This argument is not peculiar to electoral systems based on proportional representation. Most modern parliamentary systems feature a high degree of party discipline. On the other hand, the logic of the party-slate system utilized under PR means that parties can punish renegade members simply by lowering their names to the bottom of the electoral slate, thereby virtually ensuring their defeat in the next election.)

Second, PR systems usually feature relatively little volatility from election to election. Each party tends to receive a fairly stable proportion of the popular vote, and because outright majority victories are uncommon, most major parties are regular members of the government, independent of their share of the popular vote. As a result, legislatures in these systems are aided in the passage of policies that are not widely popular. It is for this reason, for example, that Katzenstein and Rogowski suggest that small European states have enacted and maintained extremely liberal trade policies.[14]

Institutions also can be insulated by changing the rules by which they operate.[15] Constitutional requirements of a balanced budget amendment, for example, make new spending initiatives more difficult. Buchanan suggests that other constitutional amendments, eliminating differential treatment in taxation rates, subsidies, and transfer payments (demogrants), also would allow "politicians who seek to serve [the] 'public interest' to survive and prosper." Similarly, Tsebelis notes that the introduction of new policy-making rules in Europe (known as the Cooperation Procedure) has insulated the Council of Ministers by eliminating the requirement of unanimity in council.[16]

Finally, institutions may be insulated by judicial mandate. Recognizing this, governments actually may seek to lose decisions in court as a means of demonstrating that their hands were tied in the passage of necessary, but unpopular, legislation. This "unenthusiastic government defender" role has been used by provincial governments in Canada seeking to avoid the political fallout for introducing minority language education laws.[17]

. . .

This project attempts to shed light on a problem that is not adequately examined in the existing literature: the political circumstances that permit the passage of sharp, significant reductions in levels of import protection. The model developed is used to explain Prime Minister Peel's decision to repeal the Corn Laws in 1846, President Roosevelt's passage of the Reciprocal Trade Agreements Act in 1934, Prime Minister Mulroney's Free Trade Agreement Implementation Act in 1988, and President Salinas's decision to initiate a North American Free Trade Agreement. The logic of the high-risk route to political tractability is applicable beyond trade liberalization and may be extended to other politically intractable policies. Indeed, the imperative to overcome intractability promises to emerge as a critical issue within the realm of comparative public policy and international political economy.

Even broader applicability is envisioned if the concept of insulation is considered. The low-risk strategy already has become critical to understanding many of the changes associated with European integration. With the transition to democracy in many former East bloc states, the debt crisis in the developing world (and, albeit to a lesser extent, in developed countries), the passage of politically intractable policies certainly will assume even greater importance in the years ahead. Such problems will require political scientists to reevaluate the workings of democratic institutions. This is said not in the same pessimistic vein that inspired Brittan, in his article "Economic Contradictions," to fear for the future of liberal democracy, but rather as a note of cautious optimism, suggesting that with effective institutional construction, politics (as Bismarck declared) can indeed be the art of the possible.

NOTES

1 Overview

1. See Anne Krueger, "The Political Economy of the Rent-Seeking Society,"*American Economic Review* 64 (1974), pp. 291–303; Stephen D. Krasner, "State Power and the Structure of International Trade," *World Politics* 28 (1976), pp. 317–47; Bruno S. Frey, *International Political Economics* (Oxford: Basil Blackwell, 1984); John A. C. Conybeare, *Trade Wars: The Theory and Practice of International Commercial Rivalry* (New York: Columbia University Press, 1987); Charles Rowley and Robert Tollison, "Rent-Seeking and Trade Protection," in *The Political Economy of Rent-Seeking,* ed. Charles Rowley, Robert Tollison, and Gordon Tullock (Boston: Kluwer Academic Press, 1988); Douglas Nelson, "Endogenous Tariff Theory: A Critical Survey," *American Journal of Political Science* 82 (1988), pp. 796–833; Robert E. Baldwin, "The Political Economy of Trade Policy," *Journal of Economic Perspectives* 3 (1989), pp. 119–35; Knut Borchardt, *Perspectives on Modern Economic History and Policy,* trans. Peter Lambert (Cambridge, England: Cambridge University Press, 1991); Cletus C. Coughlin, K. Alec Chrystal, and Geoffrey Wood, "Protectionist Trade Policies: A Survey of Theory, Evidence, and Rationale," in *International Political Economy: Perspectives on Global Power and Wealth,* ed. Jeff Frieden and David Lake, 2d ed. (New York: St. Martin's Press, 1991).

2. Dani Rodrik, "The Rush to Free Trade in the Developing World: Why So Late? Why Now? Will It Last?" (National Bureau of Economic Research working paper no. 3947, 1992), p. 1. For the qualifications, see Alexander Hamilton, "Report

on Manufactures," in *The Reports of Alexander Hamilton*, ed. Jacob E. Cooke (New York: Harper and Row, 1964); also Adam Smith, *An Inquiry into the Nature and Causes of the Wealth of Nations* (New York: P. F. Collier and Sons, 1909), bk. 4; and Robert H. Bates, Philip Brock, and Jill Tiefenthaler, "Risk and Trade Regimes: Another Exploration," *International Organization* 45 (1991), pp. 1–18.

3. See David Ricardo, *The Principles of Political Economy and Taxation* (New York: E. P. Dutton, 1960); also Gordon Tullock, "Welfare Costs of Tariffs, Monopolies, and Theft," *Western Economic Journal* 5 (1967), pp. 224–32; and Krueger, "The Political Economy of the Rent-Seeking Society."

4. The term *rent-seeking* is defined as the attempt to use the power of the state to transfer (rather than create) wealth. John A. C. Conybeare, "Tariff Protection in Developed and Developing Countries: A Case Sectoral and Longitudinal Analysis," *International Organization* 37 (1983), p. 441. See also Tullock, "Welfare Costs of Tariffs"; Gordon Tullock, "Future Directions for Rent-Seeking Research," in Rowley, Tollison, and Tullock, *The Political Economy of Rent-Seeking*; Robert Ekelund and Robert Tollison, *Mercantilism as a Rent-Seeking Society* (College Station: Texas A&M University Press, 1981); and Rowley and Tollison, "Rent-Seeking and Trade Protection."

5. Douglas R. Arnold, *The Logic of Congressional Action* (New Haven: Yale University Press, 1990), p. 3. See also Rodrik, "The Rush to Free Trade"; John Williamson, ed., *The Political Economy of Policy Reform* (Washington, D.C.: Institute for International Economics, 1994); Sam Peltzman, "Toward a More General Theory of Regulation," *Journal of Law and Economics* 15 (1976), pp. 211–40; Baldwin, "Political Economy of Trade Policy." It should be noted, however, that some groups (mostly producers in exporting sectors) will pursue free trade actively. Moreover, public apathy can be overcome. Becker suggests there is an equilibrium point between taxes (in the case of protectionism these take the form of higher consumer prices) and subsidies (import protection). If taxes necessary to finance subsidies become too great, consumer groups will mobilize to resist them. Gary Becker, "A Theory of Competition Among Pressure Groups for Political Influence," *Quarterly Journal of Economics* 98 (1983), pp. 371–400.

6. Tullock, "Future Directions for Rent-Seeking Research," p. 476.

7. Frey, *International Political Economics*, p. 26. See also E. E. Schattschneider, *Politics, Pressures, and the Tariff* (New York: Prentice-Hall, 1935).

8. Daniel Kahneman and Amos Tversky, "Choices, Values, and Frames," *American Psychologist* 4 (1984), pp. 341–50; Kahneman and Tversky, "Prospect Theory: An Analysis of Decision Under Risk," *Econometrica* 47 (1979), pp. 263–91. For experimental evidence, consult George A. Quattrone and Amos Tversky, "Contrasting Rational and Psychological Analyses of Political Choice," *American Political Science Review* 82 (1988), pp. 719–36.

9. James Q. Wilson, "The Politics of Regulation," in *The Politics of Regulation*,

ed. James Q. Wilson (New York: Basic Books, 1980). Theodore Lowi, *The End of Liberalism: Ideology, Policy, and the Crisis of Public Authority,* 2d ed. (New York: Norton, 1979).

10. Krasner, "State Power"; Margaret Weir and Theda Skocpol, "State Structures and the Possibilities for `Keynesian' Responses to the Great Depression in Sweden, Britain, and the United States," in *Bringing the State Back In,* ed. Peter B. Evans, Dietrich Rueschemeyer, and Theda Skocpol (Cambridge, England: Cambridge University Press, 1985); Alan C. Cairns, "The Embedded State: State-Society Relations in Canada," in *State and Society: Canada in Comparative Perspective,* ed. Keith Banting (Toronto: University of Toronto Press, 1986); Judith Goldstein, "Ideas, Institutions, and American Trade Policy," *International Organization* 42 (1988), pp. 179–217; G. John Ikenberry, *Reasons of State: Oil Politics and the Capacities of American Government* (Ithaca: Cornell University Press, 1988).

11. Cairns, "The Governments and Societies of Canadian Federalism," *Canadian Journal of Political Science* 10 (1977), pp. 695–725; Cairns, "The Embedded State"; Grant Jordan and Jeremy Richardson, "The British Policy Style or the Logic of Negotiation," in *Policy Styles in Western Europe,* ed. Jeremy Richardson (London: George Allen and Unwin, 1982); Richard Rose, "The Political Status of Higher Civil Servants in Britain," in *Bureaucrats and Policy Making,* ed. Ezra Sulieman (New York: Holmes and Meier, 1984).

12. William H. Riker, *The Theory of Political Coalitions* (New Haven: Yale University Press, 1962). John Waterbury, "Export-Led Growth and the Center-Right Coalition in Turkey," *Comparative Politics* 24 (1992), pp. 127–45; H. Richard Friman, "Side-Payments Versus Security Cards: Domestic Bargaining Tactics in International Economic Relations," *International Organization* 47 (1993), pp. 387–410.

13. Rodrik, "Rush to Free Trade," pp. 9–10.

14. Stephen D. Krasner, "Regimes and the Limits of Realism: Regimes as Autonomous Variables," *International Organization* 36 (1982), pp. 497–510.

15. Charles P. Kindleberger, *The World in Depression, 1929–1939* (Berkeley and Los Angeles: University of California Press, 1973). See Mark R. Brawley, *Liberal Leadership: Great Powers and Their Challengers in Peace and War* (Ithaca: Cornell University Press, 1993).

16. Arthur Stein, "Coordination and Collaboration: Regimes in an Anarchic World," *International Organization* 36 (1982), pp. 299–324; Robert Keohane, *After Hegemony* (Princeton: Princeton University Press, 1984).

17. Krasner, "State Power"; Oran R. Young, "Regime Dynamics: The Rise and Fall of International Regimes," *International Organization* 36 (1982), pp. 277–98. Peter J. Katzenstein, "Conclusion: Domestic Structures and Strategies of Foreign Economic Policy," in *Between Power and Plenty,* ed. Peter J. Katzenstein (Madison: University of Wisconsin Press, 1978).

18. See also Scott C. James and David A. Lake, "The Second Face of Hegemony:

Britain's Repeal of the Corn Laws and the American Walker Tariff of 1846," *International Organization* 43 (1989), pp. 1–29.

19. John Vincent Nye, "Revisionist Tariff History and the Theory of Hegemonic Stability," *Politics and Society* 19 (1991), pp. 209–32. Indeed, there is a great deal of literature suggesting that state actors are motivated by other than the national interest. Within the public choice tradition, see Tullock, "Welfare Costs of Tariffs" and "Future Directions for Rent-Seeking Research"; George J. Stigler, "The Theory of Economic Regulation," *Bell Journal of Economics and Management Science* 2 (1971), pp. 3–21; Krueger, "Political Economy of the Rent-Seeking Society"; Peltzman, "Toward a More General Theory of Regulation"; Rowley, Tollison, and Tullock, eds., *The Political Economy of Rent-Seeking*. From a neopluralist perspective, see Charles Lindblom, *Politics and Markets: The World's Political-Economic Systems* (New York: Basic Books, 1977); Lowi, *The End of Liberalism;* and Claus Offe, *Contradictions of the Welfare State* (London: Hutchison, 1984). For the state autonomy tradition, see Graham T. Allison, *Essence of Decision* (New York: Harper Collins, 1971); Eric A. Nordlinger, *On the Autonomy of the Democratic State* (Cambridge, Mass.: Harvard University Press, 1981); and Cairns, "The Embedded State."

20. James and Lake, "The Second Face of Hegemony."

21. Timothy J. McKeown, "Hegemonic Stability Theory and Nineteenth Century Tariff Levels in Europe," *International Organization* 37 (1983), pp. 79–80.

22. Ronald Rogowski, *Commerce and Coalitions: How Trade Affects Domestic Political Alignments* (Princeton: Princeton University Press, 1989); see also Paul Midford, "International Trade and Domestic Politics: Improving on Rogowski's Model of Political Alignments," *International Organization* 47 (1993), pp. 535–64.

23. See J. A. Thomas, "The Repeal of the Corn Laws, 1846," *Economica* 9 (1929), pp. 53–60; Thomas Ferguson, "From Normalcy to New Deal: Industrial Structure, Party Competition, and American Public Policy in the Great Depression," *International Organization* 38 (1984), pp. 41–94; Jeff Frieden, "Sectoral Conflict and Foreign Economic Policy, 1914–1940," *International Organization* 42 (1988), pp. 59–90; Helen Milner, *Resisting Protectionism: Global Industries and the Politics of International Trade* (Princeton: Princeton University Press, 1988); Milner, "Trading Places: Industries for Free Trade," *World Politics* 38 (1988), pp. 350–76; Sidney Weintraub, *Mexican Trade Policy and the North American Community* (Washington, D.C.: Center for Strategic and International Studies, 1988); Timothy J. McKeown, "The Politics of Corn Law Repeal and Theories of Commercial Policy," *British Journal of Political Science* 19 (1989), pp. 353–80.

24. Stephen Magee, "Three Simple Tests of the Stolper-Samuelson Theorem," in *Issues in International Economics,* ed. Peter Oppenheimer (Stocksfield, England: Oriel Press, 1978); Robert H. Bates, "Institutions as Investments" (Duke University Program in Political Economy, working paper no. 133, 1990); William Coleman,

Business and Politics: A Study of Collective Action, (Kingston: McGill-Queen's University Press, 1988); James and Lake, "The Second Face of Hegemony."

25. See Lindblom, *Politics and Markets;* John F. Manley, "Neo-Pluralism: A Class Analysis of Pluralism I and Pluralism II," *American Political Science Review* 77 (1983), pp. 368–83.

26. But compare Daniel Verdier, *Democracy and International Trade: Britain, France, and the United States* (Princeton: Princeton University Press, 1994). Ferguson, Frieden, and Milner all discuss the impact of free trade lobbies on American trade policy. However, while the free trade lobby assisted President Roosevelt, it was not the decisive factor in the passage and renewals of the Reciprocal Trade Agreements Act (see chapter 3). Ferguson, "From Normalcy to New Deal"; Frieden, "Sectoral Conflict and Foreign Economic Policy"; and Milner, *Resisting Protectionism* and "Trading Places."

27. Stephen D. Krasner, *Defending the National Interest: Raw Materials Investments and U.S. Foreign Policy* (Princeton: Princeton University Press, 1978). See also Krasner, "State Power."

28. David A. Lake, "The State and American Trade Strategy in the Pre-Hegemonic Era," *International Organization* 42 (1988), pp. 33–58; Lake, *Power, Protection, and Free Trade.* See also Lowi, *The End of Liberalism.*

29. See Lindblom, *Politics and Markets,* and Offe, *Contradictions of the Welfare State.*

30. Lake, "The State and American Trade Strategy," p. 38.

31. Katzenstein, "Conclusion." See also Alexander Gerschenkron, "Economic Backwardness in Historical Perspective," in *Economic Backwardness in Historical Perspective,* ed. Alexander Gerschenkron (Cambridge, Mass.: Belknap Press, 1962).

32. Krasner, *Defending the National Interest* and "State Power"; Lake, "The State and American Trade Strategy" and *Power, Protection, and Free Trade;* Frey, *International Political Economics,* p. 11 (quotation).

33. Richard F. Doner, "Limits of State Strength: Toward an Internationalist View of Economic Development," *World Politics* 44 (1992), pp. 398–431; G. John Ikenberry, "Conclusion: An Institutional Approach to American Foreign Economic Policy," *International Organization* 42 (1988), pp. 219–43, and *Reasons of State;* Cairns, "The Embedded State."

34. Thomas Risse-Kappen, "Public Opinion, Domestic Structure, and Foreign Policy in Liberal Democracies," *World Politics* 43 (1991), pp. 479–512; Lake, "The State and American Trade Strategy"; Frey, *International Political Economics;* Borchardt, *Perspectives on Modern Economic History and Policy.* See also Stigler, "The Theory of Economic Regulation," and Peltzman, "Toward a More General Theory of Regulation."

35. Peter A. Gourevitch, "Keynesian Politics: The Political Sources of Economic

Policy Choices," in *The Political Power of Economic Ideas,* ed. Peter A. Hall (Princeton: Princeton University Press, 1989), p. 89.

36. Peter A. Gourevitch, *Politics in Hard Times: Comparative Responses to International Economic Crises* (Ithaca: Cornell University Press, 1986).

37. The classic discussion of political entrepreneurship is found in Norman Frohlich, Joe A. Oppenheimer, and Oran R. Young, *Political Leadership and Collective Goods* (Princeton: Princeton University Press, 1971); see also Wilson, "The Politics of Regulation"; William H. Riker, *The Art of Political Manipulation* (New Haven: Yale University Press, 1986); Oran R. Young, "Political Leadership and Regime Formation: On the Development of Institutions in International Society," *International Organization* 45 (1991), pp. 281–308; Mark Schneider and Paul Teske, "Toward a Theory of the Political Entrepreneur: Evidence from Local Government," *American Political Science Review* 86 (1992), pp. 737–47; and Jeremy Moon, *Innovative Leadership in Democracy: Policy Change Under Thatcher* (Aldershot: Dartmouth, 1993).

38. Young, "Political Leadership and Regime Formation"; Riker, *The Art of Political Manipulation.*

39. See especially V. O. Key, "A Theory of Critical Elections," *Journal of Politics* 17 (1955), pp. 3–13; Walter Dean Burnham, *Critical Elections and the Mainsprings of American Politics* (New York: Norton, 1970); Paul Kleppner, "Critical Realignments and Electoral Systems," in *The Evolution of American Electoral Systems,* ed. Paul Kleppner et al. (Westport Conn.: Greenwood Press, 1981), p. 4 (quotation).

40. Walter Dean Burnham, "The System of 1896: An Analysis," in Kleppner et al., *The Evolution of American Electoral Systems,* pp. 157–58.

41. Bates, "Institutions as Investments."

42. Peter Hall, *Governing the Economy: The Politics of State Intervention in Britain and France* (Cambridge: Polity Press, 1986), p. 19.

43. David Feeny, "The Demand for and Supply of Institutional Arrangements," in *Rethinking Institutional Analysis and Development: Issues, Alternatives, and Choices,* ed. Vincent Ostrom, David Feeny, and Hartmut Picht (San Francisco: International Center for Economic Growth, 1988), p. 172 (first quotation); Donald V. Smiley, *The Federal Condition in Canada* (Toronto: McGraw-Hill Ryerson, 1987), pp. 178–79 (second quotation).

44. Vernon W. Ruttan and Yurijo Hayami, "Toward a Theory of Induced Institutional Innovation," *Journal of Development Studies* 20 (1984), pp. 203–23.

45. Peter B. Clark and James Q. Wilson, "Incentive Systems: A Theory of Organizations," *Administrative Science Quarterly* 6 (1961), pp. 129–66; James S. Coleman, "Foundations for a Theory of Collective Decisions," *American Journal of Sociology* 71 (1966), pp. 615–27; Robert H. Salisbury, "An Exchange Theory of Interest Groups," *Midwest Journal of Political Science* 13 (1969), pp. 1–32. On side-payments,

see Robert Putnam, "Diplomacy and Domestic Politics: The Logic of Two-Level Games," *International Organization* 42 (1988), pp. 427–60; Frederick W. Mayer, "Managing Domestic Differences in International Negotiations: The Strategic Use of Internal Side-Payments," *International Organization* 46 (1992), pp. 793–818; and Friman, "Side-Payments Versus Security Cards."

46. Bates, "Institutions as Investments."

47. Cairns, "Governments and Societies of Canadian Federalism."

48. Lake, "The State and American Trade Strategy" and *Power, Protection, and Free Trade.*

49. Arthur Stinchcombe, "Social Structure and Organizations," in *Handbook of Organizations,* ed. James G. March (Chicago: Rand-McNally, 1965); Stephen D. Krasner, "Approaches to the State," *Comparative Politics* 16 (1984), pp. 223–46; Goldstein, "Ideas, Institutions"; Judith Goldstein, *Ideas, Interests, and American Trade Policy* (Ithaca: Cornell University Press, 1993); James G. March and Johan P. Olsen, *Rediscovering Institutions* (New York: The Free Press, 1989); Kenneth A. Shepsle, "Studying Institutions: Some Lessons from the Rational Choice Approach," *Journal of Theoretical Politics* 1 (1989), pp. 131–47; Bates, "Institutions as Investments."

50. Krasner, "Approaches to the State"; Feeny, "The Demand for and Supply of Institutional Arrangements."

51. Burnham, "The System of 1896"; Stephen Skowronek, *Building a New American State* (Cambridge, England: Cambridge University Press, 1982).

52. Gourevitch, *Politics in Hard Times,* p. 9.

53. Schneider and Teske, "Toward a Theory of the Political Entrepreneur," p. 738, emphasis in original.

2   Why Did Peel Repeal the Corn Laws?

1. For a comprehensive history of the English Corn Laws, See J. S. Nicholson, *The History of the English Corn Laws* (London: Swan Sonnenschein, 1904); Norman Gras, *The Evolution of the English Corn Market* (Cambridge, Mass.: Harvard University Press, 1915); C. R. Fay, *The Corn Laws and Social England* (Cambridge, England: Cambridge University Press, 1932); and Donald Grove Barnes, *A History of the English Corn Laws from 1660–1846* (New York: Augustus M. Kelley, 1965).

2. Susan Fairlie, "The Nineteenth-Century Corn Law Reconsidered," *Economic History Review,* 2d ser., 18 (1965), pp. 544–61.

3. Sir Robert Peel, *Sir Robert Peel: From His Private Papers,* vol. 2, ed. Charles Stuart Parker (New York: Kraus Reprint, 1970), pp. 530–31.

4. Robert Stewart, *The Politics of Protection* (Cambridge, England: Cambridge University Press, 1971).

5. John Wilson Croker, *The Correspondence and Diaries of the Late Right Hon-*

ourable John Wilson Croker, vol. 2, ed. Louis J. Jennings (New York: Charles Scribner's Sons, 1884); William F. Monypenny, *The Life of Benjamin Disraeli,* vol. 2 (New York: Macmillan, 1912).

6. Lord Broughton, *Recollections of a Long Life,* vol. 6, ed. Lady Dorchester (London: John Murray, 1911); Lord Malmesbury, *Memoirs of an Ex-Minister,* vol. 1 (London: Longman, Green, 1884), p. 139 (quotation).

7. Peel, *Private Papers,* vol. 2, p. 551, emphasis in original.

8. Peel, *The Speeches of the Late Right Honourable Sir Robert Peel, Bart.* vol. 3 (London: George Routledge, 1853), p. 521.

9. Stewart, *Politics of Protection.*

10. Robert Gilpin, *War and Change in World Politics* (Cambridge, England: Cambridge University Press, 1981).

11. James and Lake, "The Second Face of Hegemony."

12. Sir Robert Peel, *Memoirs,* vol. 2, ed. Lord Mahon and Edward Cardwell (London: John Murray, 1857); Peel, *Private Papers,* vol. 2.

13. Peel, *Speeches,* vol. 3, p. 601 (quotation); James and Lake, "The Second Face of Hegemony," p. 18, 21.

14. Fay, *Corn Laws and Social England;* Asa Briggs, *The Age of Improvement: 1783–1867* (New York: David McKay, 1959); Betty Kemp, "Reflections on the Repeal of the Corn Laws," *Victorian Studies* 5 (1962), pp. 189–204; Barnes, *History of the English Corn Laws;* Fairlie, "The Nineteenth-Century Corn Law."

15. McKeown, "The Politics of Corn Law Repeal."

16. See Thomas, "The Repeal of the Corn Laws," and Richard E. Caves and Ronald W. Jones, *World Trade and Payments,* 2d ed. (Boston: Little, Brown, 1977).

17. Cheryl Schonhardt-Bailey, "Specific Factors, Capital Markets, Portfolio Diversification, and Free Trade: Domestic Determinants of the Repeal of the Corn Laws," *World Politics* 43 (1991), pp. 345–69. See also Schonhardt-Bailey, "Linking Constituency Interests to Legislative Voting Behaviour: The Role of District Economic and Electoral Composition in the Repeal of the Corn Laws," in *Computing Parliamentary History: George III to Victoria,* ed. John A. Phillips (Edinburgh: Edinburgh University Press, 1994).

18. Briggs, *Age of Improvement.*

19. Peel, *Memoirs,* vol. 2; Peel, *Private Papers,* vol. 3.

20. McKeown, "The Politics of Corn Law Repeal."

21. For examples of arguments based on pressure groups, see John Morley, *The Life of Richard Cobden,* vol. 1 (London: T. Fisher Unwin, 1905); Thomas, "The Repeal of the Corn Laws"; Fay, *The Corn Laws and Social England;* Gary Anderson and Robert Tollison, "Ideology, Interest Groups, and the Repeal of the Corn Laws," in *The Political Economy of Rent-Seeking,* ed. Charles Rowley, Robert Tollison, and Gordon Tullock (Boston: Kluwer Academic, 1988).

22. D. C. Moore, "The Corn Laws and High Farming," *Economic History Review,*

2d ser., 18 (1965), pp. 544–61; McKeown, "The Politics of Corn Law Repeal." For the Board of Trade, see Lucy Brown, *The Board of Trade and the Free Trade Movement, 1830–1842* (Oxford: Clarendon Press, 1958). For Cobden, see George Jacob Holyoake, *Sixty Years of an Agitator's Life,* vol. 1 (London: T. Fisher and Unwin, 1893).

23. Peel, *Private Papers,* vol. 2, pp. 201–2. These opinions also were expressed strongly in Peel's speeches in the Commons: especially of March 21 and December 17, 1831. Sir Robert Peel, *The Opinions of Sir Robert Peel,* ed. W. T. Haley (London: Whittaker, 1843), especially pp. 379, 384–85.

24. Peel, *Speeches,* vol. 3, p. 19.

25. Peel, *Opinions,* p. 378 (first quotation); Peel, *Memoirs,* vol. 1, p. 116 (second quotation).

26. O. F. Christie, *The Transition from Aristocracy, 1832–1867* (London: Seeley, Service, 1928); Briggs, *Age of Improvement;* Michael Brock, *The Great Reform Act* (London: Hutchison, 1973).

27. Brock, *The Great Reform Act,* p. 36.

28. Peel, *Opinions,* pp. 368–69 (March 24), p. 385 (December 17). See also Peel's letter to Lord Chandos, March 14, 1831. Peel, *Private Papers,* vol. 2, pp. 180–81.

29. Peel, *Private Papers,* vol. 3, p. 326.

30. Charles Greville, *The Greville Memoirs: A Journal of the Reign of Queen Victoria, 1837–1852,* vol. 2, ed. Henry Reeve (New York: Appleton, 1885), p. 94.

31. Peel, *Speeches,* vol. 4, p. 636; Croker, *Correspondence,* p. 268; Norman McCord, *The Anti-Corn Law League, 1838–1846,* 2d ed. (London: George Allen and Unwin, 1968), p. 201.

32. Peel, *Speeches,* vol. 4, p. 695 (May 15), p. 684 (May 4).

33. Richard Cobden, *Speeches by Richard Cobden, MP,* vol. 1, ed. John Bright and Thorold Rogers (London: Macmillan, 1870), pp. 282–83.

34. Peel, *Memoirs,* vol. 2, pp. 312–13; Cobden, *Speeches,* vol. 2, pp. 548–49.

35. Kemp, "Reflections."

36. Charles Greville, *The Greville Diary,* vol. 2, ed. Philip Wilson (Garden City, N.J.: Doubleday, Page, 1927), p. 179.

37. Goulburn cited in Peel, *Memoirs,* vol. 2, p. 202; Croker, *Correspondence,* p. 268.

38. Peel, *Memoirs,* pp. 173–74.

39. Greville, *Memoirs,* p. 96; Lord John Russell, *The Later Correspondence of Lord John Russell, 1840–1878,* vol. 1, ed. G. P. Gooch (London: Longman, Green, 1925), p. 85. See also letters by Sir Denis Le Marchant and Sir John Shelley, in Russell, *Later Correspondence.* Arbuthnot letter in Peel, *Private Papers,* vol. 3, p. 345; see also Greville, *Memoirs,* p. 53.

40. Great Britain (Hansard), House of Commons, *Parliamentary Debates,* 3d ser, vol. 78. (London: George Woodfall and Son, 1845), pp. 154–55.

41. Russell, *Later Correspondence,* p. 81.

42. Briggs, *Age of Improvement;* Barnes, *History of the English Corn Laws.*

43. Monypenny, *Life of Benjamin Disraeli,* p. 348; Peel, *Memoirs,* vol. 2, p. 247.

44. See Russell, *Later Correspondence,* pp. 82–99.

45. Peel, *Memoirs,* vol. 2, pp. 200, 251; Peel, *Private Papers,* vol. 3, pp. 291–92, 326; Greville, *Memoirs,* p. 53; Greville, *Diary,* p. 179.

46. Peel, *Memoirs,* vol. 2, pp. 248–49 (Her Majesty), p. 322 (to Aberdeen).

47. Morley, *Life of Cobden;* McCord, *The Anti-Corn Law League.*

48. Morley, *Life of Cobden,* p. 237.

49. Cobden, *Speeches,* vol. 1, p. 376; emphasis mine.

50. McCord, *The Anti-Corn Law League,* p. 203, emphasis in original.

51. Morley, *Life of Cobden,* p. 377.

52. Greville, *Memoirs.*

3   The New Deal, the Welfare State, and Free Trade

1. John Gerard Ruggie, "International Regimes, Transactions, and Change: Embedded Liberalism in the Postwar Economic Order, *International Organization* 36 (1982), pp. 379–415.

2. For nineteenth-century protectionism, see J. J. Pincus, *Pressure Groups and Politics in Antebellum Tariffs* (New York: Columbia University Press, 1977); Robert A. Pastor, *Congress and the Politics of U.S. Foreign Economic Policy, 1929–1976* (Berkeley and Los Angeles: University of California Press, 1980). For the System of '96, see Ferguson, "From Normalcy to New Deal"; also Burnham, "The System of 1896."

3. Goldstein, *Ideas, Interests,* p. 119.

4. F. W. Taussig, *The Tariff History of the United States,* 8th ed. (New York: Augustus M. Kelley, 1967).

5. William B. Kelly Jr., "Antecedents of Present Commercial Policy," in *Studies in United States Commercial Policy,* ed. William B. Kelly Jr. (Chapel Hill: University of North Carolina Press, 1963).

6. Milner, "Trading Places."

7. Quoted in William R. Allen, "The International Trade Philosophy of Cordell Hull, 1907–1933," *American Economic Review* 43 (1953), p. 115. The classic analysis of rent-seeking during the Smoot-Hawley debates is E. E. Schattschneider, *Politics, Pressures, and the Tariff* (New York: Prentice-Hall, 1935). See also Joseph Jones, *Tariff Retaliation: Repercussions of the Hawley-Smoot Bill* (Philadelphia: University of Pennsylvania Press, 1934); John Day Larkin, *Trade Agreements* (New York: Columbia University Press, 1940); Taussig, *Tariff History;* Stephen Robert Brenner, *Economic Interests and the Trade Agreements Program, 1937–1940: A Study of Institutions and Political Influence* (Ph.D. dissertation, Stanford University, 1978); Real Lavergne, *The Political Economy of U.S. Tariffs* (Toronto: The Academic Press, 1983); and Stephan Haggard, "The Institutional Foundations of Hegemony: Ex-

plaining the Reciprocal Trade Agreements Act of 1934," *International Organization* 42 (1988), pp. 91–119.

8. Brenner provides the best overview of the RTAA in *Economic Interests*. Other useful works include William S. Culbertson, *Reciprocity* (New York: Whittlesay House, 1937); Arthur Upgren, *Reciprocal Trade Agreements* (Minneapolis: University of Minnesota Press, 1937); Henry J. Tasca, *The Reciprocal Trade Policy of the United States* (Ph.D. dissertation, University of Pennsylvania, 1938); Francis Sayre, *The Way Forward: The American Trade Agreements Program* (New York: Macmillan, 1939); Larkin, *Trade Agreements;* Cordell Hull, *The Memoirs of Cordell Hull,* vol. 1. (New York: Macmillan, 1948); Arthur M. Schlesinger Jr., *The Coming of the New Deal* (Boston: Houghton Mifflin, 1958); Taussig, *Tariff History;* Pastor, *U.S. Foreign Economic Policy;* Lavergne, *The Political Economy of U.S. Tariffs;* Haggard, "The Institutional Foundations"; and Carolyn Rhodes, *Reciprocity, U.S. Trade Policy, and the GATT Regime* (Ithaca: Cornell University Press, 1993).

9. Allen, "Trade Philosophy of Cordell Hull"; Schlesinger, *The Coming of the New Deal;* Raymond A. Bauer, Ithiel de la Sola Pool, and Lewis Anthony Dexter, *American Business and Public Policy,* 2d ed. (Chicago: Aldine-Atherton Inc., 1972); Kindleberger, *World in Depression;* Pastor, *U.S. Foreign Economic Policy;* Lake, *Power, Protection, and Free Trade;* Daniel Bennett Smith, *Toward Internationalism* (New York: Garland, 1990); Eric M. Uslaner, "Political Parties, Ideas, Interests, and Free Trade in the United States" (paper presented at the Conference on Party and Trade: Political Perspectives on External Trade, Washington, D.C., 1992); Gilbert R. Winham, *The Evolution of International Trade Agreements* (Toronto: University of Toronto Press, 1992). Between 1934 and 1947, reciprocal trade agreements were reached with twenty-seven countries that together accounted for the majority of U.S. trade. Indeed, although complete data are not available for agreements reached after 1939, in that year 66 percent of all dutiable imports into the United States were on products that had been covered by agreements reached between 1934 and 1947. Similarly, 54 percent of U.S. exports in 1937 were to countries with which agreements had been reached by 1940. Brenner, *Economic Interests,* pp. 157–58.

10. Haggard, "Institutional Foundations," p. 117; Senate Committee on Finance, *Hearings, on H.R. 8687, Reciprocal Trade Agreements* (Washington, D.C.: U.S. Government Printing Office, 1934); House Committee on Ways and Means, *Hearings, on H.R. 8430, Reciprocal Trade Agreements* (Washington, D.C.: U.S. Government Printing Office, 1934); Senate Committee on Finance, *Hearings, on H.J. Res. 96, Extension of Reciprocal Trade Agreements Act* (Washington, D.C.: U.S. Government Printing Office, 1937); House Committee on Ways and Means, *Hearings, on H.J. Res. 96, Extension of Reciprocal Trade Agreements Act* (Washington, D.C.: U.S. Government Printing Office, 1937) and *Hearings, on H.J. Res. 407, Extension of Reciprocal Trade Agreements Act* (Washington, D.C.: U.S. Government Printing Office,

1940); Senate Committee on Finance, *Hearings, on H.J. Res. 407, Extension of Reciprocal Trade Agreements Act* (Washington, D.C.: U.S. Government Printing Office, 1940); American Liberty League, "A Program for Congress" (Document 83, 1935); Hull, *Memoirs;* Schlesinger, *The Coming of the New Deal;* Brenner, *Economic Interests;* Robert Dallek, *Franklin D. Roosevelt and American Foreign Policy, 1932–1945* (New York: Oxford University Press, 1979); Smith, *Toward Internationalism;* Rhodes, *Reciprocity.*

11. Kindleberger, *The World in Depression.* See also Tasca, *Reciprocal Trade Policy,* and Sayre, *The Way Forward.*

12. Goldstein, "Ideas, Institutions"; Lake, *Power, Protection, and Free Trade;* Conybeare, *Trade Wars.*

13. Ferguson, "From Normalcy to New Deal"; Frieden, "Sectoral Conflict."

14. Haggard, "Institutional Foundations."

15. Franklin D. Roosevelt, *The Public Papers and Addresses of Franklin D. Roosevelt,* vol. 5, ed. Samuel I. Rosenman (New York: Random House, 1938); Richard Kirkendall, "The New Deal and American Politics," in *Fifty Years Later: The New Deal Evaluated,* ed. Harvard Sitkoff (Philadelphia: Temple University Press, 1985).

16. Brenner, *Economic Interests,* pp. 178–79. See also E. Pendleton Herring, "Second Session of the Seventy-Third Congress, January 3, 1934, to June 18, 1934," *American Political Science Review* 28 (1934), pp. 852–65; Ellis W. Hawley, "The New Deal and Business," in *The New Deal: The National Level,* ed. John Braeman, Robert H. Bremner, and David Brody (Columbus: Ohio State University Press, 1975). For the Economy Bill, see James T. Patterson, *Congressional Conservatism and the New Deal* (Lexington: University of Kentucky Press, 1967).

17. David W. Brady, *Critical Elections and Congressional Policy Making* (Stanford: Stanford University Press, 1988).

18. Raymond Moley, *After Seven Years* (New York: Harper and Brothers, 1939), p. 369; Schlesinger, *The Coming of the New Deal,* p. 260.

19. See Kenneth Finegold and Theda Skocpol, "State, Party, and Industry: From Business Recovery to the Wagner Act in America's New Deal," in *Statemaking and Social Movements,* ed. Charles Bright and Susan Harding (Ann Arbor: University of Michigan Press, 1984).

20. Gourevitch, *Politics in Hard Times.*

21. Kirkendall, "The New Deal and Agriculture," in Braeman, Bremner, and Brody, *The New Deal.* See also Henry A. Wallace, *Democracy Reborn,* ed. Russell Lord (New York: Reynal and Hitchcock, 1944). Important discussions of the AAA include Wallace, *Democracy Reborn;* Basil Rauch, *The History of the New Deal, 1933–1938* (New York: Creative Age Press, 1944); James MacGregor Burns, *Roosevelt: The Lion and the Fox* (New York: Harcourt, Brace, 1956); Schlesinger, *The Coming of the New Deal;* and Dallek, *Roosevelt and American Foreign Policy.*

22. Finegold and Skocpol, "State, Party, and Industry."

23. James R. Moore, "Sources of New Deal Economic Policy: The International Dimension," *Journal of American History* 61 (1974), pp. 728–44.

24. Smith, *Toward Internationalism.*

25. See Schlesinger, *The Coming of the New Deal;* Kindleberger, *The World in Depression;* Moore, "Sources of New Deal Economic Policy"; Dallek, *Roosevelt and American Foreign Policy;* Frieden, "Sectoral Conflict"; and Smith, *Toward Internationalism.*

26. Roosevelt, *Public Papers,* vol. 3; Franklin D. Roosevelt, *Complete Presidential Press Conferences of Franklin D. Roosevelt,* vols. 3–4 (New York: Da Capo, 1972).

27. Jones, *Tariff Retaliation.*

28. Roosevelt, *Public Papers,* vol. 2, p. 15 (quotation); Moley, *After Seven Years;* Rexford G. Tugwell, *FDR: Architect of an Era* (New York: Macmillan, 1967). See also Herring, "Second Session of the Seventy-Third Congress"; Patterson, *Congressional Conservatism;* James Holt, "The New Deal and the American Anti-Statist Tradition," in Braeman, Bremner, and Brody, *The New Deal.*

29. Edward Berkowitz and Kim McQuaid, *Creating the Welfare State* (New York: Praeger, 1980).

30. George Wolfskill, *The Revolt of the Conservatives: A History of the American Liberty League, 1934–1940* (Boston: Houghton Mifflin, 1962); Frederick Rudolph, "The American Liberty League, 1934–1940," *American History Review* 56 (1950), pp. 19–33.

31. Berkowitz and McQuaid, *Creating the Welfare State;* Finegold and Skocpol, "State, Party, and Industry"; Herbert Stein, *The Fiscal Revolution in America,* rev. ed. (Washington, D.C.: AEI Press, 1990).

32. Raymond Moley, *The First New Deal* (New York: Harcourt, Brace and World, 1966); Franklin D. Roosevelt, *Roosevelt and Frankfurter: Their Correspondence, 1928–1945,* ed. Max Freedman (Boston: Little, Brown, 1967), p. 210.

33. Roosevelt, *Public Papers,* vol. 3, pp. 372–73; Moley, *After Seven Years* and *The First New Deal.*

34 Ferguson, "From Normalcy to New Deal," p. 86.

35. See Moley, *After Seven Years;* Burns, *The Lion and the Fox;* Schlesinger, *The Coming of the New Deal;* Berkowitz and McQuaid, *Creating the Welfare State;* Theda Skocpol and John Ikenberry, "The Political Formation of the American Welfare State in Historical and Comparative Perspective," *Comparative Social Research* 6 (1983), pp. 87–148.

36. Hawley, "The New Deal and Business"; Wolfskill, *The Revolt of the Conservatives,* p. 19.

37. Burns, *The Lion and the Fox.*

38. Moley, *After Seven Years* (quotation). See also Burns, *The Lion and the Fox;* Patterson, *Congressional Conservatism;* Hawley, "The New Deal and Business"; Walter S. Salant, "The Spread of Keynesian Doctrines and Practices in the United

States," in *The Political Power of Economic Ideas,* ed. Peter A. Hall (Princeton: Princeton University Press, 1989); and Stein, *Fiscal Revolution.*

39. Arthur Altmeyer, *The Formative Years of Social Security* (Madison: University of Wisconsin Press, 1966); Berkowitz and McQuaid, *Creating the Welfare State.*

40. Theda Skocpol and Kenneth Finegold, "Explaining New Deal Labor Policy," *American Political Science Review* 84 (1990), pp. 1297–304; Milton Derber, "The New Deal and Labor," in Braeman, Bremner, and Brody, *The New Deal;* Finegold and Skocpol, "State, Party, and Industry."

41. Kirkendall, "The New Deal and American Politics."

42. Moley, *The First New Deal,* p. 526.

43. Michael Patrick Allen, "Capitalist Response to State Intervention: Theories of the State and Political Finance in the New Deal," *American Sociological Review* 56 (1991), pp. 679–89.

44. Tasca, *Reciprocal Trade Policy;* Brenner, *Economic Interests;* Ferguson, "From Normalcy to New Deal"; Gourevitch, *Politics in Hard Times;* Frieden, "Sectoral Conflict"; Haggard, "Institutional Foundations"; Uslaner, "Political Parties."

45. Ferguson, "From Normalcy to New Deal," pp. 87–89; Gourevitch, *Politics in Hard Times,* p. 152; and Uslaner, "Political Parties."

46. Harold Van B. Cleveland, "The International Monetary System in the Interwar Period," in *Balance of Power or Hegemony,* ed. Benjamin M. Rowland (New York: New York University Press, 1976); Dallek, *Roosevelt and American Foreign Policy;* and Frieden, "Sectoral Conflict."

47. House Ways and Means Committee, *Hearings,* 1934; Senate Finance Committee, *Hearings,* 1937; American Liberty League, "A Program for Congress"; Hull, *Memoirs;* Schlesinger, *The Coming of the New Deal;* Dallek, *Roosevelt and American Foreign Policy;* Smith, *Toward Internationalism.*

48. House Ways and Means Committee, *Hearings,* 1937, 1940; Senate Finance Committee, *Hearings,* 1937, 1940; Brenner, *Economic Interests.*

49. Hull, *Memoirs,* p. 370.

50. For more on Hull's role in pressing for free trade within the administration, see Moley, *After Seven Years;* Hull, *Memoirs;* Allen, "Trade Philosophy of Cordell Hull"; Rexford G. Tugwell, *In Search of Roosevelt* (Cambridge, Mass.: Harvard University Press, 1972) and *The Diary of Rexford G. Tugwell,* ed. Michael Vincent Namorato (New York: Greenwood, 1992); Kindleberger, *World in Depression;* Harold L. Ickes, *The Secret Diary of Harold L. Ickes,* vol. 2 (New York: Da Capo, 1974); Brenner, *Economic Interests;* Smith, *Toward Internationalism;* John G. Ikenberry, "A World Economy Restored: Expert Consensus and the Anglo-American Postwar Settlement," *International Organization* 46 (1992), pp. 289–321; and Rhodes, *Reciprocity.*

51. Ferguson, "From Normalcy to New Deal," p. 92. The commitment to multilateralism was qualified somewhat, however, because the State Department was se-

verely limited in its ability to negotiate reciprocity in agricultural commodities. Verdier suggests: "These limitations were expressly intended to keep the farmers on board, an aim even more important to the Roosevelt administration than free trade" (Verdier, *Democracy and International Trade,* p. 188).

52. Ferguson, "From Normalcy to New Deal," p. 92.

4   The Two-Level Gamble

1. For accounts of the National Policy and its legacy of high tariffs, western settlement, European immigration, regional tension, import-substituting industrialization, and industrial uncompetitiveness, see Canada, Senate Standing Committee on Foreign Affairs, *Canada's Trade Relations with the United States* (Ottawa: Minister of Supply and Services, 1982); Maureen Appel Molot and Glen Williams, "The Political Economy of Continentalism," in *Canadian Politics in the 1980s,* ed. Michael S. Whittington and Glen Williams, 2d ed. (Toronto: Methuen, 1984); Frank Stone, *Canada, the GATT, and the International Trade System* (Montreal: The Institute for Research on Public Policy, 1984); Sidney Weintraub, "Canada Acts on Free Trade," *Journal of Interamerican Studies and World Affairs* 28 (1986), pp. 101–18; and Glen Williams, *Not for Export,* rev. ed. (Toronto: McClelland and Stewart, 1986).

2. For analysis of Canadian involvement in international trade negotiations in the post–World War II era, including the Kennedy and Tokyo rounds of GATT, see Canada, Senate Department of External Affairs, *Foreign Policy for Canadians* (Ottawa: Information Canada, 1970); Canada, *Report of the Royal Commission on the Economic Union and Development Prospects for Canada* (Ottawa: Minister of Supply and Services, 1985); Gilbert R. Winham, *Trading with Canada* (New York: Priority Press, 1988) and "Bureaucratic Politics and Canadian Trade Negotiation," *International Journal* 34 (1978), pp. 64–89; Stone, *Canada, the GATT;* Colleen Hamilton and John Whalley, "The GATT and Canadian Interests," in *Canada and the Multilateral Trading System,* ed. John Whalley (Toronto: University of Toronto Press, 1985); Michael M. Hart, *Canadian Economic Development and the International Trading System* (Toronto: University of Toronto Press, 1985); John Whalley, Colleen Hamilton, and Roderick Hill, *Canadian Trade Policies and the World Economy* (Toronto: University of Toronto Press, 1985); and G. Bruce Doern and Brian W. Tomlin, *Faith and Fear: The Free Trade Story* (Toronto: Stoddart, 1991).

3. See Donald Barry, "Eisenhower, St. Laurent, and Free Trade, 1953," *International Perspectives* (March–April 1987), pp. 8–10.

4. Brian Mulroney, *Where I Stand* (Toronto: McClelland and Stewart, 1983); Peter Aucoin, "Organizational Change in the Machinery of Canadian Government: From Rational Management to Brokerage Politics," *Canadian Journal of Political Science* 19 (1986), pp. 3–27.

5. Canada, Prime Minister's Office, "Communications Strategy for Canada-U.S.

Bilateral Trade Initiative," in *The Free Trade Papers,* ed. Duncan Cameron (Toronto: James Lorimer, 1986), pp. 7, 4. See also Richard Johnston et al., *Letting the People Decide* (Montreal: McGill–Queen's University Press, 1992), pp. 143–44.

6. Duncan Cameron, "Introduction," in *The Free Trade Papers,* ed. Duncan Cameron (Toronto: James Lorimer, 1986); Cameron, "Resisting Free Trade," *Canadian Journal of Political and Social Theory* 12 (1988), pp. 202–11; Robert A. Young, "Political Scientists, Economists, and the Canada-U.S. Free Trade Agreement," *Canadian Public Policy* 15 (1989), pp. 49–56; Graham Fraser, *Playing for Keeps* rev. ed. (Toronto: McClelland and Stewart, 1990); Pierre Martin, "Free Trade and Party Politics in Quebec," in *The NAFTA Puzzle: Political Parties and Trade in North America,* ed. Charles F. Doran and Gregory P. Marchildon (Boulder: Westview, 1994).

7. See Johnston et al., *Letting the People Decide.*

8. Cameron, "Introduction"; David Langille, "The Business Council on National Issues and the Canadian State," *Studies in Political Economy* 24 (1987), pp. 41–85; François Rocher, "Canadian Business, Free Trade, and the Rhetoric of Economic Continentalization," *Studies in Political Economy* 35 (1991), pp. 135–54; R. Jack Richardson, "Free Trade: Why Did It Happen?" *Canadian Review of Sociology and Anthropology* 29 (1992), pp. 307–28.

9. Michael Lusztig, "The Limits of Rent-Seeking: Why Protectionists Become Free Traders," Political Economy Research Group, *Papers in Political Economy* (working paper no. 61, University of Western Ontario, London, Ontario, 1995).

10. William G. Watson, "Canada-U.S. Free Trade: Why Now?" *Canadian Public Policy* 13 (1987), pp. 337–49.

11. See especially Paul Wonnacott and Ronald J. Wonnacott, *Free Trade Between the U.S. and Canada* (Cambridge, Mass.: Harvard University Press, 1967).

12. Anthony Downs, *An Economic Theory of Democracy* (New York: Harper and Row, 1957).

13. Alan C. Cairns, "The Electoral System and the Party System in Canada, 1921–1965," *Canadian Journal of Political Science* 1 (1968), pp. 55–80.

14. The 1980 National Energy Program is but one example of a policy with extremely different implications across regions. See Eric M. Uslaner, *Shale Barrel Politics* (Stanford: Stanford University Press, 1989); Patrick James and Robert Michelin, "The Canadian National Energy Program and Its Aftermath: Perspectives on an Era of Confrontation," *American Review of Canadian Studies* 19 (1989), pp. 59–81; Jeffrey Church, "Comment on 'Energy Politics in Canada, 1980–1981: Threat Power in a Sequential Game,'" *Canadian Journal of Political Science* 26 (1993), pp. 60–64. See also several works by Patrick James: "The Canadian National Energy Program and Its Aftermath," *Canadian Public Policy* 16 (1990), pp. 174–90; "Energy Politics in Canada, 1980–1981: Threat Power in a Sequential Game," *Canadian Journal of Political Science* 26 (1993), pp. 31–59; and his "Reply to 'Comment on "Energy

Politics in Canada, 1980–1981: Threat Power in a Sequential Game,'" *Canadian Journal of Political Science* 26 (1993), pp. 65–68.

15. Riker, *Theory of Political Coalitions.*

16. Janine Brodie, "The 'Free Trade' Election," *Studies in Political Economy* 28 (1989), 175–82; Gilles Breton and Jane Jenson, "After Free Trade and Meech Lake: Quoi de Neuf?" *Studies in Political Economy* 34 (1991), pp. 199–217.

17. Smiley, *Federal Condition in Canada.* For similar accounts, see Peter Leslie and Keith Brownsey, "Constitutional Reform and Continental Free Trade: A Review of Issues in Canadian Federalism in 1987," *Publius* 18 (1988), pp. 153–74; Garth Stevenson, "The Agreement and the Dynamics of Canadian Federalism," in *Trade-Offs on Free Trade,* ed. Marc Gold and David Leyton-Brown (Toronto: Carswell, 1988); Richard Simeon, "Parallelism in the Meech Lake Accord and the Free Trade Agreement," and Patrick J. Monahan, "Discussion," both in *Re-Forming Canada? The Meaning of the Meech Lake Accord and the Free Trade Agreement for the Canadian State,* ed. John D. Whyte and Ian Peach (Kingston Ont.: Queen's Institute of Intergovernmental Relations, 1989); Smiley, "Meech Lake and Free Trade: Studies in Canadian Federalism," *Canadian Public Administration* 32 (1989), pp. 470–81; Pierre E. Trudeau, "Say Goodbye to the Dream of One Canada," in *Meech Lake and Canada: Perspectives from the West,* ed. Roger Gibbins (Edmonton: Academic, 1989); Doern and Tomlin, *Faith and Fear;* and Johnston et al., *Letting the People Decide.*

18. Smiley, *Federal Condition in Canada;* Doern and Tomlin, *Faith and Fear.*

19. Doern and Tomlin, *Faith and Fear.*

20. Mulroney, *Where I Stand,* p. 90 (long quotation); Mulroney, Speech at Sept Iles, Quebec, August 6, 1984.

21. Charles Taylor, "Shared and Divergent Values," in *Options for a New Canada,* ed. Ronald L. Watts and Douglas M. Brown (Toronto: University of Toronto Press, 1991).

22. Smiley, "Meech Lake and Free Trade."

23. Smiley, *The Federal Condition.* The First National Policy was the aforementioned one of 1879. The Second National Policy, according to Smiley, was the Keynesian postwar settlement.

24. There are a number of useful works on the NEP. See Gordon C. Watkins and Michael A. Walker, eds., *Reaction: The National Energy Program* (Vancouver: Fraser Institute, 1981); John N. McDougall, *Fuels and the National Policy* (Toronto: Butterworths, 1982); G. Bruce Doern and Glen Toner, *The Politics of Energy* (Toronto: Methuen, 1985); Kenneth Norrie, "Energy, Canadian Federalism, and the West," in *Canadian Federalism,* ed. Harold Waller, Filippo Sabetti, and Daniel Elazar (Lanham, Md.: University Press of America, 1988); James and Michelin, "Canadian National Energy Program"; James, "Energy Politics in Canada"; Church, "Comment."

25. Norrie, "Energy, Canadian Federalism, and the West"; *Alberta Report,* March 9, 1987; Peter Lougheed, "The Rape of the National Energy Program Will Never Happen Again," in *Free Trade, Free Canada,* ed. Earle Grey (Woodville, Ont.: Canadian Speeches, 1988).

26. The Canadian Senate was constituted on the principle of equal regional representation. Each of the four great regions—Ontario, Quebec, the Atlantic, and the West—was represented by twenty-four senators. From the time of the NEP, Alberta rejected the concept of Canada as a collection of equal regions and began to press for provincial equality in the Senate specifically, and under the Constitution more generally. For more on this subject, see Michael Lusztig, "Federalism and Institutional Design: The Perils and Politics of a Triple-E Senate in Canada," *Publius* 25 (1995): 35–50.

27. See Lougheed, "Rape of the National Energy Program."

28. For a history of the constitutional reform process in Canada to 1982, see Michael B. Stein, "Canadian Constitutional Reform, 1927–1982: A Comparative Case Analysis over Time," in *Canadian Federalism,* ed. Harold Waller, Filippo Sabetti, and Daniel J. Elazar (Lanham, Md.: University Press of America, 1988).

29. For a comprehensive analysis of the 1982 constitutional process, see Keith Banting and Richard Simeon, eds., *And No One Cheered* (Toronto: Methuen, 1983), and John Whyte, Roy Romanow, and Howard Leeson, *Canada Notwithstanding* (Toronto: Carswell, 1984).

30. Thomas Courchene, "Market Nationalism," *Policy Options* 7 (1986), pp. 7–12; Martin, "Free Trade and Party Politics."

31. Carney quoted in Roger Gibbins, "Canadian Federalism: The Entanglement of Meech Lake and the Free Trade Agreement," *Publius* 19 (1989), p. 196; Lougheed, "Rape of the National Energy Program," p. 152.

32. Alberta, Department of Federal and Intergovernmental Affairs, "The Canada–United States Free Trade Agreement—Questions and Answers" (1987) and "Straight Talk on Free Trade" (1987); British Columbia, Ministry of Economic Development, "Briefing on Canada/United States Trade Negotiations" (January 1987) and "British Columbia Consultations on the Canada/U.S. Bilateral Trade Negotiations" (May 1987).

33. Monahan, *Meech Lake: The Inside Story* (Toronto: University of Toronto Press, 1991), especially pp. 49–51. See also Andrew Cohen, *A Deal Undone* (Vancouver: Douglas and McIntyre, 1990).

34. Monahan, *Meech Lake.*

35. Ibid., p. 84.

36. *Toronto Star,* April 27, 1987; *Globe and Mail,* May 2, 1987.

37. Canada, House of Commons, *Debates,* p. 12120.

38. See Cohen, *A Deal Undone,* ch. 11; Monahan, *Meech Lake,* ch. 8.

39. Quoted in Monahan, *Meech Lake,* p. 223.

40. Courchene, "Market Nationalism"; see also Martin, "Free Trade and Party Politics"; Hudson Meadwell and Pierre Martin, "Is Free Trade Nationalism an Antinomy?" (paper presented at the annual meeting of the Canadian Political Science Association, Ottawa, Ontario, 1993); Patrick James and Michael Lusztig, "Canada: Predicting Quebec's Economic and Political Future Within North America" (paper presented at the annual meeting of the American Political Science Association, Chicago, Ill., 1995).

41. Leslie and Brownsey, "Constitutional Reform and Continental Free Trade," pp. 164–65.

42. Hon. James Horsman, former Alberta minister of federal and intergovernmental affairs, interview by author, December 30, 1992.

43. Michael M. Hart, senior adviser, Trade Policy Studies, Department of External Affairs and International Trade, interview by author, January 6, 1993; Doern and Tomlin, *Faith and Fear,* p. 52.

44. See Canada, Department of External Affairs, *Canadian Trade Policy for the 1980s* (Ottawa: Minister of Supply and Services, 1983) and *Competitiveness and Security* (Ottawa: Minister of Supply and Services, 1985); Doern and Tomlin, *Faith and Fear;* and Michael Hart, *Decision at Midnight: Inside the Canada-U.S. Free Trade Negotiations* (Vancouver: University of British Columbia Press, 1994).

45. James Gillies, *Where Business Fails* (Montreal: The Institute for Research on Public Policy, 1981); Doern and Tomlin, *Faith and Fear;* Jock A. Finlayson, director of research, Business Council on National Issues, interview by author, January 6, 1993; Cameron, "Introduction"; Williams, *Not for Export;* Lusztig, "The Limits of Rent-Seeking."

46. Senior official, Department of External Affairs, interview by author, December 30, 1992; Smiley, "Meech Lake and Free Trade."

47. Hart, interview; Martin, "Free Trade and Party Politics."

48. Gil Rémillard, "Keynote Address to the Conference—Mont Gabriel Quebec," translated by Peter Leslie, in *Rebuilding the Relationship: Quebec and Its Confederation Partners,* ed. Peter Leslie (Kingston, Ont.: Queen's University Institute of Intergovernmental Relations, 1987). For a thorough analysis of the contents of the accord, see Peter Hogg, *Meech Lake Constitutional Accord Annotated* (Toronto: Carswell, 1988).

49. Benoît Bouchard, "Address to the Conference—Mont Gabriel Quebec," in Leslie, *Rebuilding the Relationship;* Cohen, *A Deal Undone,* p. 82.

50. Cohen, *A Deal Undone,* p. 90.

51. *Globe and Mail,* April 25, 1987; *Toronto Star,* April 25, 1987.

52. Getty cited in *Globe and Mail,* April 30, 1987; provinces' reactions cited in *Globe and Mail,* April 27, 1987, and *Toronto Star,* April 30, 1987.

53. *Toronto Star,* April 26, 1987.

54. *Globe and Mail,* April 27, 1987; *Toronto Star,* April 28, 1987; British Columbia,

Ministry of Economic Development, "Briefing on Canada/United States Trade Negotiations."

55. See, for example, *Alberta Report,* May 11, 1987.

56. *Globe and Mail,* May 8, 1987.

57. Smiley, "Meech Lake and Free Trade"; Cohen, *A Deal Undone.*

58. Alan C. Cairns, "Citizens (Outsiders) and Governments (Insiders) in Constitution-Making: The Case of Meech Lake," in *Disruptions: Constitutional Struggles from the Charter to Meech Lake,* ed. Douglas Williams (Toronto: McLelland and Stewart, 1991).

59. For a discussion of the Charlottetown Accord of 1992, see Kenneth McRoberts and Patrick Monahan, eds., *The Charlottetown Accord, the Referendum, and the Future of Canada* (Toronto: University of Toronto Press, 1993); Michael Lusztig, "Constitutional Paralysis: Why Canadian Constitutional Initiatives Are Doomed to Fail," *Canadian Journal of Political Science* 27 (1994), pp. 747–71.

60. Johnston et al., *Letting the People Decide.*

5 NAFTA and Solidarity

1. Jorge Casteñada, "Salinas's International Relations Gamble," *Journal of International Affairs* 43 (1990), pp. 407–22; Diane E. Davis, "Mexico's New Politics: Changing Perspectives on Free Trade," *World Policy Journal* 9 (1992), pp. 655–71.

2. Neil Nevitte, "Bringing Values 'Back In': Value Change and North American Integration" (paper presented at the Toward a North American Community? conference in Calgary, Alberta, 1993), p. 9; Ronald Inglehart, Neil Nevitte, and Miguel Basáñez, *Convergencia en Norte America: Comercio, política, y cultura* (Mexico: Siglo, 1994).

3. Dale Story, "Trade Policy in the Third World: A Case Study of the Mexican GATT Decision," *International Organization* 36 (1982), pp. 767–94; Gerardo Bueno, "The Structure of Protectionism in Mexico," in *The Structure of Protection in Developing Countries,* ed. Bela Balassa et al. (Baltimore: Johns Hopkins University Press, 1971); Weintraub, *Mexican Trade Policy;* Miguel D. Ramirez, "Stabilization and Trade Reform in Mexico," *Journal of Developing Areas* 27 (1993), p. 175.

4. Bueno, "Structure of Protectionism," p. 180.

5. Albert O. Hirschman, "The Political Economy of Import-Substituting Industrialization in Latin America," in *A Bias for Hope,* ed. Albert O. Hirschman (New Haven: Yale University Press, 1971).

6. Blanca Heredia, "Profits, Politics, and Size: The Political Transformation of Mexican Business," in *The Right and Democracy in Latin America,* ed. Douglas A. Chalmers, Maria do Carmo Campello de Souza, and Atilio A. Boron (New York: Praeger, 1992), p. 289; see also Basáñez, "Is Mexico Headed Toward Its Fifth Crisis?" in *Political and Economic Liberalization in Mexico: At a Critical Juncture?* ed. Riordan Roett (Boulder, Colo.: Lynne Rienner, 1993), p. 99.

7. Hirschman, "Import-Substituting Industrialization"; Weintraub, *Mexican Trade Policy;* Adriaan Ten Kate, "Trade Liberalization and Economic Stabilization in Mexico: Lessons of Experience," *World Development* 20 (1992), pp. 659–72.

8. Luis Rubio, "Economic Reform and Political Change in Mexico," in Roett, *Political and Economic Liberalization in Mexico,* p. 36. See also Weintraub, *Mexican Trade Policy;* Story, "Trade Policy in the Third World"; Roderic Ai Camp, *Entrepreneurs and Politics in Twentieth Century Mexico* (New York: Oxford University Press, 1989); Davis, "Mexico's New Politics."

9. M. Delal Baer, "North American Free Trade," *Foreign Affairs* 70 (1991); Denise Dresser, "Bringing the Poor Back In: Poverty Alleviation and Regime Legitimacy in Mexico" (paper presented at the twenty-seventh congress of the Latin American Studies Association, Los Angeles, California, 1992); Alejandro Álvarez Béjar and Gabriel Mendoza Pichardo, "Mexico, 1988–1991: A Successful Adjustment Program?" translated by John F. Uggen, *Latin American Perspectives* 20 (1993), pp. 32–45; Clark W. Reynolds, "Power, Value, and Distribution in the NAFTA," in Roett, *Political and Economic Liberalization in Mexico.*

10. Nora Lustig, *Mexico: The Remaking of an Economy* (Washington, D.C.: The Brookings Institution, 1992), pp. 117–20; Ramirez, "Stabilization and Trade Reform," p. 181.

11. Weintraub, *Mexican Trade Policy,* p. 19; Sidney Weintraub and M. Delal Baer, "The Interplay Between Economic and Political Opening: The Sequence in Mexico," *Washington Quarterly* 15 (1992), p. 192.

12. Baer, "North American Free Trade," p. 96; Ramirez, "Stabilization and Trade Reform," p. 183.

13. Diana Alarcón and Terry McKinley, "Beyond Import Substitution: The Restructuring Projects of Mexico and Brazil," *Latin American Perspectives* 19 (1992), pp. 72–87; Béjar and Pichardo, "Mexico, 1988–1991." See also Daniel Drache, "Assessing the Benefits of Free Trade," in *The Political Economy of North American Free Trade,* ed. Ricardo Grinspun and Maxwell A. Cameron (Montreal: McGill–Queen's University Press, 1993).

14. Béjar and Pichardo, "Mexico, 1988–1991," p. 37. *Maquiladoras* are free trade zones along the Mexico–United States border. They tend to attract labor-intensive firms taking advantage of Mexico's low-wage workforce.

15. Similarly, Canada initiated the CUFTA negotiations. See Manuel Pastor Jr., "Mexican Trade Liberalization and NAFTA," *Latin American Research Review* 29 (1994), pp. 153–73.

16. See Conybeare, *Trade Wars.*

17. Davis, "Mexico's New Politics," p. 656.

18. Judith Adler Hellman, "Mexican Perceptions of Free Trade: Support and Opposition to NAFTA," in *The Political Economy of North American Free Trade,* ed. Ricardo Grinspun and Maxwell A. Cameron (Montreal: McGill–Queen's University

Press, 1993); Manuel Pastor Jr. and Carol Wise, "The Origins and Sustainability of Mexico's Free Trade Policy," *International Organization* 48 (1994), pp. 459–89.

19. Lustig, *Mexico,* ch. 5; Sidney Weintraub, "The Economy on the Eve of Free Trade," *Current History* 92 (1993), pp. 67–72; Reynolds, "Power, Value, and Distribution"; Baer, "North American Free Trade."

20. Guy Poitras and Raymond Robinson, "The Politics of NAFTA in Mexico," *Journal of Interamerican Studies and World Affairs* 36 (1994): 1–35. See also Pastor and Wise, "Mexico's Free Trade Policy."

21. Poitras and Robinson, "The Politics of NAFTA in Mexico," p. 9.

22. Susan Kaufman Purcell and John F. H. Purcell, "State and Society in Mexico: Must a Stable Polity Be Institutionalized?" *World Politics* 32 (1980), pp. 194–227.

23. Stephen D. Morris, "Political Reformism in Mexico: Salinas at the Brink," *Journal of Interamerican Studies and World Affairs* 34 (1992), p. 31.

24. The military is only of passing interest as it was dissolved as a formal sector of the party in 1940, although it has maintained an informal link to the coalition. Evelyn P. Stevens, "Mexico's PRI: The Institutionalization of Corporatism," in *Authoritarianism and Corporatism,* ed. James M. Molloy (Pittsburgh: University of Pittsburgh Press, 1977).

25. David Brooks, "The End of the Miracle," *NACLA's Latin America and Empire Report* 21 (1987), p. 16.

26. Nora Hamilton, *The Limits of State Autonomy: Post-Revolutionary Mexico* (Princeton: Princeton University Press, 1982).

27. Stevens, "Mexico's PRI."

28. Soledad Loaeza, "The Role of the Right in Political Change in Mexico, 1982–1988," in *The Right and Democracy in Latin America,* ed. Douglas A. Chalmers, Maria do Carmo Campello de Souza, and Atilio A. Boron (New York: Praeger, 1992).

29. For the Chambers Law, see Stevens, "Mexico's PRI"; John F. H. Purcell and Susan Kaufman Purcell, "Mexican Business and Public Policy," in Molloy, *Authoritarianism and Corporatism in Latin America;* David R. Mares, "Explaining Choice of Development Strategies: Suggestions from Mexico, 1970–1982," *International Organization* 39 (1985), pp. 667–97. See also Heredia, "Profits, Politics, and Size."

30. Purcell and Purcell, "Mexican Business and Public Policy"; Robert R. Kaufman, "Democratic and Authoritarian Responses to the Debt Issue: Argentina, Brazil, Mexico," *International Organization* 39 (1985), pp. 473–503; Stevens, "Mexico's PRI"; Purcell and Purcell, "State and Society in Mexico."

31. Purcell and Purcell, "Mexican Business and Public Policy"; Judith Gentleman, "Prospects for Stability and Change in Mexico," *Latin American Research Review* 23 (1988), pp. 188–98; Purcell and Purcell, "State and Society in Mexico."

32. Mancur Olson, *The Logic of Collective Action* (Cambridge, Mass.: Harvard University Press, 1965).

33. Loaeza, "The Role of the Right"; Heredia, "Profits, Politics, and Size," p. 297 (quotation).

34. During the 1980s, the PAN was most successful in urban and more industrialized districts, as well as those featuring higher levels of education. Joseph L. Klesner, "Modernization, Economic Crisis, and Electoral Alignment in Mexico," *Mexican Studies* 9 (1993), p. 204. See also Camp, "The Cross in the Polling Booth: Religion, Politics, and the Laity in Mexico," *Latin American Research Review* 29 (1994), pp. 69–100. For the PRD, see *Economist*, June 9, 1990; Baer, "Mexico's Second Revolution"; Klesner, "Modernization, Economic Crisis."

35. Reynolds, "Power, Value, and Distribution," pp. 73–74 (quotation); Basáñez, "Is Mexico Headed Toward Its Fifth Crisis?" pp. 106–7.

36. *Economist*, June 9, 1990; Robert A. Pastor, "Salinas Takes a Gamble," *New Republic*, September 10 and 17, 1990; Pastor, "Post-Revolutionary Mexico: The Salinas Opening," *Journal of Interamerican Studies and World Affairs* 32 (1990), pp. 1–22; Jorge Chabat, "Mexico's Foreign Policy in 1990: Electoral Sovereignty and Integration with the United States," *Journal of Interamerican Studies and World Affairs* 33 (1991), pp. 1–25.

37. Guy Poitras and Raymond Robinson, "The Politics of NAFTA in Mexico," *Journal of Interamerican Studies and World Affairs* 36 (1994), pp. 1–35. For the peasant insurrection in Chiapas, see *New York Times*, January 3, 1994. For more on opposition to the NAFTA in Mexico, see Carlos A. Heredia, "NAFTA and Democratization in Mexico," *Journal of International Affairs* 48 (1994), pp. 13–38.

38. Salinas quoted in Pastor, "Post-Revolutionary Mexico," p. 19; Baer, "North American Free Trade," p. 97. See also Casteñada, "Salinas's International Relations Gamble," p. 419; Pastor, "Post-Revolutionary Mexico," p. 15, and "Salinas Takes a Gamble," p. 31; Peter H. Smith, "The Political Impact of Free Trade on Mexico," *Journal of Interamerican Studies and World Affairs* 34 (1992), pp. 10–11. For the opinion polls, see *Los Angeles Times*, October 10, 1991, and Johnston et al., *Letting the People Decide*. Basáñez, "Winners and Losers of NAFTA in Mexico" (paper presented at the NAFTA Now conference, St. Louis, Missouri, 1994).

39. Baer, "North American Free Trade"; Davis, "Mexico's New Politics"; Reynolds, "Power, Value, and Distribution"; Weintraub, "The Economy on the Eve of Free Trade."

40. Ramirez, "Stabilization and Trade Reform," pp. 176–77; Peter S. Cleaves and Charles J. Stephens, "Business and Economic Policy in Mexico," *Latin American Research Review* 26 (1991), p. 189; Béjar and Pichardo, "Mexico, 1988–1991."

41. *Economist*, November 6, 1993; Kate, "Trade Liberalization," p. 666; Lustig, *Mexico*, pp. 50–54; Reynolds, "Power, Value, and Distribution," pp. 79–80; Chabat, "Mexico's Foreign Policy in 1990," pp. 3–4.

42. Gourevitch, *Politics in Hard Times*; Goldstein, "Ideas, Institutions."

43. Baer, "North American Free Trade" and "Mexico's Second Revolution";

Smith, "Impact of Free Trade on Mexico," p. 10 (first quotation); Dresser, "Bringing the Poor Back In," p. 10 (second quotation).

44. See, for example, Carlos Salinas, *Political Participation, Public Investment, and Support for the System: A Comparative Study of Rural Communities in Mexico* (San Diego: Center for U.S.-Mexican Studies, 1982); also Martin C. Needler, "Economic Policy and Political Survival," *Mexican Studies* 9 (1993), pp. 139–43.

45. Dresser, "Bringing the Poor Back In"; Morris, "Political Reformism in Mexico: Salinas at the Brink"; Stephen D. Morris, "Political Reformism in Mexico," *Latin American Research Review* 28 (1993), pp. 191–205; Mexico, Secretariat of Commerce and Industrial Development, *Mexique-Canada: Une Nouvelle Ère de relations* (Ottawa, 1993); Jonathan Fox, "The Difficult Transition from Clientelism to Citizenship: Lessons from Mexico," *World Politics* 46 (1994), pp. 151–84.

46. Riordan Roett, "At the Crossroads: Liberalization in Mexico," in Roett, *Political and Economic Liberalization in Mexico,* p. 9.

47. Reynolds, "Power, Value, and Distribution," p. 85; Camp, "Political Liberalization: The Last Key to Economic Modernization in Mexico," in Roett, *Political and Economic Liberalization in Mexico,* n. 57; Carlos Salinas, "A New Hope for the Hemisphere?" *New Perspective Quarterly* 8 (1991), pp. 7–8.

48. Fox, "The Difficult Transition," p. 166; Peter M. Ward, "Social Welfare Policy and Political Opening in Mexico," *Journal of Latin American Studies* 25 (1993), p. 626; Programming and Budget team member quoted in Dresser, "Bringing the Poor Back In," p. 7.

49. Klesner, "Modernization, Economic Crisis"; party official quoted in *Economist,* August 24, 1991; *Este Pais,* October 1991.

50. Quotation from Morris, "Political Reformism in Mexico: Salinas at the Brink," p. 33; Poitras and Robinson, "The Politics of NAFTA in Mexico."

51. Smith, "Impact of Free Trade on Mexico," pp. 10–11.

52. Weintraub and Baer, "Interplay Between Economic and Political Opening," pp. 189–90. See also Heredia, "Profits, Politics, and Size"; Loaeza, "The Role of the Right"; and Rubio, "Economic Reform and Political Change."

53. Calvin P. Blair, "Mexico's National Program for Industrial Promotion and Foreign Trade, 1984–1988," *Mexican Forum* 5 (1985), pp. 1–6; Cleaves and Stephens, "Business and Economic Policy."

54. *Economist,* June 27, 1992; Nancy A. Nichols, "From Complacency to Competitiveness," *Harvard Business Review* 9–10 (1993), pp. 162–72.

55. Matilde Luna, Ricardo Tirado, and Franciso Valdés, "Businessmen and Politics in Mexico, 1982–1986," in *Government and Private Sector in Contemporary Mexico,* ed. Sylvia Maxfield and Ricardo Anzaldua Montoya (San Diego: Center for U.S.-Mexican Studies, 1987); Camp, *Entrepreneurs and Politics;* Ramirez, "Stabilization and Trade Reform"; Judith Teichman, "Dismantling the Mexican State and the Role of the Private Sector," in *The Political Economy of North American Free Trade,*

ed. Ricardo Grinspun and Maxwell A. Cameron (Montreal: McGill–Queen's University Press, 1993).

56. For a fuller discussion see Lusztig, "The Limits of Rent-Seeking."

57. Poitras and Robinson, "The Politics of NAFTA in Mexico," pp. 14–15, 15.

58. *Economist*, October 6, 1990; Mexican Investment Board, *Mexico Investment Update*, 4th quarter, 1994; Mexico, Secretariat of Commerce and Industrial Development, *Mexique-Canada*.

59. Maria de los Angeles Pozas, *Industrial Restructuring in Mexico: Corporate Adaptation, Technological Innovation, and Changing Patterns of Industrial Relations in Monterrey* (San Diego: Center for U.S.-Mexican Studies, 1993), p. 30.

60. Poitras and Robinson, "The Politics of NAFTA in Mexico," p. 20; *Economist*, November 27, 1990; Baer, "North American Free Trade" and "Mexico's Second Revolution"; Lustig, *Mexico*; Rubio, "Economic Reform and Political Change."

61. See Nicholas Kaldor, "Welfare Propositions of Economics and Interpersonal Comparisons of Utility," *Economic Journal* 49 (1939), pp. 549–52; T. Scitovszky, "A Note on Welfare Propositions in Economics," *Review of Economic Studies* 8 (1941), pp. 77–88.

62. Pastor, "Salinas Takes a Gamble," p. 32; Weintraub, "The Economy on the Eve of Free Trade," p. 72; Pozas, *Industrial Restructuring in Mexico*, 30; Mexican Investment Board, *Mexico Investment Update*, 1st quarter, 1994.

63. Mexico, Secretariat of Commerce and Industrial Development, *Mexique-Canada*, p. 18; Ruggie, "International Regimes."

64. Baer, "Mexico's Second Revolution," p. 56 (quotation).

6 Conclusion

1. Putnam, "Diplomacy and Domestic Politics"; George Tsebelis, *Nested Games: Rational Choice in Comparative Politics* (Berkeley and Los Angeles: University of California Press, 1990). See also Peter B. Evans, *Double-Edged Diplomacy: International Politics and Domestic Politics* (Berkeley and Los Angeles: University of California Press, 1993); Jongryn Mo, "The Logic of Two-Level Games with Endogenous Domestic Coalitions," *Journal of Conflict Resolution* 38 (1994), pp. 402–22.

2. A literature on the difficulties of enacting such policies is emerging within comparative public policy and international political economy. Recent works include Arnold, *The Logic of Congressional Action*; Rodrik, "The Rush to Free Trade"; Dani Rodrik, "The Limits of Trade Policy Reform in Developing Countries," *Journal of Economic Perspectives* 6 (1992), pp. 87–105; and Williamson, *The Political Economy of Policy Reform*.

3. Samuel Brittan, "The Economic Contradictions of Democracy," *British Journal of Political Science* 5 (1975), pp. 129–60, and "Inflation and Democracy," in *The Political Economy of Inflation*, ed. Fred Hirsch and John Goldthorpe (Cambridge, Mass.: Harvard University Press, 1978); Daniel Bell, *The Cultural Contradictions of*

Capitalism (New York: Basic Books, 1976); Colin Crouch, "Inflation and the Political Organization of Economic Interests," in *The Political Economy of Inflation*, ed. Hirsch and Goldthorpe (Cambridge, Mass.: Harvard University Press, 1978); Crouch, "The State, Capital, and Liberal Democracy," in *The State and Economy in Contemporary Capitalism*, ed. Colin Crouch (New York: St Martin's Press, 1979); Mancur Olson, *The Rise and Decline of Nations: Economic Growth, Stagflation, and Social Rigidities* (New Haven: Yale University Press, 1982).

4. Bell, *Cultural Contradictions;* Brittan, "Inflation and Democracy"; Crouch, "The State, Capital, and Liberal Democracy."

5. Brittan, "Economic Contradictions."

6. Nouriel Roubini and Jeffrey Sachs, "Political and Economic Determinants of Budget Deficits in the Industrial Democracies," *European Economic Review* 33 (1989), pp. 903–38.

7. Leonard Silk, "Dangers of Slow Growth," *Foreign Affairs* 72 (1993), pp. 167–82.

8. Silk, "Dangers of Slow Growth"; see also Alan Murray, "The Global Economy Bungled," *Foreign Affairs* 72 (1993), pp. 158–66.

9. Laszlo Bruszt, "Transformative Politics: Social Costs and Social Peace in East Central Europe," *East European Politics and Societies* 6 (1992), pp. 55–72; Jim Leitzel, "Russian Economic Reform: Is Economics Helpful?" *Eastern Economic Journal* 19 (1993), pp. 365–78.

10. Weintraub and Baer, "The Interplay Between Economic and Political Opening"; Wlodzimierz Brus, "Marketisation and Democratisation: The Sino-Soviet Divergence," *Cambridge Journal of Economics* 17 (1993), pp. 423–40.

11. See Haggard, "Institutional Foundations."

12. N. F. R. Crafts, "Institutions and Economic Growth: Recent British Experience in an International Context," *West European Politics* 15 (1992), pp. 16–38; Wayne Sandholtz, "Choosing Union: Monetary Politics and Maastricht," *International Organization* 47 (1993), pp. 1–40; Putnam, "Diplomacy and Domestic Politics," pp. 427–29.

13. Ronald Rogowski, "Trade and the Variety of Democratic Institutions," *International Organization* 41 (1987), pp. 203–23.

14. Peter J. Katzenstein, *Small States in World Markets: Industrial Policy in Europe* (Ithaca: Cornell University Press, 1985); Rogowski, "Trade and the Variety of Democratic Institutions."

15. This point has long been recognized by analysts of trade policy. See I. M. Destler, *American Trade Politics*, 2d ed. (Washington, D.C.: Institute for International Economics, 1992); Susanne Lohmann and Sharyn O'Halloran, "Divided Government and U.S. Trade Policy: Theory and Evidence," *International Organization* 48 (1994), esp. pp. 599–600.

16. James M. Buchanan, "How Can Constitutions Be Designed so that Politicians Who Seek to Serve 'Public Interest' Can Survive and Prosper?" *Constitutional*

Political Economy 4 (1993), pp. 1–6; George Tsebelis, "The Power of the European Parliament as Conditional Agenda Setter," *American Political Science Review* 88 (1994), pp. 128–42.

17. Christopher Manfredi, "Litigation and Institutional Design: The Charter of Rights and Freedoms and Micro-Constitutional Politics" (paper presented at the annual meeting of the Canadian Political Science Association, Ottawa, Ontario, 1993 [quotation]), "'Appropriate and Just in the Circumstances': Public Policy and the Enforcement of Rights Under the Canadian Charter of Rights and Freedoms" (paper presented at the annual meeting of the American Political Science Association, Chicago, Illinois, 1992), and *Judicial Power and the Charter: Canada and the Paradox of Liberal Constitutionalism* (Toronto: McClelland and Stewart, 1993).

BIBLIOGRAPHY

Alarcón, Diana, and Terry McKinley. "Beyond Import Substitution: The Restructuring Projects of Mexico and Brazil." *Latin American Perspectives* 19 (1992): 72–87.

Alberta. Department of Federal and Intergovernmental Affairs. "The Canada–United States Free Trade Agreement—Questions and Answers." 1987.

———. "Straight Talk on Free Trade." 1987.

Alberta Report. Various.

Allen, Michael Patrick. "Capitalist Response to State Intervention: Theories of the State and Political Finance in the New Deal." *American Sociological Review* 56 (1991): 679–89.

Allen, William R. "The International Trade Philosophy of Cordell Hull, 1907–1933." *American Economic Review* 43 (1953): 101–16.

Allison, Graham T. *Essence of Decision.* New York: Harper Collins, 1971.

Altmeyer, Arthur. *The Formative Years of Social Security.* Madison: University of Wisconsin Press, 1966.

American Liberty League. "A Program for Congress." Document 83, 1935.

Anderson, Gary, and Robert Tollison. "Ideology, Interest Groups, and the Repeal of the Corn Laws." In *The Political Economy of Rent-Seeking,* ed. Charles Rowley, Robert Tollison, and Gordon Tullock. Boston: Kluwer Academic, 1988.

Arnold, R. Douglas. *The Logic of Congressional Action.* New Haven: Yale University Press, 1990.

Aucoin, Peter. "Organizational Change in the Machinery of Canadian Government: From Rational Management to Brokerage Politics." *Canadian Journal of Political Science* 19 (1986): 3–27.

Baer, M. Delal. "Mexico's Second Revolution: Pathways to Liberalization." In Roett, *Political and Economic Liberalization in Mexico.*

———. "North American Free Trade." *Foreign Affairs* 70 (1991).

Baldwin, Robert E. "The Political Economy of Trade Policy." *Journal of Economic Perspectives* 3 (1989): 119–35.

Banting, Keith, and Richard Simeon, eds. *And No One Cheered.* Toronto: Methuen, 1983.

Barnes, Donald Grove. *A History of the English Corn Laws from 1660–1846.* New York: Augustus M. Kelley, 1965.

Barry, Donald. "Eisenhower, St. Laurent, and Free Trade, 1953." *International Perspectives* (March–April 1987): 8–10.

Basáñez, Miguel. "Is Mexico Headed Toward Its Fifth Crisis?" In Roett, *Political and Economic Liberalization in Mexico.*

———. "Winners and Losers of NAFTA in Mexico." Paper presented at the NAFTA Now Conference, St. Louis, Missouri, 1994.

Bates, Robert H. "Institutions as Investments." Duke University Program in Political Economy. Working paper no. 133, 1990.

Bates, Robert H., Philip Brock, and Jill Tiefenthaler. "Risk and Trade Regimes: Another Exploration." *International Organization* 45 (1991): 1–18.

Bauer, Raymond A., Ithiel de la Sola Pool, and Lewis Anthony Dexter. *American Business and Public Policy.* 2d ed. Chicago: Aldine-Atherton Inc., 1972.

Becker, Gary. "A Theory of Competition Among Pressure Groups for Political Influence." *Quarterly Journal of Economics* 98 (1983): 371–400.

Béjar, Alejandro Álvarez, and Gabriel Mendoza Pichardo. "Mexico, 1988–1991: A Successful Adjustment Program?" Translated by John F. Uggen. *Latin American Perspectives* 20 (1993): 32–45.

Bell, Daniel. *The Cultural Contradictions of Capitalism.* New York: Basic Books, 1976.

Berkowitz, Edward, and Kim McQuaid. *Creating the Welfare State.* New York: Praeger, 1980.

Blair, Calvin P. "Mexico's National Program for Industrial Promotion and Foreign Trade, 1984–1988." *Mexican Forum* 5 (1985): 1–6.

Borchardt, Knut. *Perspectives on Modern Economic History and Policy.* Translated by Peter Lambert. Cambridge, England: Cambridge University Press, 1991.

Bouchard, Benoît. "Address to the Conference—Mont Gabriel Quebec." In *Rebuilding the Relationship: Quebec and Its Confederation Partners,* ed. Peter Leslie. Kingston, Ont.: Queen's University Institute of Intergovernmental Relations, 1987.

Brady, David W. *Critical Elections and Congressional Policy Making.* Stanford: Stanford University Press, 1988.

Brawley, Mark R. *Liberal Leadership: Great Powers and Their Challengers in Peace and War.* Ithaca: Cornell University Press, 1993.

Brenner, Stephen Robert. *Economic Interests and the Trade Agreements Program, 1937–1940: A Study of Institutions and Political Influence.* Ph.D. dissertation, Stanford University, 1978.

Breton, Gilles, and Jane Jenson. "After Free Trade and Meech Lake: Quoi de Neuf?" *Studies in Political Economy* 34 (1991): 199–217.

Briggs, Asa. *The Age of Improvement: 1783–1867.* New York: David McKay, 1959.

British Columbia. Ministry of Economic Development. "Briefing on Canada/United States Trade Negotiations." January 1987.

———. "British Columbia Consultations on the Canada/U.S. Bilateral Trade Negotiations." May 1987.

Brittan, Samuel. "The Economic Contradictions of Democracy." *British Journal of Political Science* 5 (1975): 129–60.

———. "Inflation and Democracy." In *The Political Economy of Inflation,* ed. Fred Hirsch and John Goldthorpe. Cambridge, Mass.: Harvard University Press, 1978.

Brock, Michael. *The Great Reform Act.* London: Hutchison, 1973.

Brodie, Janine. "The 'Free Trade' Election." *Studies in Political Economy* 28 (1989): 175–82.

Brooks, David. "The End of the Miracle." NACLA*'s Latin America and Empire Report* 21 (1987): 14–20.

Broughton, Lord. *Recollections of a Long Life.* Vol. 6. Edited by Lady Dorchester. London: John Murray, 1911.

Brown, Lucy. *The Board of Trade and the Free Trade Movement, 1830–1842.* Oxford: Clarendon Press, 1958.

Brus, Wlodzimierz. "Marketisation and Democratisation: The Sino-Soviet Divergence." *Cambridge Journal of Economics* 17 (1993): 423–40.

Bruszt, Laszlo. "Transformative Politics: Social Costs and Social Peace in East Central Europe." *East European Politics and Societies* 6 (1992): 55–72.

Buchanan, James M. "How Can Constitutions Be Designed so that Politicians Who Seek to Serve 'Public Interest' Can Survive and Prosper?" *Constitutional Political Economy* 4 (1993): 1–6.

Bueno, Gerardo. "The Structure of Protectionism in Mexico." In *The Structure of Protection in Developing Countries,* ed. Bela Balassa et al. Baltimore: Johns Hopkins University Press, 1971.

Burnham, Walter Dean. *Critical Elections and the Mainsprings of American Politics.* New York: Norton, 1970.

———. "The System of 1896: An Analysis." In *The Evolution of American Electoral Systems,* ed. Paul Kleppner et al. Westport, Conn.: Greenwood Press, 1981.

Burns, James MacGregor. *Roosevelt: The Lion and the Fox.* New York: Harcourt, Brace, 1956.

Cairns, Alan C. "Citizens (Outsiders) and Governments (Insiders) in Constitution-Making: The Case of Meech Lake." In *Disruptions: Constitutional Struggles from the Charter to Meech Lake,* ed. Douglas Williams. Toronto: McClelland and Stewart, 1991.

———. "The Electoral System and the Party System in Canada, 1921–1965." *Canadian Journal of Political Science* 1 (1968): 55–80.

———. "The Embedded State: State-Society Relations in Canada." In *State and Society: Canada in Comparative Perspective,* ed. Keith Banting. Toronto: University of Toronto Press, 1986.

———. "The Governments and Societies of Canadian Federalism." *Canadian Journal of Political Science* 10 (1977): 695–725.

Cameron, Duncan. "Introduction." In *The Free Trade Papers,* ed. Duncan Cameron. Toronto: James Lorimer, 1986.

———. "Resisting Free Trade." *Canadian Journal of Political and Social Theory* 12 (1988): 202–11.

Camp, Roderic Ai. "The Cross in the Polling Booth: Religion, Politics, and the Laity in Mexico." *Latin American Research Review* 29 (1994): 69–100.

———. *Entrepreneurs and Politics in Twentieth Century Mexico.* New York: Oxford University Press, 1989.

———. "Political Liberalization: The Last Key to Economic Modernization in Mexico." In Roett, *Political and Economic Liberalization in Mexico.*

Canada. House of Commons. *Debates.* 34th Parliament, 2d sess. Ottawa: Minister of Supply and Services, 1990.

Canada. Prime Minister's Office. "Communications Strategy for Canada-U.S. Bilateral Trade Initiative." In *The Free Trade Papers,* ed. Duncan Cameron. Toronto: James Lorimer, 1986.

Canada. *Report of the Royal Commission on the Economic Union and Development Prospects for Canada.* Ottawa: Minister of Supply and Services, 1985.

Canada. Department of External Affairs. *Canadian Trade Policy for the 1980s.* Ottawa: Minister of Supply and Services, 1983.

———. *Competitiveness and Security.* Ottawa: Minister of Supply and Services, 1985.

———. *Foreign Policy for Canadians.* Ottawa: Information Canada, 1970.

———. Senior official. Interview by author, December 30, 1992.

Canada. Senate. Standing Committee on Foreign Affairs. *Canada's Trade Relations with the United States.* Ottawa: Minister of Supply and Services, 1982.

Casteñada, Jorge. "Salinas's International Relations Gamble." *Journal of International Affairs* 43 (1990): 407–22.

Caves, Richard E., and Ronald W. Jones. *World Trade and Payments.* 2d ed. Boston: Little, Brown, 1977.

Chabat, Jorge. "Mexico's Foreign Policy in 1990: Electoral Sovereignty and Integration with the United States." *Journal of Interamerican Studies and World Affairs* 33 (1991): 1–25.

Christie, O. F. *The Transition from Aristocracy, 1832–1867.* London: Seeley, Service, 1928.

Church, Jeffrey. "Comment on 'Energy Politics in Canada, 1980–1981: Threat Power in a Sequential Game.'" *Canadian Journal of Political Science* 26 (1993): 60–64.

Clark, Peter B., and James Q. Wilson. "Incentive Systems: A Theory of Organizations." *Administrative Science Quarterly* 6 (1961): 129–66.

Cleaves, Peter S., and Charles J. Stephens. "Business and Economic Policy in Mexico." *Latin American Research Review* 26 (1991): 187–202.

Cobden, Richard. *Speeches by Richard Cobden, MP.* Vols. 1 and 2. Edited by John Bright and Thorold Rogers. London: Macmillan, 1870.

Cohen, Andrew. *A Deal Undone.* Vancouver: Douglas and McIntyre, 1990.

Coleman, James S. "Foundations for a Theory of Collective Decisions." *American Journal of Sociology* 71 (1966): 615–27.

Coleman, William. *Business and Politics: A Study of Collective Action.* Kingston, Ont.: McGill–Queen's University Press, 1988.

Conybeare, John A. C. "Tariff Protection in Developed and Developing Countries: A Case Sectoral and Longitudinal Analysis." *International Organization* 37 (1983): 441–67.

———. *Trade Wars: The Theory and Practice of International Commercial Rivalry.* New York: Columbia University Press, 1987.

Coughlin, Cletus, K. Alec Chrystal, and Geoffrey Wood. "Protectionist Trade Policies: A Survey of Theory, Evidence, and Rationale." In *International Political Economy: Perspectives on Global Power and Wealth,* ed. Jeff Frieden and David Lake. 2d ed. New York: St. Martin's Press, 1991.

Courchene, Thomas. "Market Nationalism." *Policy Options* 7 (1986): 7–12.

Crafts, N. F. R. "Institutions and Economic Growth: Recent British Experience in an International Context." *West European Politics* 15 (1992): 16–38.

Croker, John Wilson. *The Correspondence and Diaries of the Late Right Honourable John Wilson Croker.* Vol. 2. Edited by Louis J. Jennings. New York: Charles Scribner's Sons, 1884.

Crouch, Colin. "Inflation and the Political Organization of Economic Interests." In *The Political Economy of Inflation,* ed. Fred Hirsch and John Goldthorpe. Cambridge, Mass.: Harvard University Press, 1978.

———. "The State, Capital, and Liberal Democracy." In *The State and Economy in Contemporary Capitalism,* ed. Colin Crouch. New York: St. Martin's Press, 1979.

Culbertson, William S. *Reciprocity.* New York: Whittlesay House, 1937.

Dallek, Robert. *Franklin D. Roosevelt and American Foreign Policy, 1932–1945.* New York: Oxford University Press, 1979.

Davis, Diane E. "Mexico's New Politics: Changing Perspectives on Free Trade." *World Policy Journal* 9 (1992): 655–71.

Derber, Milton. "The New Deal and Labor." In *The New Deal: The National Level,* ed. John Braeman, Robert H. Bremner, and David Brody. Columbus: Ohio State University Press, 1975.

Destler, I. M. *American Trade Politics.* 2d ed. Washington, D.C.: Institute for International Economics, 1992.

Doern, G. Bruce, and Brian W. Tomlin. *Faith and Fear: The Free Trade Story.* Toronto: Stoddart, 1991.

Doern, G. Bruce, and Glen Toner. *The Politics of Energy.* Toronto: Methuen, 1985.

Doner, Richard F. "Limits of State Strength: Toward an Internationalist View of Economic Development." *World Politics* 44 (1992): 398–431.

Downs, Anthony. *An Economic Theory of Democracy.* New York: Harper and Row, 1957.

Drache, Daniel. "Assessing the Benefits of Free Trade." In *The Political Economy of North American Free Trade,* ed. Ricardo Grinspun and Maxwell A. Cameron. Montreal: McGill–Queen's University Press, 1993.

Dresser, Denise. "Bringing the Poor Back In: Poverty Alleviation and Regime Legitimacy in Mexico." Paper presented at the twenty-seventh congress of the Latin American Studies Association, Los Angeles, California, 1992.

The Economist. Various.

Ekelund, Robert, and Robert Tollison. *Mercantilism as a Rent-Seeking Society.* College Station: Texas A&M University Press, 1981.

Este Pais. Various.

Evans, Peter B. *Double-Edged Diplomacy: International Politics and Domestic Politics.* Berkeley and Los Angeles: University of California Press, 1993.

Fairlie, Susan. "The Nineteenth-Century Corn Law Reconsidered." *Economic History Review,* 2d ser. 18 (1965): 544–61.

Fay, C. R. *The Corn Laws and Social England.* Cambridge, England: Cambridge University Press, 1932.

Feeny, David. "The Demand for and Supply of Institutional Arrangements." In *Rethinking Institutional Analysis and Development: Issues, Alternatives, and Choices,* ed. Vincent Ostrom, David Feeny, and Hartmut Picht. San Francisco: International Center for Economic Growth, 1988.

Ferguson, Thomas. "From Normalcy to New Deal: Industrial Structure, Party Competition, and American Public Policy in the Great Depression." *International Organization* 38 (1984): 41–94.

Finegold, Kenneth, and Theda Skocpol. "State, Party, and Industry: From Business Recovery to the Wagner Act in America's New Deal." In *Statemaking and Social Movements*, ed. Charles Bright and Susan Harding. Ann Arbor: University of Michigan Press, 1984.

Finlayson, Jock A. Interview by author, January 6, 1993.

Fox, Jonathan. "The Difficult Transition from Clientelism to Citizenship: Lessons from Mexico." *World Politics* 46 (1994): 151–84.

Fraser, Graham. *Playing for Keeps.* Rev. ed. Toronto: McClelland and Stewart, 1990.

Frey, Bruno S. *International Political Economics.* Oxford: Basil Blackwell, 1984.

Frieden, Jeff. "Sectoral Conflict and Foreign Economic Policy, 1914–1940." *International Organization* 42 (1988): 59–90.

Friman, H. Richard. "Side-Payments Versus Security Cards: Domestic Bargaining Tactics in International Economic Relations." *International Organization* 47 (1993): 387–410.

Frohlich, Norman, Joe A. Oppenheimer, and Oran R. Young. *Political Leadership and Collective Goods.* Princeton: Princeton University Press, 1971.

Gentleman, Judith. "Prospects for Stability and Change in Mexico." *Latin American Research Review* 23 (1988): 188–98.

Gerschenkron, Alexander. "Economic Backwardness in Historical Perspective." In *Economic Backwardness in Historical Perspective*, ed. Alexander Gerschenkron. Cambridge, Mass.: Belknap Press, 1962.

Gibbins, Roger. "Canadian Federalism: The Entanglement of Meech Lake and the Free Trade Agreement." *Publius* 19 (1989): 185–98.

Gillies, James. *Where Business Fails.* Montreal: The Institute for Research on Public Policy, 1981.

Gilpin, Robert. *War and Change in World Politics.* Cambridge, England: Cambridge University Press, 1981.

The Globe and Mail. Various.

Goldstein, Judith. "Ideas, Institutions, and American Trade Policy." *International Organization* 42 (1988): 179–217.

———. *Ideas, Interests, and American Trade Policy.* Ithaca: Cornell University Press, 1993.

Gourevitch, Peter A. "Keynesian Politics: The Political Sources of Economic Policy Choices." In *The Political Power of Economic Ideas*, ed. Peter A. Hall. Princeton: Princeton University Press, 1989.

———. *Politics in Hard Times: Comparative Responses to International Economic Crises.* Ithaca: Cornell University Press, 1986.

Gras, Norman. *The Evolution of the English Corn Market.* Cambridge, Mass.: Harvard University Press, 1915.

Great Britain (Hansard). House of Commons. *Parliamentary Debates.* 3d ser. vol. 78. London: George Woodfall and Son, 1845.

Greville, Charles. *The Greville Diary.* Vol. 2. Edited by Philip Wilson. Garden City, N.J.: Doubleday, Page, 1927.

―――. *The Greville Memoirs: A Journal of the Reign of Queen Victoria, 1837–1852.* Vol. 2. Edited by Henry Reeve. New York: Appleton, 1885.

Haggard, Stephan. "The Institutional Foundations of Hegemony: Explaining the Reciprocal Trade Agreements Act of 1934." *International Organization* 42 (1988): 91–119.

Hall, Peter. *Governing the Economy: The Politics of State Intervention in Britain and France.* Cambridge: Polity Press, 1986.

Hamilton, Alexander. "Report on Manufactures." In *The Reports of Alexander Hamilton,* ed. Jacob E. Cooke. New York: Harper and Row, 1964.

Hamilton, Colleen, and John Whalley. "The GATT and Canadian Interests." In *Canada and the Multilateral Trading System,* ed. John Whalley. Toronto: University of Toronto Press, 1985.

Hamilton, Nora. *The Limits of State Autonomy: Post-Revolutionary Mexico.* Princeton: Princeton University Press, 1982.

Hart, Michael M. *Canadian Economic Development and the International Trading System.* Toronto: University of Toronto Press, 1985.

―――. *Decision at Midnight: Inside the Canada-U.S. Free Trade Negotiations.* Vancouver: University of British Columbia Press, 1994.

―――. Interview by author, January 6, 1993.

Hawley, Ellis W. "The New Deal and Business." In *The New Deal: The National Level,* ed. John Braeman, Robert H. Bremner, and David Brody. Columbus: Ohio State University Press, 1975.

Hellman, Judith Adler. "Mexican Perceptions of Free Trade: Support and Opposition to NAFTA." In *The Political Economy of North American Free Trade,* ed. Ricardo Grinspun and Maxwell A. Cameron. Montreal: McGill-Queen's University Press, 1993.

Heredia, Blanca. "Profits, Politics, and Size: The Political Transformation of Mexican Business." In *The Right and Democracy in Latin America,* ed. Douglas A. Chalmers, Maria do Carmo Campello de Souza, and Atilio A. Boron. New York: Praeger, 1992.

Heredia, Carlos A. "NAFTA and Democratization in Mexico." *Journal of International Affairs* 48 (1994): 13–38.

Herring, E. Pendleton. "Second Session of the Seventy-Third Congress, January 3, 1934, to June 18, 1934." *American Political Science Review* 28 (1934): 852–65.

Hirschman, Albert O. "The Political Economy of Import-Substituting Industrialization in Latin America." In *A Bias for Hope,* ed. Albert O. Hirschman. New Haven: Yale University Press, 1971.

Hogg, Peter. *Meech Lake Constitutional Accord Annotated.* Toronto: Carswell, 1988.

Holt, James. "The New Deal and the American Anti-Statist Tradition." In *The New*

Deal: The National Level, ed. John Braeman, Robert H. Bremner, and David Brody. Columbus: Ohio State University Press, 1975.

Holyoake, George Jacob. *Sixty Years of an Agitator's Life.* Vol. 1. London: T. Fisher and Unwin, 1893.

Horsman, James. Interview by author, December 30, 1992.

Hull, Cordell. *The Memoirs of Cordell Hull.* Vol. 1. New York: Macmillan, 1948.

Ickes, Harold L. *The Secret Diary of Harold L. Ickes.* Vol. 2. New York: Da Capo, 1974.

Ikenberry, G. John. "Conclusion: An Institutional Approach to American Foreign Economic Policy." *International Organization* 42 (1988): 219–43.

———. *Reasons of State: Oil Politics and the Capacities of American Government.* Ithaca: Cornell University Press, 1988.

———. "A World Economy Restored: Expert Consensus and the Anglo-American Postwar Settlement." *International Organization* 46 (1992): 289–321.

Inglehart, Ronald, Neil Nevitte, and Miguel Basáñez. *Convergencia en Norte America: Comercio, política, y cultura.* Mexico: Siglo, 1994.

James, Patrick. "The Canadian National Energy Program and Its Aftermath." *Canadian Public Policy* 16 (1990): 174–90.

———. "Energy Politics in Canada, 1980–1981: Threat Power in a Sequential Game." *Canadian Journal of Political Science* 26 (1993): 31–59.

———. "A Reply to 'Comment on "Energy Politics in Canada, 1980–1981: Threat Power in a Sequential Game."'" *Canadian Journal of Political Science* 26 (1993): 65–68.

James, Patrick, and Michael Lusztig. "Canada: Predicting Quebec's Economic and Political Future Within North America." Paper presented at the annual meeting of the American Political Science Association, Chicago, Ill., 1995.

James, Patrick, and Robert Michelin. "The Canadian National Energy Program and Its Aftermath: Perspectives on an Era of Confrontation." *American Review of Canadian Studies* 19 (1989): 59–81.

James, Scott C., and David A. Lake. "The Second Face of Hegemony: Britain's Repeal of the Corn Laws and the American Walker Tariff of 1846." *International Organization* 43 (1989): 1–29.

Johnston, Richard, André Blais, Henry E. Brady, and Jean Crête. *Letting the People Decide.* Montreal: McGill–Queen's University Press, 1992.

Jones, Joseph. *Tariff Retaliation: Repercussions of the Hawley-Smoot Bill.* Philadelphia: University of Pennsylvania Press, 1934.

Jordan, Grant, and Jeremy Richardson. "The British Policy Style or the Logic of Negotiation." In *Policy Styles in Western Europe,* ed. Jeremy Richardson. London: George Allen and Unwin, 1982.

Kahneman, Daniel, and Amos Tversky. "Choices, Values, and Frames." *American Psychologist* 4 (1984): 341–50.

———. "Prospect Theory: An Analysis of Decision Under Risk." *Econometrica* 47 (1979): 263–91.

Kaldor, Nicholas. "Welfare Propositions of Economics and Interpersonal Comparisons of Utility." *Economic Journal* 49 (1939): 549–52.

Kate, Adriaan Ten. "Trade Liberalization and Economic Stabilization in Mexico: Lessons of Experience." *World Development* 20 (1992): 659–72.

Katzenstein, Peter J. "Conclusion: Domestic Structures and Strategies of Foreign Economic Policy." In *Between Power and Plenty,* ed. Peter J. Katzenstein. Madison: University of Wisconsin Press, 1978.

———. *Small States in World Markets: Industrial Policy in Europe.* Ithaca: Cornell University Press, 1985.

Kaufman, Robert R. "Democratic and Authoritarian Responses to the Debt Issue: Argentina, Brazil, Mexico." *International Organization* 39 (1985): 473–503.

Kelly, William B., Jr. "Antecedents of Present Commercial Policy." In *Studies in United States Commercial Policy,* ed. William B. Kelly Jr. Chapel Hill: University of North Carolina Press, 1963.

Kemp, Betty. "Reflections on the Repeal of the Corn Laws." *Victorian Studies* 5 (1962): 189–204.

Keohane, Robert. *After Hegemony.* Princeton: Princeton University Press, 1984.

Key, V. O. "A Theory of Critical Elections." *Journal of Politics* 17 (1955): 3–13.

Kindleberger, Charles P. *The World in Depression, 1929–1939.* Berkeley and Los Angeles: University of California Press, 1973.

Kirkendall, Richard. "The New Deal and Agriculture." In *The New Deal: The National Level,* ed. John Braeman, Robert H. Bremner, and David Brody. Columbus: Ohio State University Press, 1975.

———. "The New Deal and American Politics." In *Fifty Years Later: The New Deal Evaluated,* ed. Harvard Sitkoff. Philadelphia: Temple University Press, 1985.

Kleppner, Paul. "Critical Realignments and Electoral Systems." In *The Evolution of American Electoral Systems,* ed. Paul Kleppner et al. Westport, Conn.: Greenwood Press, 1981.

Klesner, Joseph L. "Modernization, Economic Crisis, and Electoral Alignment in Mexico." *Mexican Studies* 9 (1993): 187–223.

Krasner, Stephen D. "Approaches to the State." *Comparative Politics* 16 (1984): 223–46.

———. *Defending the National Interest: Raw Materials Investments and U.S. Foreign Policy.* Princeton: Princeton University Press, 1978.

———. "Regimes and the Limits of Realism: Regimes as Autonomous Variables." *International Organization* 36 (1982): 497–510.

———. "State Power and the Structure of International Trade." *World Politics* 28 (1976): 317–47.

Krueger, Anne. "The Political Economy of the Rent-Seeking Society." *American Economic Review* 64 (1974): 291–303.

Lake, David A. *Power, Protection, and Free Trade.* Ithaca: Cornell University Press, 1988.

———. "The State and American Trade Strategy in the Pre-Hegemonic Era." *International Organization* 42 (1988): 33–58.

Langille, David. "The Business Council on National Issues and the Canadian State." *Studies in Political Economy* 24 (1987): 41–85.

Larkin, John Day. *Trade Agreements.* New York: Columbia University Press, 1940.

Lavergne, Real. *The Political Economy of U.S. Tariffs.* Toronto: The Academic Press, 1983.

Leitzel, Jim. "Russian Economic Reform: Is Economics Helpful?" *Eastern Economic Journal* 19 (1993): 365–78.

Leslie, Peter, and Keith Brownsey. "Constitutional Reform and Continental Free Trade: A Review of Issues in Canadian Federalism in 1987." *Publius* 18 (1988): 153–74.

Lindblom, Charles. *Politics and Markets: The World's Political-Economic Systems.* New York: Basic Books, 1977.

Loaeza, Soledad. "The Role of the Right in Political Change in Mexico, 1982–1988." In *The Right and Democracy in Latin America,* ed. Douglas A. Chalmers, Maria do Carmo Campello de Souza, and Atilio A. Boron. New York: Praeger, 1992.

Lohmann, Susanne, and Sharyn O'Halloran. "Divided Government and U.S. Trade Policy: Theory and Evidence." *International Organization* 48 (1994): 595–632.

Los Angeles Times. Various.

Lougheed, Peter. "The Rape of the National Energy Program Will Never Happen Again." In *Free Trade, Free Canada,* ed. Earle Grey. Woodville, Ont.: Canadian Speeches, 1988.

Lowi, Theodore. *The End of Liberalism: Ideology, Policy, and the Crisis of Public Authority.* 2d ed. New York: Norton, 1979.

Luna, Matilde, Ricardo Tirado, and Franciso Valdés. "Businessmen and Politics in Mexico, 1982–1986." In *Government and Private Sector in Contemporary Mexico,* ed. Sylvia Maxfield and Ricardo Anzaldua Montoya. San Diego: Center for U.S.-Mexican Studies, 1987.

Lustig, Nora. *Mexico: The Remaking of an Economy.* Washington, D.C.: The Brookings Institution, 1992.

Lusztig, Michael. "Constitutional Paralysis: Why Canadian Constitutional Initiatives Are Doomed to Fail." *Canadian Journal of Political Science* 27 (1994): 747–71.

———. "Federalism and Institutional Design: The Perils and Politics of a Triple-E Senate in Canada." *Publius* 25 (1995): 35–50.

———. "The Limits of Rent-Seeking: Why Protectionists Become Free Traders."

Political Economy Research Group, *Papers in Political Economy,* working paper no. 61. University of Western Ontario, London, Ontario, 1995.

Magee, Stephen. "Three Simple Tests of the Stolper-Samuelson Theorem." In *Issues in International Economics,* ed. Peter Oppenheimer. Stocksfield, England: Oriel Press, 1978.

Malmesbury, Lord. *Memoirs of an Ex-Minister.* Vol. 1. London: Longman, Green, 1884.

Manfredi, Christopher. "'Appropriate and Just in the Circumstances': Public Policy and the Enforcement of Rights Under the Canadian Charter of Rights and Freedoms." Paper presented at the Annual Meeting of the American Political Science Association, Chicago, Illinois, 1992.

————. *Judicial Power and the Charter: Canada and the Paradox of Liberal Constitutionalism.* Toronto: McClelland and Stewart, 1993.

————. "Litigation and Institutional Design: The Charter of Rights and Freedoms and Micro-Constitutional Politics." Paper presented at the annual meeting of the Canadian Political Science Association, Ottawa, Ontario, 1993.

Manley, John F. "Neo-Pluralism: A Class Analysis of Pluralism I and Pluralism II." *American Political Science Review* 77 (1983): 368–83.

March, James G., and Johan P. Olsen. *Rediscovering Institutions.* New York: The Free Press, 1989.

Mares, David R. "Explaining Choice of Development Strategies: Suggestions from Mexico, 1970–1982." *International Organization* 39 (1985): 667–97.

Martin, Pierre. "Free Trade and Party Politics in Quebec." In *The NAFTA Puzzle: Political Parties and Trade in North America,* ed. Charles F. Doran and Gregory P. Marchildon. Boulder, Colo.: Westview, 1994.

Mayer, Frederick W. "Managing Domestic Differences in International Negotiations: The Strategic Use of Internal Side-Payments." *International Organization* 46 (1992): 793–818.

McCord, Norman. *The Anti-Corn Law League, 1838–1846.* 2d ed. London: George Allen and Unwin, 1968.

McDougall, John N. *Fuels and the National Policy.* Toronto: Butterworths, 1982.

McKeown, Timothy J. "Hegemonic Stability Theory and Nineteenth Century Tariff Levels in Europe." *International Organization* 37 (1983): 73–91.

————. "The Politics of Corn Law Repeal and Theories of Commercial Policy." *British Journal of Political Science* 19 (1989): 353–80.

McRoberts, Kenneth, and Patrick Monahan, eds. *The Charlottetown Accord, the Referendum, and the Future of Canada.* Toronto: University of Toronto Press, 1993.

Meadwell, Hudson, and Pierre Martin. "Is Free Trade Nationalism an Antinomy?" Paper presented at the annual meeting of the Canadian Political Science Association, Ottawa, Ontario, 1993.

Mexican Investment Board. *Mexico Investment Update.* Various.

Mexico. Secretariat of Commerce and Industrial Development. *Mexique-Canada: Une Nouvelle Ère de relations.* Ottawa, 1993.

Midford, Paul. "International Trade and Domestic Politics: Improving on Rogowski's Model of Political Alignments." *International Organization* 47 (1993): 535–64.

Milner, Helen. *Resisting Protectionism: Global Industries and the Politics of International Trade.* Princeton: Princeton University Press, 1988.

———. "Trading Places: Industries for Free Trade." *World Politics* 38 (1988): 350–76.

Mo, Jongryn. "The Logic of Two-Level Games with Endogenous Domestic Coalitions." *Journal of Conflict Resolution* 38 (1994): 402–22.

Moley, Raymond. *After Seven Years.* New York: Harper and Brothers, 1939.

———. *The First New Deal.* New York: Harcourt, Brace and World, 1966.

Molot, Maureen Appel, and Glen Williams. "The Political Economy of Continentalism." In *Canadian Politics in the 1980s,* ed. Michael S. Whittington and Glen Williams. 2d ed. Toronto: Methuen, 1984.

Monahan, Patrick J. "Discussion." In *Re-Forming Canada? The Meaning of the Meech Lake Accord and the Free Trade Agreement for the Canadian State,* ed. John D. Whyte and Ian Peach. Kingston, Ont.: Queen's University Institute of Intergovernmental Relations, 1989.

———. *Meech Lake: The Inside Story.* Toronto: University of Toronto Press, 1991.

Monypenny, William F. *The Life of Benjamin Disraeli.* Vol. 2. New York: Macmillan, 1912.

Moon, Jeremy. *Innovative Leadership in Democracy: Policy Change Under Thatcher.* Aldershot, England: Dartmouth, 1993.

Moore, D. C. "The Corn Laws and High Farming." *Economic History Review,* 2d ser., 18 (1965): 544–61.

Moore, James R. "Sources of New Deal Economic Policy: The International Dimension." *Journal of American History* 61 (1974): 728–44.

Morley, John. *The Life of Richard Cobden.* Vol. 1. London: T. Fisher Unwin, 1905.

Morris, Stephen D. "Political Reformism in Mexico." *Latin American Research Review* 28 (1993): 191–205.

———. "Political Reformism in Mexico: Salinas at the Brink." *Journal of Interamerican Studies and World Affairs* 34 (1992): 27–57.

Mulroney, Brian. Speech at Sept Iles, Quebec, August 6, 1984.

———. *Where I Stand.* Toronto: McClelland and Stewart, 1983.

Murray, Alan. "The Global Economy Bungled." *Foreign Affairs* 72 (1993): 158–66.

Needler, Martin C. "Economic Policy and Political Survival." *Mexican Studies* 9 (1993): 139–43.

Nelson, Douglas. "Endogenous Tariff Theory: A Critical Survey." *American Journal of Political Science* 82 (1988): 796–833.

Nevitte, Neil. "Bringing Values 'Back In': Value Change and North American Integration." Paper presented at the Toward a North American Community? conference in Calgary, Alberta, 1993.

New York Times. Various.

Nichols, Nancy A. "From Complacency to Competitiveness." *Harvard Business Review* 9–10 (1993): 162–72.

Nicholson, J. S. *The History of the English Corn Laws.* London: Swan Sonnenschein, 1904.

Nordlinger, Eric A. *On the Autonomy of the Democratic State.* Cambridge, Mass.: Harvard University Press, 1981.

Norrie, Kenneth. "Energy, Canadian Federalism, and the West." In *Canadian Federalism,* ed. Harold Waller, Filippo Sabetti, and Daniel Elazar. Lanham, Md.: University Press of America, 1988.

Nye, John Vincent. "Revisionist Tariff History and the Theory of Hegemonic Stability." *Politics and Society* 19 (1991): 209–32.

Offe, Claus. *Contradictions of the Welfare State.* London: Hutchison, 1984.

Olson, Mancur. *The Logic of Collective Action.* Cambridge, Mass.: Harvard University Press, 1965.

———. *The Rise and Decline of Nations: Economic Growth, Stagflation, and Social Rigidities.* New Haven: Yale University Press, 1982.

Pastor, Manuel, Jr. "Mexican Trade Liberalization and NAFTA." *Latin American Research Review* 29 (1994): 153–73.

Pastor, Manuel, Jr., and Carol Wise. "The Origins and Sustainability of Mexico's Free Trade Policy." *International Organization* 48 (1994): 459–89.

Pastor, Robert A. *Congress and the Politics of U.S. Foreign Economic Policy, 1929–1976.* Berkeley and Los Angeles: University of California Press, 1980.

———. "Post-Revolutionary Mexico: The Salinas Opening." *Journal of Interamerican Studies and World Affairs* 32 (1990): 1–22.

———. "Salinas Takes a Gamble." *New Republic,* September 10 and 17, 1990.

Patterson, James T. *Congressional Conservatism and the New Deal.* Lexington: University of Kentucky Press, 1967.

Peel, Sir Robert. *Memoirs,.* Vols. 1 and 2. Edited by Lord Mahon and Edward Cardwell. London: John Murray, 1857.

———. *The Opinions of Sir Robert Peel.* Edited by W. T. Haley. London: Whittaker, 1843.

———. *Sir Robert Peel: From His Private Papers.* Vols. 2 and 3. Edited by Charles Stuart Parker. New York: Kraus Reprint, 1970.

———. *The Speeches of the Late Right Honourable Sir Robert Peel, Bart.* Vols. 3 and 4. London: George Routledge, 1853.

Peltzman, Sam. "Toward a More General Theory of Regulation." *Journal of Law and Economics* 15 (1976): 211–40.

Pincus, J. J. *Pressure Groups and Politics in Antebellum Tariffs.* New York: Columbia University Press, 1977.

Poitras, Guy, and Raymond Robinson. "The Politics of NAFTA in Mexico." *Journal of Interamerican Studies and World Affairs* 36 (1994): 1–35.

Pozas, Maria de los Angeles. *Industrial Restructuring in Mexico: Corporate Adaptation, Technological Innovation, and Changing Patterns of Industrial Relations in Monterrey.* San Diego: Center for U.S.-Mexican Studies, 1993.

Purcell, John F. H., and Susan Kaufman Purcell. "Mexican Business and Public Policy." In *Authoritarianism and Corporatism in Latin America,* ed. James M. Molloy. Pittsburgh: University of Pittsburgh Press, 1977.

Purcell, Susan Kaufman, and John F. H. Purcell. "State and Society in Mexico: Must a Stable Polity Be Institutionalized?" *World Politics* 32 (1980): 194–227.

Putnam, Robert. "Diplomacy and Domestic Politics: The Logic of Two-Level Games." *International Organization* 42 (1988): 427–60.

Quattrone, George A., and Amos Tversky. "Contrasting Rational and Psychological Analyses of Political Choice." *American Political Science Review* 82 (1988): 719–36.

Ramirez, Miguel D. "Stabilization and Trade Reform in Mexico." *Journal of Developing Areas* 27 (1993): 173–90.

Rauch, Basil. *The History of the New Deal, 1933–1938.* New York: Creative Age Press, 1944.

Rémillard, Gil. "Keynote Address to the Conference—Mont Gabriel Quebec." Translated by Peter Leslie. In *Rebuilding the Relationship: Quebec and Its Confederation Partners,* ed. Peter Leslie. Kingston, Ont.: Queen's University Institute of Intergovernmental Relations, 1987.

Reynolds, Clark W. "Power, Value, and Distribution in the NAFTA." In Roett, *Political and Economic Liberalization in Mexico.*

Rhodes, Carolyn. *Reciprocity, U.S. Trade Policy, and the GATT Regime.* Ithaca: Cornell University Press, 1993.

Ricardo, David. *The Principles of Political Economy and Taxation.* New York: E. P. Dutton, 1960.

Richardson, R. Jack. "Free Trade: Why Did It Happen?" *Canadian Review of Sociology and Anthropology* 29 (1992): 307–28.

Riker, William H. *The Art of Political Manipulation.* New Haven: Yale University Press, 1986.

———. *The Theory of Political Coalitions.* New Haven: Yale University Press, 1962.

Risse-Kappen, Thomas. "Public Opinion, Domestic Structure, and Foreign Policy in Liberal Democracies." *World Politics* 43 (1991): 479–512.

Rocher, François. "Canadian Business, Free Trade, and the Rhetoric of Economic Continentalization." *Studies in Political Economy* 35 (1991): 135–54.

Rodrik, Dani. "The Limits of Trade Policy Reform in Developing Countries." *Journal of Economic Perspectives* 6 (1992): 87–105.

———. "The Rush to Free Trade in the Developing World: Why So Late? Why Now? Will It Last?" Washington, D.C.: National Bureau of Economic Research, working paper no. 3947, 1992.

Roett, Riordan. "At the Crossroads: Liberalization in Mexico." In Roett, *Political and Economic Liberalization in Mexico.*

Roett, Riordan, ed. *Political and Economic Liberalization in Mexico: At a Critical Juncture?* Boulder, Colo.: Lynne Reinner, 1993.

Rogowski, Ronald. *Commerce and Coalitions: How Trade Affects Domestic Political Alignments.* Princeton: Princeton University Press, 1989.

———. "Trade and the Variety of Democratic Institutions." *International Organization* 41 (1987): 203–23.

Roosevelt, Franklin D. *Complete Presidential Press Conferences of Franklin D. Roosevelt.* Vols. 3 and 4. New York: Da Capo, 1972.

———. *The Public Papers and Addresses of Franklin D. Roosevelt.* Vols. 2, 3, and 5. Edited by Samuel I. Rosenman. New York: Random House, 1938.

———. *Roosevelt and Frankfurter: Their Correspondence, 1928–1945.* Edited by Max Freedman. Boston: Little, Brown, 1967.

Rose, Richard. "The Political Status of Higher Civil Servants in Britain." In *Bureaucrats and Policy Making,* ed. Ezra Sulieman. New York: Holmes and Meier, 1984.

Roubini, Nouriel, and Jeffrey Sachs. "Political and Economic Determinants of Budget Deficits in the Industrial Democracies." *European Economic Review* 33 (1989): 903–38.

Rowley, Charles, and Robert Tollison. "Rent-Seeking and Trade Protection." In *The Political Economy of Rent-Seeking,* ed. Charles Rowley, Robert Tollison, and Gordon Tullock. Boston: Kluwer Academic, 1988.

Rowley, Charles, Robert Tollison, and Gordon Tullock, eds. *The Political Economy of Rent-Seeking.* Boston: Kluwer Academic Press, 1988.

Rubio, Luis. "Economic Reform and Political Change in Mexico." In Roett, *Political and Economic Liberalization in Mexico.*

Rudolph, Frederick. "The American Liberty League, 1934–1940." *American History Review* 56 (1950): 19–33.

Ruggie, John Gerard. "International Regimes, Transactions, and Change: Embedded Liberalism in the Postwar Economic Order." *International Organization* 36 (1982): 379–415.

Russell, Lord John. *The Later Correspondence of Lord John Russell, 1840–1878.* Vol. 1. Edited by G. P. Gooch. London: Longman, Green, 1925.

Ruttan, Vernon W., and Yurijo Hayami. "Toward a Theory of Induced Institutional Innovation." *Journal of Development Studies* 20 (1984): 203–23.

Salant, Walter S. "The Spread of Keynesian Doctrines and Practices in the United

States." In *The Political Power of Economic Ideas,* ed. Peter A. Hall. Princeton: Princeton University Press, 1989.

Salinas, Carlos. "A New Hope for the Hemisphere?" *New Perspective Quarterly* 8 (1991): 4–9.

———. *Political Participation, Public Investment, and Support for the System: A Comparative Study of Rural Communities in Mexico.* San Diego: Center for U.S.-Mexican Studies, 1982.

Salisbury, Robert H. "An Exchange Theory of Interest Groups." *Midwest Journal of Political Science* 13 (1969): 1–32.

Sandholtz, Wayne. "Choosing Union: Monetary Politics and Maastricht." *International Organization* 47 (1993): 1–40.

Sayre, Francis. *The Way Forward: The American Trade Agreements Program.* New York: Macmillan, 1939.

Schattschneider, E. E. *Politics, Pressures, and the Tariff.* New York: Prentice-Hall, 1935.

Schlesinger, Arthur M., Jr. *The Coming of the New Deal.* Boston: Houghton Mifflin, 1958.

Schneider, Mark, and Paul Teske. "Toward a Theory of the Political Entrepreneur: Evidence from Local Government." *American Political Science Review* 86 (1992): 737–47.

Schonhardt-Bailey, Cheryl. "Linking Constituency Interests to Legislative Voting Behaviour: The Role of District Economic and Electoral Composition in the Repeal of the Corn Laws." In *Computing Parliamentary History: George III to Victoria,* ed. John A. Phillips. Edinburgh: Edinburgh University Press, 1994.

———. "Specific Factors, Capital Markets, Portfolio Diversification, and Free Trade: Domestic Determinants of the Repeal of the Corn Laws." *World Politics* 43 (1991): 345–69.

Scitovszky, T. "A Note on Welfare Propositions in Economics." *Review of Economic Studies* 8 (1941): 77–88.

Shepsle, Kenneth A. "Studying Institutions: Some Lessons from the Rational Choice Approach." *Journal of Theoretical Politics* 1 (1989): 131–47.

Silk, Leonard. "Dangers of Slow Growth." *Foreign Affairs* 72 (1993): 167–82.

Simeon, Richard. "Parallelism in the Meech Lake Accord and the Free Trade Agreement." In *Re-Forming Canada? The Meaning of the Meech Lake Accord and the Free Trade Agreement for the Canadian State,* ed. John D. Whyte and Ian Peach. Kingston, Ont.: Queen's University Institute of Intergovernmental Relations, 1989.

Skocpol, Theda, and John Ikenberry. "The Political Formation of the American Welfare State in Historical and Comparative Perspective." *Comparative Social Research* 6 (1983): 87–148.

Skocpol, Theda, and Kenneth Finegold. "Explaining New Deal Labor Policy." *American Political Science Review* 84 (1990): 1297–304.

Skowronek, Stephen. *Building a New American State*. Cambridge, England: Cambridge University Press, 1982.

Smiley, Donald V. *The Federal Condition in Canada*. Toronto: McGraw-Hill Ryerson, 1987.

———. "Meech Lake and Free Trade: Studies in Canadian Federalism." *Canadian Public Administration* 32 (1989): 470–81.

Smith, Adam. *An Inquiry into the Nature and Causes of the Wealth of Nations*. New York: P. F. Collier and Sons, 1909.

Smith, Daniel Bennett. *Toward Internationalism*. New York: Garland, 1990.

Smith, Peter H. "The Political Impact of Free Trade on Mexico." *Journal of Interamerican Studies and World Affairs* 34 (1992): 1–25.

Stein, Arthur. "Coordination and Collaboration: Regimes in an Anarchic World." *International Organization* 36 (1982): 299–324.

Stein, Herbert. *The Fiscal Revolution in America*. Rev. ed. Washington, D.C.: AEI Press, 1990.

Stein, Michael B. "Canadian Constitutional Reform, 1927–1982: A Comparative Case Analysis over Time." In *Canadian Federalism,* ed. Harold Waller, Filippo Sabetti, and Daniel J. Elazar. Lanham, Md.: University Press of America, 1988.

Stevens, Evelyn P. "Mexico's PRI: The Institutionalization of Corporatism." In *Authoritarianism and Corporatism,* ed. James M. Molloy. Pittsburgh: University of Pittsburgh Press, 1977.

Stevenson, Garth. "The Agreement and the Dynamics of Canadian Federalism." In *Trade-Offs on Free Trade,* ed. Marc Gold and David Leyton-Brown. Toronto: Carswell, 1988.

Stewart, Robert. *The Politics of Protection*. Cambridge, England: Cambridge University Press, 1971.

Stigler, George J. "The Theory of Economic Regulation." *Bell Journal of Economics and Management Science* 2 (1971): 3–21.

Stinchcombe, Arthur. "Social Structure and Organizations." In *Handbook of Organizations,* ed. James G. March. Chicago: Rand-McNally, 1965.

Stone, Frank. *Canada, the GATT, and the International Trade System*. Montreal: The Institute for Research on Public Policy, 1984.

Story, Dale. "Trade Policy in the Third World: A Case Study of the Mexican GATT Decision." *International Organization* 36 (1982): 767–94.

Tasca, Henry J. *The Reciprocal Trade Policy of the United States*. Ph.D. dissertation, University of Pennsylvania, 1938.

Taussig, F. W. *The Tariff History of the United States*. 8th ed. New York: Augustus M. Kelley, 1967.

Taylor, Charles. "Shared and Divergent Values." In *Options for a New Canada,* ed. Ronald L. Watts and Douglas M. Brown. Toronto: University of Toronto Press, 1991.

Teichman, Judith. "Dismantling the Mexican State and the Role of the Private Sector." In *The Political Economy of North American Free Trade,* ed. Ricardo Grinspun and Maxwell A. Cameron. Montreal: McGill–Queen's University Press, 1993.

Toronto Star. Various.

Thomas, J. A. "The Repeal of the Corn Laws, 1846." *Economica* 9 (1929): 53–60.

Trudeau, Pierre E. "Say Goodbye to the Dream of One Canada." In *Meech Lake and Canada: Perspectives from the West,* ed. Roger Gibbins. Rev. ed. Edmonton: Academic, 1989.

Tsebelis, George. *Nested Games: Rational Choice in Comparative Politics.* Berkeley and Los Angeles: University of California Press, 1990.

———. "The Power of the European Parliament as Conditional Agenda Setter." *American Political Science Review* 88 (1994): 128–42.

Tugwell, Rexford G. *The Diary of Rexford G. Tugwell.* Edited by Michael Vincent Namorato. New York: Greenwood, 1992.

———. *FDR: Architect of an Era.* New York: Macmillan, 1967.

———. *In Search of Roosevelt.* Cambridge, Mass.: Harvard University Press, 1972.

Tullock, Gordon. "Future Directions for Rent-Seeking Research." In *The Political Economy of Rent-Seeking,* ed. Charles Rowley, Robert Tollison, and Gordon Tullock. Boston: Kluwer Academic Press, 1988.

———. "Welfare Costs of Tariffs, Monopolies, and Theft." *Western Economic Journal* 5 (1967): 224–32.

U.S. Congress. House. Committee on Ways and Means. *Hearings on H.R. 8430, Reciprocal Trade Agreements.* Washington, D.C.: U.S. Government Printing Office, 1934.

———. *Hearings on H.J. Res. 96, Extension of Reciprocal Trade Agreements Act.* Washington, D.C.: U.S. Government Printing Office, 1937.

———. *Hearings on H.J. Res. 407, Extension of Reciprocal Trade Agreements Act.* Washington, D.C.: U.S. Government Printing Office, 1940.

U.S. Congress. Senate. Committee on Finance. *Hearings on H.R. 8687, Reciprocal Trade Agreements.* Washington, D.C.: U.S. Government Printing Office, 1934.

———. *Hearings on H.J. Res. 96, Extension of Reciprocal Trade Agreements Act.* Washington, D.C.: U.S. Government Printing Office, 1937.

———. *Hearings on H.J. Res. 407, Extension of Reciprocal Trade Agreements Act.* Washington, D.C.: U.S. Government Printing Office, 1940.

Upgren, Arthur. *Reciprocal Trade Agreements.* Minneapolis: University of Minnesota Press, 1937.

Uslaner, Eric M. "Political Parties, Ideas, Interests, and Free Trade in the United States." Paper presented at the Conference on Party and Trade: Political Perspectives on External Trade, Washington, D.C., 1992.

———. *Shale Barrel Politics.* Stanford: Stanford University Press, 1989.

Van B. Cleveland, Harold. "The International Monetary System in the Interwar Period." In *Balance of Power or Hegemony,* ed. Benjamin M. Rowland. New York: New York University Press, 1976.

Verdier, Daniel. *Democracy and International Trade: Britain, France, and the United States.* Princeton: Princeton University Press, 1994.

Wallace, Henry A. *Democracy Reborn.* Edited by Russell Lord. New York: Reynal and Hitchcock, 1944.

Ward, Peter M. "Social Welfare Policy and Political Opening in Mexico." *Journal of Latin American Studies* 25 (1993): 613–28.

Waterbury, John. "Export-Led Growth and the Center-Right Coalition in Turkey." *Comparative Politics* 24 (1992): 127–45.

Watkins, Gordon C., and Michael A. Walker, eds. *Reaction: The National Energy Program.* Vancouver: Fraser Institute, 1981.

Watson, William G. "Canada-U.S. Free Trade: Why Now?" *Canadian Public Policy* 13 (1987): 337–49.

Weintraub, Sidney. "Canada Acts on Free Trade." *Journal of Interamerican Studies and World Affairs* 28 (1986): 101–18.

———. "The Economy on the Eve of Free Trade." *Current History* 92 (1993): 67–72.

———. *Mexican Trade Policy and the North American Community.* Washington, D.C.: Center for Strategic and International Studies, 1988.

Weintraub, Sidney, and M. Delal Baer. "The Interplay Between Economic and Political Opening: The Sequence in Mexico." *Washington Quarterly* 15 (1992): 187–201.

Weir, Margaret, and Theda Skocpol. "State Structures and the Possibilities for 'Keynesian' Responses to the Great Depression in Sweden, Britain, and the United States." In *Bringing the State Back In,* ed. Peter B. Evans, Dietrich Rueschemeyer, and Theda Skocpol. Cambridge, England: Cambridge University Press, 1985.

Whalley, John, Colleen Hamilton, and Roderick Hill. *Canadian Trade Policies and the World Economy.* Toronto: University of Toronto Press, 1985.

Whyte, John, Roy Romanow, and Howard Leeson. *Canada Notwithstanding.* Toronto: Carswell, 1984.

Williams, Glen. *Not for Export.* Rev. ed. Toronto: McLelland and Stewart, 1986.

Williamson, John, ed. *The Political Economy of Policy Reform.* Washington, D.C.: Institute for International Economics, 1994.

Wilson, James Q. "The Politics of Regulation." In *The Politics of Regulation,* ed. James Q. Wilson. New York: Basic Books, 1980.

Winham, Gilbert R. "Bureaucratic Politics and Canadian Trade Negotiation." *International Journal* 34 (1978): 64–89.

———. *The Evolution of International Trade Agreements.* Toronto: University of Toronto Press, 1992.

———. *Trading with Canada.* New York: Priority Press, 1988.

Wolfskill, George. *The Revolt of the Conservatives: A History of the American Liberty League, 1934–1940.* Boston: Houghton Mifflin, 1962.

Wonnacott, Paul, and Ronald J. Wonnacott. *Free Trade Between the U.S. and Canada.* Cambridge, Mass.: Harvard University Press, 1967.

Young, Oran R. "Political Leadership and Regime Formation: On the Development of Institutions in International Society." *International Organization* 45 (1991): 281–308.

———. "Regime Dynamics: The Rise and Fall of International Regimes." *International Organization* 36 (1982): 277–98.

Young, Robert A. "Political Scientists, Economists, and the Canada-U.S. Free Trade Agreement." *Canadian Public Policy* 15 (1989): 49–56.

INDEX